# Encyclopedia
# of Cheese
# and
# Cheese Cookery

# Encyclopedia of Cheese and Cheese Cookery

by Betty Wason

Foreword by Phil Alpert, President, Cheeses of All Nations

# A Salute to Cheese

GALAHAD BOOKS • NEW YORK CITY

# INTRODUCTION

In A SALUTE TO CHEESE, Betty Wason tells everything you need to know about cheese from its making to its serving and enjoyment. Gourmets may find recipes in Part IV that are new to them. Travelers can delight in the folklore and legends about cheese that Miss Wason has gathered from almost every country in the world. And, finally, budding epicureans and young cooks will welcome this useful and informative introduction to what I consider the world's finest food. Novice and expert alike can revel in the Glossary of the World's Cheeses, which was compiled especially for this book. It is the most complete list of cheese names and characteristics available anywhere.

Cheese, as one of the great discoveries of early man, must have been as much appreciated for its taste in those dim dark days as it is right now. And because cheese is convenient, storable and portable, it is a food whose secrets have been passed down from

5

generation to generation, changing and evolving from the original simple curds of our roaming ancestors to sophisticated variations designed to please every member of the family of man.

Interest in cheese and its gourmet qualities seems to grow in direct proportion to the number of passports issued by the United States Government each year. And that means that the "audience" for cheese has increased tremendously in the past decade. However, aside from a few technical works, there has been very little published either here or in Europe that reflects advances in cheese making, new varieties of cheeses, or pulls together in one volume the information this new audience needs. It is this need which A SALUTE TO CHEESE fills so admirably.

Further, I have seen few books on cheese as readable and entertaining as this one, and hope you will read every page of it instead of flipping through just for the recipes or serving suggestions. The author, an authority in the field, tells you what cheese to serve with what wine, fruit or bread, and even what quantities to buy for every occasion from dessert service to big cocktail parties.

There is a restaurant in France which serves cheese not only as dessert but as the whole dinner as well! From beginning to end you're treated to a pageant of cheese in a symphony of sights, tastes and odors that surpasses any son-et-lumière spectacle you'll find in Europe. One by one the great boards of cheese arrive. The first, resting on cool leaves, are the gentle, mild cheeses. You taste each — with sips of wine in between. Next come the tangy, the hard, the aromatic cheeses. And some hours later you wind up in a crescendo of the great blues — Stilton, Gorgonzola, Roquefort.

My parting wish for you is that you may enjoy such a dinner without stirring from your own table or your own home. Gather your family and your friends about, take Betty Wason as a guide, and have a cheese tour of the world in one meal.

Cheese and cheers,

Phil Alpert

Cheeses of All Nations
New York City

6

# Contents

# Acknowledgments

All my life I have been a cheese lover, but until I did the research for this book, I had no idea cheese was such a complex and fascinating subject. Much of the information in the following pages has come from books — I have used André Simon's *Cheeses of the World* almost as a bible and have pored over the booklet called "Cheese Varieties and Descriptions" published by the United States Department of Agriculture until the pages are limp.

But the only way for anyone really to learn about cheese is to taste it, and for the opportunity to taste it I am particularly grateful to Phil Alpert of Cheeses of All Nations, who, again and again, has supplied me with selections of rare and exotic cheeses to sample, instructing me on the proper way to taste each cheese in order to savor its distinctive qualities most fully. He also lent me from his files of cheese material, accumulated

9

over some forty years in the cheese business, a big pile of magazine and newspaper articles, from which I culled additional technical information.

Still another person who gave me invaluable assistance was Heinz Hofer of the Switzerland Cheese Association, who not only was kind enough to clarify the fine points of cheese-making for me in the course of several interviews but even volunteered to check certain sections of the manuscript for accuracy. As the various methods of manufacturing cheese are so complex and hard for the layman to understand, I feel I owe Mr. Hofer a particular debt of gratitude.

Several years ago, I was given a book called *The Roquefort Adventure*, written by Henri Pourrat, shortly before leaving for Europe on a trip that I had hoped would take me to the famous caves on Mont Combalou in southern France. Unhappily, my itinerary became so complex that I had to skip the visit to Roquefort, which now I very much regret; the book, at least, proved to be an extremely valuable reference source on the ancient history of this superb cheese.

My passionate interest in archaeology proved to be a further help in delving into the early history of cheese-making, for in several museums in Spain I saw tools of cheese-making dating from the Bronze Age, and in archaeology books, in my library plus translations of the classic Greek and Roman writers, I came across many interesting anecdotes about cheese in ancient times.

Although I failed to visit the cheese-curing caves at Roquefort, on that same trip to Europe I did at least manage later to visit a spotlessly modern cheese factory in Denmark, and still another debt must be acknowledged to the Danish Ministry of Agriculture, which arranged that visit. There I saw the various steps followed in the manufacture of Danish cheeses, which made it easier for me to understand something of the intricacies of cheese-making when I set about writing this book.

Finally I must acknowledge the yeoman efforts of my assistant, Jeanne Meyer, who not only helped me in the testing of recipes but whose quick eyes were also ever on the lookout for interesting cheeses that should be mentioned in the book — or incorporated into tempting and unusual dishes.

# THE wonders OF CHEESE

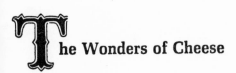

# The Wonders of Cheese

What a world of flavors the one word "cheese" suggests! Soft buttery slices of a young Monterey Jack . . . the crumbly sharp bite of Coon . . . the pungency of Roquefort, the smooth, yellow, afternoon mildness of Edam. Do you want a cheese to slip into your picnic basket to be nibbled under the sun on a hilltop slope? What's better than a wedge of Switzerland's Emmentaler (the big-holed cheese we call "Swiss")? Or perhaps you are planning an intimate candlelit dinner: The perfect dessert is a Camembert, runny-soft as clotted cream, spread on crisp, bland water biscuits and served with chilled Emperor grapes, snifters of cognac, and black, black coffee.

Some cheeses by their very strangeness suggest faraway places and exotic climes. I can't resist Feta, the chalk-white, salty

13

sheep's cheese of Greece, for it always reminds me of idyllic afternoons in Athens when I nibbled at this deceptively mild cheese between sips of Greek retsina wine or ouzo. With Feta one should always have ruby-dark Kalamata olives that have been marinated in olive oil and red-wine vinegar — and one should sit at a café table lazily watching the world go by with the incredible beauty of the Parthenon in the distance, its marble columns reflecting the pink light of the afternoon sun.

Stilton for some is the ultimate cheese — green-veined Stilton, its creamy complexion softening to brown around the edges, mellow in the mouth, the perfect partner for a glass of rare vintage port. Others sing the praises of Brie, buttery smooth and white-crusted, as flat as a small pie, with a flavor no words can adequately describe. Still made in France much as it has been since the tenth century, Brie was officially recognized as a "royal cheese" by the Congress of Vienna in 1815, when that august body was presided over by Prince Metternich, with Prince Talleyrand among the thirty European ambassadors casting votes in its favor.

## WHAT IS CHEESE?

No one has ever been able to count the number of kinds of cheese in the world, though many have tried. The United States Department of Agriculture has figured out a compressed list of eighteen basic types, but twenty or more varieties can be grouped under each type, and still one would not have scratched the surface. How to categorize the cheeses spiced with cumin or fennel, those with resinous or smoky flavors, the wheels of cheese marinated in wine or beer or even whiskey, those rubbed to glistening finishes with olive oil or braided into rope-like knots, or the cheeses layered with grape skins or hops or spicy red peppers to create special flavors as they are cured?

How, one may ask, is it possible to make so many different products from a single ingredient? For all cheese begins as milk.

The answer is both simple and complex. The watery part of the milk, the whey, separates from the firmer part, the curd, by the action of either rennet (or another micro-organism) or heat or both. The whey is drained from the curd, and the curd is made into cheese. (But some cheeses are also made from whey!)

# THE UNRIPENED CHEESES, SIMPLEST OF ALL

In my childhood, we had a big black cast-iron stove in our kitchen, and, whenever the milk turned sour (it was raw milk, not pasteurized), we poured the sour milk into wide pans and placed them on the back of the stove, where there was very gentle heat. After a few hours, the milk would have turned into thick clabber. By the next day, the curd of the clabber would have separated from the whey; my mother would cut the curd into chunks with a knife and pour it into a cheesecloth bag to drain over a bowl in the sink. After the whey had been drained off, the "pot cheese" that was left was broken into fine particles with a fork, salted lightly, and blended with sweet cream. This substance was what we still call "cottage cheese," and here and there a few American farm families continue to make their own to this day. In New England, I am told, melted butter is sometimes added to the curd instead of cream. What is sold in many markets as white "farmer's cheese" is the same as "pot cheese" but with less of the whey drained out and with the curd broken into finer particles and pressed into a mold.

Every milk-producing country in the world has its own version of cottage cheese, known by various names. In France it is *fromage blanc*, in Germany *Quarkkäse*, in Italy *ricotta*, in England "pot cheese," in Scotland "Aberdeen Crowdie." A similar cheese, known as "hatted kit," once was considered a great delicacy. To make it, according to a recipe in an eighteenth-century Scottish cookbook, one should "warm two quarts of buttermilk, carry it in a basin to the cow and milk one pint of milk into it. Stir the milk well and leave for about 24 hours. Next day take your basin once more to the cow for a second pint of milk. It will in time form into the shape of a hat which you take off and drain through a fine sieve. Pile the curds into a mold and leave long enough to shape. Serve with fresh cream."

Hatted kit, like cottage cheese, Quarkkäse, and farmer's cheese, belongs to the category of fresh unripened cheese.

Cream cheese is not ripened, either — that is, fresh cream cheese is not. Here we get into a problem of nomenclature, for in France many ripened soft cheeses bear the name *crème*, and, in the western part of our own country, a variation of mild Cheddar is (or used to be) sometimes called "cream cheese" — probably because it is made with cream-rich milk.

Also there are some "cream cheeses" that are made from pure

cream and others made from mixtures of cream and whole milk. The French *coeur à la crème* is made from a thickened clabber of rich whole milk, mixed with cream and drained in heart-shaped wicker baskets. Our American cream cheese is also a mixture of whole milk and cream, as is the American Neufchâtel — though the latter is lower in butterfat than is cream cheese. Today a lactic-acid culture is usually added to make the milk-cream mixture turn to clabber — the same culture that is used to produce commercial sour cream and yogurt. The one thing that distinguishes fresh cream cheese from cottage and pot cheeses is that the curd is not subjected to heat — the natural action of lactic acid causes the cream to separate from the milk, thickening it to a rich clabber that can be easily skimmed off, then drained. Because the curd is not subjected to heat, it is much softer. A few fresh cream cheeses are lightly salted (the French *demi-sel*, for example), but all are highly perishable and delicate in flavor.

(Ricotta is available in several forms. The kind we find in American supermarkets is made domestically of skimmed cow's milk, but in Italy Ricotta is made of the whey of sheep's milk or of clabbered skimmed sheep's milk blended with whey. Some is as soft as our cottage cheese, though of finer, firmer quality, some is semifirm, and some is hard enough to grate.)

People have been making simple unripened cheeses for at least 6,000 years. References to cheese have been found in Sumerian cuneiform tablets of 4000 B.C.; and simple little cheese pots — bowls with holes punched in the bottoms, through which the whey could drain — have been found in ancient Egyptian tombs, as well as in later Bronze Age excavations throughout the Mediterranean lands. Not long ago, in the Museo de Prehistoria in Valencia, Spain, I saw such ancient cheese molds or pots, which had been found in settlements dating back to 1000 B.C. In the same museum are reproductions of rock drawings 8,000 years old, found in this same region, which show men driving herds of cattle to pasture — a pictorial record that demonstrates that milk and its chief product cheese were important articles of diet in the earliest civilizations of man.

## HOW RIPENED CHEESE IS MADE

A shepherd who stored his supply of milk in a new goatskin and left the goatskin lying in the hot sun probably discovered, untold ages ago, the secret of ripening cheese. For it is the action of rennet, a substance found in the stomach lining of young mammals, that causes the most dramatic change in the chemical content of milk. Rennet causes the solid particles, the casein and the butterfat, to break away from the watery content of the milk and form into a solid mass. In the days when the dressed stomachs of young kids or lambs were used as drinking vessels (goatskin bladders are still used as wine jugs by many European peasants), cheese would form naturally from milk carried in such canteens, and, when the whey was poured off, a curd would remain that was solid enough to be shaped with the hands. To this day, in certain parts of Turkey and Pakistan, cheese is cured in goatskin or sheepskin bags.

Of how many centuries — or millennia — ago this secret of how to "cure and ripen" cheese was discovered there is no record, but it was well known in Homer's time; the Greek poet, in describing the cave of the Cyclops in *The Odyssey*, tells how Ulysses and his men found rows of cheeses in baskets on a ledge along the wall. When the one-eyed Cyclops entered in the afternoon to milk his ewes, part of the sheep's milk was put aside to be drunk, the rest was promptly "curdled," and the one-eyed giant took out the cheese curd to mold it with his hands, placing it in baskets to dry. Presumably he kept a culture on hand for the purpose of making cheese, just as yeast "starters" were kept for making bread.

Adding rennet to the milk is the most important step in making any ripened cheese. Such variable factors as the length of time the rennet is left in the milk, the temperature of the milk during the curing period, and the way the curd is cut (whether in large or in fine particles) and thereafter drained largely determine the texture of the cheese that will finally result. For example, in making Camembert, the rennet is added when the milk is at a temperature of 78° or 80°F. and is left in the milk for five hours. But to make Port du Salut, the temperature of the milk is raised to 95° and the rennet left in for only half an hour before the curd is cut and drained.

The kind of rennet or other organism added to the milk to cause this process is still another variable. In Portugal, some cheeses are ripened with a rennet extracted from a member of the thistle family. In today's cheese factories, other bacteria that will hasten the process of "curdling" may be used in place of rennet.

17

# MILK, THE FIRST VARIABLE

Today practically all the cheeses in the United States and most of those in the rest of the world are made of cow's milk, with a few made from the milk of sheep (ewes) and goats.

But it has not always been so. Hippocrates wrote of cheese made from mare's milk (presumably the original Caciocavallo, or Kashkaval, which means literally "horse cheese"), and in certain parts of the world cheese is still made from reindeer's milk and the milk of water buffaloes. (Both Mozzarella and Provolone were, until recent times, made of buffalo's milk.)

Any milk can be made into cheese, and it is reasonable to assume that camel cheese may once have been a prized delicacy, for in ancient Persia "milch camels" frequently were listed as important parts of princesses' dowries. Yak butter in Tibet is a kind of cheese. The Laplanders cherish smoked reindeer cheese. According to ancient Chinese literature, the milk of apes was sometimes drunk in China. Who knows, there may once even have been an ape cheese!

Some cheese is made from skimmed sweet milk, some from skimmed sour milk, some from whole milk, and some from whole milk with cream added. Frequently a mixture of two or more milks will be used, perhaps a mixture of sheep's and cow's milk or of sheep's, goat's *and* cow's milk. Quite frequently there is a mixture of milk from the very same cows, the pailfuls of the previous night's milking being blended with the fresh milk drawn in the morning. As curdling occurs more quickly in milk that has stood for twelve hours or more, a mixture of this kind can be cured more quickly than can entirely fresh milk. Sour milk or buttermilk will curdle much more quickly than will fresh, and sour milk is therefore often mixed with fresh milk.

It is easy enough to understand that a cheese made from sheep's or goat's milk would have quite a different flavor from a cow's-milk cheese even if exactly the same methods of production were observed. But even milk from different cows varies enormously, not only in richness of butterfat, but also in subtle nuances of flavor that are in turn transmitted to the cheeses. In this respect, milk is to cheese what grapes are to wine. After most of Europe's vineyards had been destroyed by the phylloxera disease in the 1880s, new disease-resistant varieties of grapes were imported from the United States, but, lo and behold, the wines of each vineyard, from the new grape strains, turned out to be almost identical to those produced on the same soil before. And just as local soil and climate conditions affect the taste and bouquet of the wine, the pasturage on which cows graze, the air they breathe, the water they drink, and their supplemental food affect the milk — and in turn the cheese. Mountain or Alpine cheeses in Switzerland differ from cheeses produced from the milk of cows pastured in valleys far below. The Swiss forbid the feeding of silage to cows whose milk will be used to make Emmentaler and Gruyère because they believe that silage (fermented alfalfa and other grasses stored in silos) gives cheese a bitter aftertaste.

André Simon, in his book *Cheeses of the World*, tells how a woman living in Middlesex (England) attempted to make cheese like the famed product of Gloucester, using a dairymaid from Gloucester to supervise the entire operation. But the cheese that resulted was entirely different from Gloucester cheese. The English farmer who recorded this fact told how he himself had tried to make Cheshire cheese from the milk of cows in Essex, with the same dismal results.

This relationship with environmental conditions is why even excellent American imitations of European cheeses come out a little different. They may be good, and to the untrained palate they may even taste the same — but to the expert the difference is usually obvious.

Sometimes the imitation turns out to be better than the original, which has happened a number of times in Europe; many think the Tilsiter cheeses of Switzerland and Norway are better than the Tilsiterkäse originally made in East Prussia (by Dutch immigrants from The Netherlands). Liederkranz, one of the proudest of American cheeses, was created by Emil Frey, a German immigrant who was trying to produce an imitation of Schlosskäse Bismarck. His cheese was not the same as the German cheese he tried to imitate — it was better, so good that the choral society to which Frey belonged began singing its praises, and, in gratitude for their support, Frey called his new cheese "Liederkranz," literally "wreath of song," after the glee club. His cheese was unique and so superb that it gained international renown; and, because it had a German name, many Americans foolishly thought it must be an imported cheese to be so good!

There are many excellent cheeses being made in the United States today, and there could be more if cheese manufacturers were not in such a hurry. But more on that later.

## THE BIRTH OF THE BLUES

In the beginning, there was no attempt to create temptingly different varieties of cheese. It simply happened.

Take Roquefort, the oldest and most renowned of the blue-veined cheeses.

Now one knows how long ago the first Roquefort was created. According to a popular, but probably apocryphal, tale, a shepherd boy one day left his sandwich of bread and cheese inside the entrance to a cave to go chasing after a pretty maiden. Young love being what it is, he soon forgot all about the sandwich, until he found it weeks later, the bread blue with mold, and the cheese moldy too. Because he was young and hungry, he ate the cheese, mold and all — and discovered that the moldy part was the most delicious. So goes the tale. It is more likely that the blue-veined cheese of Roquefort is older than the stuff we now call "bread."

Certain it is that there were sheep-herders living in the mountain fastness on which the small town of Roquefort is perched long before the dawn of history — before the period of the oldest decipherable written records. Not far from Roquefort lie the Lascaux caverns, with their extraordinarily beautiful cave paintings of bulls, wild horses, and deer. The long underground passage-graves built by a megalithic people who lived there possibly 6,000 years ago have been found in the mountains in clusters. And, in the caverns where today Roquefort cheese is still cured, carved antlers of both deer and mouflons (the ancestors of domesticated rams), Stone Age axes, and other such remnants of this early people have been found on the cave floors — as well as crude cheese molds somewhat like those I saw in the museum in Spain. In Roman times, the people in the Roquefort region were known as "Rutenes," the "red ones," a hardy race as noted for their fierce independence as for the cheese they produced from sheep's milk. Pliny the Elder wrote of "the cheese that bears away the prize" from the region of Nîmes, which was the central city of the Roquefort region in Roman times. "Unfortunately," wrote Pliny of this cheese of Nîmes, "its time is short, it is good only at the height of its freshness"; and, if it was blue-veined, he did not mention the fact.

Whether or not it contained the streaks of blue so prized in today's Roquefort would have depended entirely on whether or not the cheese of Nîmes was cured in the Roquefort caverns, for the blue-green veining is caused by an organism existing in the caves that attaches itself to the cheese. At least, that is the way it was in the beginning. Today, to make sure that the cheese will have plenty of blue, bread molded with the *Penicillium roqueforti* culture is layered with the curd of the cheese as it matures in the moist recesses of the caves.

But a tale recorded by a medieval monk makes clear that no bread was used to induce the mold in Roquefort cheese in his day.

It was during the ninth century when the Emperor Charlemagne, who had been in Spain fighting the Saracens (the "Moors," we call them today), stopped off at a monastery in Aveyron, the department in which Roquefort lies, on his way back to his capital at Aix-la-Chapelle. The bishop of the monastery was embarrassed when Charlemagne arrived, dusty, weary, and hungry. It was a fast day, and the monks had nothing to offer their monarch but some of the local cheese made from the milk of ewes. The cheese was creamy and fresh, with a marbling of blue-green through the center. Charlemagne, when the cheese was set before him, started to pick out the bluish part with the point of his knife.

"My Lord," exclaimed the bishop, "permit me to tell you that what you are taking out is the best part of all."

The emperor spread the blue-veined cheese on his bread, tasted it, and promptly ordered that every year he be sent two loads of this marvelous cheese, "and be sure there's blue in it." According to the chronicle related by the monk, the bishop protested: "But, sire, we can't be sure every cheese will have blue inside. Not all the cheeses turn out so well."

"Then split each cheese, to search for the blue before sending it to me. For your trouble, I will give you one of my farms."

From that time on, Roquefort was recognized as one of the world's great cheeses, and all the people in the region were ordered to bring the milk of their ewes to the mountain called "Combalou," so that it could be made into cheese and cured in the magic atmosphere of the caves, in order to fill Charlemagne's order.

I have come across references to Gorgonzola as "an Italian imitation of Roquefort cheese," which is ridiculous. First of all, Roquefort is made solely from the milk of ewes during the lambing season. Gorgonzola is a cow's-milk cheese, though it is sometimes made from a mixture of cow's and goat's milk. Furthermore, the high humidity of the Roquefort caves (thanks to an underground lake) and the thin, clear air of the high, rugged mountain slopes, where only balsam firs grow from crevices in the rocks, both have their effects on the flavor of the ripening cheese. Distinguishing the two veined cheeses still further is the fact that a different kind of mold forms on Gorgonzola, one peculiar to the Italian caves where this cheese is aged, a mold that is at first reddish brown, becoming green-brown, then green-blue, as it penetrates the creamy white interior of the cheese.

Roquefort is usually heralded as the only blue-veined cheese made from sheep's milk, but that is not literally true. In the Balkans, a number of veined sheep's-milk cheeses are produced. Spain has its Cabrales, a blue-veined sheep cheese wrapped in vine leaves. Even in France several "blues" are made with mixtures of sheep's and cow's milk. Roquefort, however, is the only blue-veined sheep's-milk cheese of international repute available in the world's markets. All genuine Roquefort cheese — all the cheese cured in the caverns of Roquefort — bears a symbol of a sheep printed in red.

France produces many other blue-veined cheeses made from cow's milk or from mixtures of cow's, sheep's and goat's milk, besides a number of delicious little goat cheeses that have thick blue mold clinging to the outer rinds, though the cheeses inside are pure chalky white.

Today most of the blue-veined cheeses, wherever produced, are deliberately inoculated with *Penicillium roqueforti* instead of the veining being left to nature. Even Stilton, which was not made before 1730, is inoculated and therefore can be said to have begun life as a cow's-milk imitation of Roquefort. The vast differences in flavor and texture between Stilton and Roquefort and between Stilton and Danablu, which is also a cow's-milk cheese, speak eloquently of the influence of native soil and climate in developing the final character of a cheese.

## NOT GREEN, JUST IMMATURE

In many respects, cheeses can be compared to people. Some improve with age; others simply turn rotten. To a large extent, the result depends on early environment, how the cheese is treated, what inoculations it receives, the conditions that surround it as it matures.

Blue-veined cheeses become that way because microorganisms, bacteria, or fungoids (several ways of saying the same thing) are either absorbed or planted in them.

Many cheeses have special flavoring agents added to the drained curd. Caraway seeds, cumin, black or red pepper, or green herbs (there is a thyme cheese made in Turkey, and many countries make sage cheeses) may be added. Cheeses that are bright yellow in color usually are that way because a coloring substance called "annatto" has been stirred into the curd. In olden times, the color was supplied by marigold juice or carrot juice.

The Swiss Schabzieger, which we call by the easier name "Sapsago," is a pale, greenish yellow because of the addition of crushed clover leaves. It is sometimes called "green cheese."

The term "green cheese," however, generally means a cheese that has not been fully ripened. The old saying that "the moon is made of green cheese" probably arose because the drained or pressed curd, while it is lying in curing cellars, often has a mottled look, much like the surface of the moon.

There is a great deal of confusion even within the cheese industry itself over the exact meanings of the terms "curing," "ripening," and "aging."

"Curing" generally refers to that formative period when a cheese develops its own special character, a period that may be a few hours, several days, or several months — depending on the cheese variety. (See Index listing for the section where a fuller explanation of what happens during curing is given.) It takes an experienced cheesemaker to determine when a cheese has completed this formative stage and is ready for transfer to ripening cellars, because of such variables as seasonal or other differences in the milk, changes in the atmosphere, and temperament on the part of microorganisms added to the curd.

"Ripening" is the process of maturing that follows the curing stage, although, to make things more difficult for the consumer, the term is often used as if it were synonymous with "curing." Technically, for example, an "unripened cheese" means a fresh cheese that has not undergone any curing process. Yet a cured cheese that has not been properly ripened is not called an "unripened cheese" but a "green cheese"!

To add to the confusion, the term "aging" is sometimes used

as a synonym for "ripening," or again it may refer to the entire period from the time the curd is inoculated with rennet until it reaches the consumer's hands, or it may refer to a "post-ripening" period when a cheese is purposely stored longer to become sharper and firmer. Many packages of cheese to be found in American supermarkets bear the notice "aged 60 days." As the curing period of a firm cheese may be as long as sixty days and then a ripening period must follow that could be anywhere from three months to a year, the "aged 60 days" label is not necessarily any indication that the cheese is fully mature.

Cheese-making is a highly complicated art, one that requires not only great technical skill but also a special feeling for the product, a sixth sense, if you will, for when a particular cheese has reached its prime.

Even a cheese that is fully cured and fully ripened will continue to develop subtle changes when stored in cellars maintained especially for the purpose. And again it takes an expert to judge when a particular cheese will not improve by additional aging and when, in fact, it may be on the verge of putrefaction. (There are, it must be remarked, some cheese lovers, especially among the Europeans, who actually prefer cheeses so old that they are crawling with maggots. Such cheese is not harmful; those who have stomachs strong enough to go on eating with relish after picking out wriggling little creatures from the cheese are perfectly safe in indulging their strange whims. I suspect, however, that it will be a long time before cheese of this degree of "ripeness" will be in demand on the American market.)

As a semifirm or firm cheese ages in a cellar, it becomes firmer, drier, and sharper in flavor. Its color, too, changes: The creamy white of a Stilton or Gorgonzola will become brownish, especially around the edges; a bright yellow cheese will become darker yellow. The very hard grating cheeses fade from pale, clear beige to dull, greenish white.

In trying to become personally acquainted with as many cheeses as possible, I have been dismayed several times, after describing a cheese as "buttery (or creamy) in texture, mellow in flavor," to taste another sample of the same cheese that has been aged longer and to find the texture crumbly (or flaky) and the flavor sharp, even pungent.

For those who prefer blander flavors and softer textures,

the young (but fully cured and ripened) cheeses will be more attractive. Those who like their cheeses sharp and "assertive" will prefer the more mature types.

It's like the age-old argument about women. Some men think a virginal slip of a girl, dewy-eyed and innocent, is the most irresistible creature in the world. Other men find a worldly, knowledgeable woman of forty more seductive. It's all a matter of taste! (And there are those, too, of course, who like to experiment with all kinds, nibbling here and there.)

After a semifirm or hard cheese has been fully ripened, it can be aged up to two, occasionally three, years. Sbrinz, a cheese of Switzerland, is considered at its finest at three years and is sometimes aged even longer. But few cheeses are deliberately stored in ripening cellars for longer than three years, even though certain varieties are usable when older if they have been kept under optimum conditions.

One cheese merchant in New York City, Jerry Colitt, owner of Old Denmark on Fifty-seventh Street, maintains a special cellar for aging fine cheeses, which he buys in quantity from his native Denmark. Some he deliberately ages for two years or longer, offering them as "vintage" cheeses, much as a wine merchant keeps prize wines locked away until they have mellowed to perfection. Of some 7,000 pounds of cheese in the Old Denmark cellars, only about 4,000 are considered mellow enough for Mr. Colitt's more critical customers; the rest are kept aside to ripen slowly to complete maturity.

The only one of the world's cheeses deliberately aged for longer than three years is the cheese called "Saanen" produced in Switzerland. Saanen is always aged six or seven years. In olden times, a wheel of it might be put away in a cellar at the birth of a child, to be brought out when the young man or woman was betrothed. It is claimed that certain Saanen cheeses have remained edible for 100 years.

Remember, though, that even the firm cheeses do not necessarily improve with long aging. There are certain Goudas that develop a piquant, delightfully sharp taste after aging for as long as two years — but that does not mean that the Gouda you have bought at the supermarket will do anything but dry up if you keep it for six months.

How can the novice determine which cheeses are well aged, which overripe, which simply rotten? Just as, in learning about wines, one must drink them regularly and critically and thus train the palate to know the differences, so, with cheese, one must try many, and gradually the taste buds will become the best judge. In the meantime, it is best to patronize a reputable cheese store (or delicatessen or gourmet shop carrying a wide selection of cheeses), and one should not hesitate, when a cheese seems unpleasant, to take it back. A cheese man will respect you more when he sees that you have critical taste.

## CURING: GIVING A CHEESE ITS CHARACTER

It is when the whey is drained from the curd that the first distinguishing step in cheese-making occurs, for the amount of whey pressed out will determine whether it is to be a "soft," a "semisoft," a "semifirm," a "firm," or a "hard" cheese. These terms are used within the industry to distinguish the main classifications of cheese according to texture.

All soft cheeses, even the "soft ripened cheeses," are quite perishable. In fact, it can be stated as a general rule that the firmer and less moist the cheese, the longer its life; and conversely, the more whey that has been permitted to remain in the curd, the more rapidly will the cheese deteriorate. For this reason, it is never wise to buy soft cheeses in any but small quantities, and it is important to be particularly fussy in choosing such cheeses, not taking any that are shrunken, brownish around the edges, or with an offensively ammonial smell.

The soft cheeses, on the other hand, are some of the most exciting to learn about, for each has its own unique charm.

In making a soft ripened cheese, a little of the whey is allowed to remain in the curd. Then this soft curd is shaped by hand or poured into small molds, which may be round, square, rectangular, triangular, or crescent-shaped. Rarely does a soft ripened cheese weigh more than ten ounces, and most come in five- to six-ounce sizes. Such a cheese may remain in a curing cellar for as brief a time as two weeks — but brief as it is, this period is vital, for it is in the curing cellar that the cheese acquires its unique flavor and aroma. Some of the cheeses are deliberately smeared or inoculated with special bacteria; others "breathe" them from the air, just as the blue-veined cheeses absorb their molds.

Pont-l'Evêque, a soft ripened cheese of Normandy, has never been successfully imitated by cheese-makers in any other part of the world because the fungoid that gives the cheese its distinctive bouquet exists only in that one small locality, in the cellars where the cheeses are cured.

After Liederkranz achieved world renown and larger factories were needed for its production, the cheese-making operation was removed from Monroe, New York, where it began, to Van Wert, Ohio. The producers purchased the best available, richest milk from nearby dairy farmers and carefully followed the same formula in making the cheese that they had used before, but the result was disastrous. The soft cheese produced in the new, spotlessly clean factory had no flavor at all. Experiment after experiment was tried, to no avail. Then one of the employees who had come to Van Wert from Monroe had a brilliant flash. Perhaps there was something about the room in the Monroe factory that had caused that important mold to form on the outside of the cheese. The bacteria-infested shelves from the old factory were brought to Van Wert, where they were carefully scraped and the moldy stuff from the wood was smeared on the clean walls of the new curing room. It made the difference! Once again the cheese developed its characteristic aroma.

Sometimes the soft cheeses, instead of being poured into molds, are placed on reeds or matting or are wrapped in vine leaves or even pine bark. Because cheese is so receptive to outside influences during its curing process, the flavors of such protective wrappings will be subtly absorbed and will add still other distinguishing characteristics to particular cheeses.

For semisoft cheeses, more of the whey is drained or pressed from the curd before curing, and both the curing and ripening periods are longer. These cheeses, too, will absorb flavors from their environments, and, if they are inoculated with special flavor-creating bacteria during the curing process, those bacteria will become part of the cheese.

To make cheeses in the semifirm-to-hard range, every bit of the whey must be pressed out by hand or mechanical presses. The curing period may last two months or longer (to make natural Gruyère, the curing period is generally three months); the ripening period that follows may range from eight months to a year. A good natural Cheddar is usually ripened for at least nine months.

Most semisoft and all semifirm or hard natural cheeses must develop firm protective outer rinds. In some cases — by no means all — the pressed, shaped wheels of cheese are dipped into warm-water baths or warm brine to cause the casein in the curd to harden slightly on the outside. After the cheese is removed from this bath, it often is rubbed all over with fat (lard, butter, or olive oil) or covered with wax or paraffin, as the case may be. In making an American Cheddar like Colorado Blackie or Coon cheese, black wax is applied to a cheesecloth covering to form a protective outer wrapping. This wax-hardened wrapping has become a symbol of the excellence of such splendid American cheeses, and the cheeses would not seem the same without it!

During the first few weeks that the semifirm-to-hard cheeses remain in curing cellars, they must be turned repeatedly, at first every day, then every few days. This turning is important in forming an evenly shaped, smooth outer rind. In certain cases the fermentation that occurs within the cheese during curing causes it to swell on top while remaining flat on the bottom. In other cases, the cheese must be turned so that air reaches all sides evenly. During this period, the outside of the cheese is often rubbed with salt, a process called "dry-salting." The salt, of course, also serves as a preservative.

The various cheese-manufacturing processes differ so enormously that it is impossible to describe or identify them all. I recall with mouth-watering pleasure a visit to a cheese factory in Denmark, where six different varieties of cheese were produced. Methods of treatment differed for each of the cheeses. In the room where cheeses still had to be turned regularly, I noted that plate-shaped wheels of Samsø, about twelve inches in diameter and three to four inches thick, were mottled in color, with distinct layers of ocher and pale, creamy white discernible from top to bottom. Yet in the next room, where the Samsø cheeses had been graduated from the curing to the ripening stage, the outer rinds of the cheeses had become firm and ocher-colored, whereas the interiors (as I was shown with a cut wedge) were of an even, creamy gold from top to bottom. When fully matured (Samsø is usually ripened for six months), the cheese is a rich, butter gold, with a few irregular small holes, firm enough to eat in wedges or slices, smooth and luscious to the tongue.

Some cheeses, instead of being dry-salted, are kept moist by immersion in a salt brine. Feta is kept in a salt brine indefinitely, even after it is fully cured. Other cheeses may be immersed in wine, cider, beer, or even whiskey while in the curing stage.

The term "curing cellars" is still used in modern terminology, though today such "cellars" are not necessarily below ground at all; they are well-insulated rooms where the temperature and humidity can be controlled at will. In the days before mechanical controls were invented, caves and cellars dug deep in the earth were the best storage spots because of the thick insulation provided by nature, as anyone who has entered a cave on a blistering-hot day can attest.

Today, some cheeses are deliberately moved from rooms with one temperature to rooms with lower (or higher) temperatures during the curing process, to bring about certain desired results.

## PUTTING THE HOLES IN SWISS CHEESE

Why do some cheeses have holes and others not?

The holes are caused by the fermentation that occurs in the curd when a firmly pressed cheese is being cured. It was explained earlier that heat is sometimes used to encourage the separating of the curd from the whey — and sometimes not. Many textbooks on cheese technology use the term "cooked curd" to describe cheeses that have had heat applied in this way, but this term is misleading, for the degree of heat is so low that the curd does not actually cook. The purpose of the heat is only to separate the whey from the curd more completely. This separated curd is then cut (for Swiss Cheese a "harp" is used to form very fine particles), drained in cheesecloth, and then pressed, today by mechanical presses, until the curd is firm and almost dry.

When the curd that has undergone such a process is stored in a warm curing cellar, gas begins to form, and the gas makes bubbles, and the bubbles create the holes. The more violent the fermentation, the larger the holes.

In ancient times, few cheeses had such holes. No one knows for a certainty, but it is believed that the first Swiss cheeses with holes began to appear during the Middle Ages at a time when cheese-makers were trying to figure out ways to make bigger and bigger wheels of cheese.

Then as now, the cost of maintaining highways was borne

by tolls collected at gates all along the way, and a cheese merchant carrying his wares from farm to city might have to pay as many as twenty tolls before he reached the market place. The tolls for cheese were levied according to the number of cheeses in a cart, rather than according to weight, so that the larger a cheese, the less toll a cheese merchant would have to pay in proportion. The Swiss, who had been making cheese for 2,000 years, were especially cunning about turning out big cheeses, and, even in those days, some of their wheels weighed from 100 to 200 pounds each. And when these huge cheeses were stored for curing in certain deep, warm, well-protected mountain caves, big holes began to pop up here and there in the interiors. Because the Swiss cheese was excellent, the holes became its characteristic mark, and customers began to demand the big-holed cheese.

Today some people think the sizes of the holes in what we call "Swiss Cheese" (and the French and English call "Gruyère" and the Swiss themselves call "Emmentaler") has a direct relation to quality. That is not true. In fact, the Swiss Cheese most prized by a connoisseur may be one that has virtually no holes at all but only small cracks here and there. In England, cheese customers prefer both Emmentaler and natural Gruyère with smaller holes, and, before they leave Switzerland, smaller-holed cheeses are selected for the English market, whereas those cheeses marked for export to the United States are selected from among the cheeses with much bigger holes.

To make a single 200-pound Emmentaler cheese requires about 1,200 quarts of partly skimmed milk from cows pastured in both valley and Alpine meadows, a blend of evening milk with fresh morning milk. The warmed, drained curd is pressed into huge round molds until solidified, then passed in procession from a cool cellar to a salting cellar to a prewarming cellar to, finally, a "fermentation" cellar warm enough to cause the gas bubbles to begin popping. This curing requires six to ten weeks, with the huge wheels turned and salted several times a week. After curing, the cheese is ripened for three months, sometimes longer.

Natural Gruyère is smaller than Emmentaler, averaging about seventy-five pounds per wheel. It is higher in butterfat, is made mostly from the milk of Alpine cows, and has much smaller holes. Both the curing and the ripening of Gruyère take longer; sometimes the wheels are ripened for a full year before being placed on the market. (This natural Gruyère must not be confused with the small foil-wrapped wedges of process Gruyère found in most supermarkets. The latter are a blend of shredded natural Gruyère and Switzerland Swiss, or Emmentaler, which are cooked together at high temperatures, then pressed into wedges and foil-wrapped. They have nothing like the same texture and flavor as the original cheese.) France also makes several natural cheeses bearing the name "Gruyère," including a delicious Crème de Gruyère, a semisoft cheese. The French versions are very good and are properly ripened, but they are imitations of the Swiss original.

The best of the American Swiss cheeses are made in the State of Wisconsin, which is today the largest cheese-producing state in the nation. A colony of settlers from the Canton of Glarus in Switzerland first came to Wisconsin in the 1840s, and, in the town that they called "New Glarus," they set about making cheese just as they had made it in the old country. In 1850, Adam Blumer of New Glarus suggested that the Swiss dairymen pool their milk to start a cheese factory, and within another decade the Swiss cheeses of New Glarus and of nearby Monroe had become famous. To this day, the old Swiss traditions are cherished in the region, and, at cheese festivals, girls and young men in traditional Swiss costumes perform to Old World dances and yodel in good Alpine fashion.

Unfortunately, there are many cheeses called "Swiss" on the American market that have been produced in factories whose owners care more about profits than quality. Chemical additives are sometimes used to hasten "aging" and to cause more active fermentation, in order to produce larger holes. When sliced and prepackaged, even an excellent cheese looses much of its original flavor and aroma, and, when the cheese is inferior to begin with, the final product is pretty sorry. The holes in such cheese might as well have been put in by BB guns for all they mean.

## PASTEURIZED PROCESS CHEESE: WHAT IT IS AND IS NOT

When a firm, ripened, natural cheese can be kept in an edible state for two or more years, it's hard to understand why men should have labored so hard to produce the bland, rubbery process cheeses that now take up so much space at supermarket dairy counters. But as far back as 1895 efforts were being made in both Germany and Switzerland to put up cheese in cans. By 1911, the first process cheese was developed commercially in Switzerland. The next year, 1912, a cheese peddler out of Chicago named James L. Kraft was experimenting with a process he called "pasteurizing" cheese. Kraft's first efforts were far from successful, but he kept on trying, and in 1917, when the United States entered World War I on the side of the Allies, Kraft was able to sell the army tons of a bland, soft, canned cheese for the use of the "doughboys" on the Western Front. In 1920, Kraft introduced the first rindless process cheese on the market, a five-pound loaf, which was advertised nationally with all the hullabaloo of a Hollywood premiere. Five years later, he had succeeded in making smaller packages of his "pasteurized" cheese.

Process cheese is made by grinding together in fine particles two or more kinds of cheese, then heating and stirring the mixture into a bubbling homogeneous, plastic mass. As many as 400 pounds of cheese may be stirred in a single, giant steam-jacketed kettle in which the cheese is heated to a temperature of at least 150°F., then held at this temperature for from thirty seconds to five minutes. The cheese then is cooled to room temperature and poured into cartons or plastic containers, which are hermetically sealed.

The cheese is almost sterile, it will keep for very long periods of time, and its bland, innocuous flavor makes it acceptable to those multitudes with uncritical tastes, including children. Nutritionally it has been a boon to mothers who must slap together lunch-box sandwiches day after day and to cooks in institutional kitchens who must prepare gallon-sized casseroles of macaroni and cheese. The unfortunate thing is that millions of people do not know the difference between these rubbery substitutes and fine natural cheese, and successive generations grow up without learning to appreciate the strange, wonderful world of flavors a taste for good cheese offers.

"Pasteurized process cheese food" was developed later, in the 1930s. It is a blend of natural cheese with such products as nonfat dry milk, whey solids, skim milk, whey albumin, and water. By law it has to contain no more than 51 per cent natural cheese by volume. Because it contains such a high proportion of liquid, it is softer and melts more easily. Frequently other

ingredients like pimientos, pineapple, bits of bacon, and caraway seeds are added, or a smoky flavor may be artifically in-
duced.

"Process cheese spreads" may be even higher in moisture content, some as high as 80 per cent (which means only 20 per cent
cheese). These spreads usually have had artificial stabilizers
(like vegetable gum) added to give them consistencies similar
to that of fresh cheese.

The term "pasteurized" connotes a superior product, which
this process substance is not. Natural cheeses may and often
are made from pasteurized milk, but "pasteurized cheese" is
always a blend of cheeses that have been heated to very high
temperatures, and the high temperatures in themselves rob the
finished products of flavor. Because these pasteurized cheeses
have been made almost sterile with high temperatures, they
cannot ripen further. This sterility of course prevents or at
least delays spoilage, but it's the ripening of natural cheese
that produces the wonderful mellowness.

## CHEESE AND HISTORY

Cheese was a subject of fascination to Roman gourmets in
the days of the great Caesars, and over the roads of the Roman
Empire many a wagon carried wheels of cheese to be sold in
the Imperial City.

Pliny the Elder, the Roman historian, in his ten-volume *Natural History*, wrote of a *caseus helveticus*, a Swiss cheese that
was in great demand in Rome. He described the cheese as hard
enough to grate into powder, and cheese experts believe it was
the original of what is now called "Sbrinz;" or it could have
been the forerunner of Saanen, the cheese said sometimes to
have remained edible for 100 years.

(The big-holed cheese we call "Swiss" was not known to the
Romans, however. The earliest written mention of Gruyère
cheese is from the year 1115, when the aging Count of Gruyère
decided to build an abbey to demonstrate his pious devotion to
the God he soon expected to meet in heaven. To pay for his
monastery, he placed a tax on every wheel of cheese produced
in his domain, and the famed Abbey of Rougemont was built
with the profits on Gruyère cheese. Emmentaler cheese was first
called by that name in the sixteenth century, after the Valley
of Emmental, where it was and still is produced.)

The Romans also imported cheeses from France, England, and the Dalmatian coast. Besides the sheep cheese of Nîmes mentioned by Pliny, a cheese of Toulouse was highly rated by Roman gastronomes, including the Emperor Augustus, who liked it on black bread, accompanied by figs and fried little fishes. Cantal cheese from the Haute-Auvergne was another French cheese singled out for mention by Pliny — and this golden, savory cheese is still produced today in France much as it was 2,000 years ago.

When the Romans reached England, they were so impressed by the excellence of Cheshire cheese (which was already famous among the Angles of that little isle) that they built a wall around the city of Chester to protect the cheese-making industry.

Very likely, sheep cheeses from the biblical lands also were served at Roman tables, for many a reference to cheese appears in the Bible, and wasn't it shepherds watching over their flocks who first saw the Star? Semiramis, queen to Ninus, the legendary founder of Nineveh, was said to have been nurtured on cheese brought to her by birds when she was a child, and Pliny reports that the prophet Zoroaster lived on a single cheese in the wilderness for twenty years. It must have been a cheese of the same mammoth size as those that David took to the armies of Saul, for David carried only ten cheeses to feed 1,000 men.

The Greeks of the Golden Age made much of cheesecake, with each city-state boasting its own special recipe for this delicacy, and to this day at least a dozen kinds of tiropeta (which literally translates as "cheese cake" or "cheese pastry") are made in Greece, some fried, some baked, some molded and chilled without any cooking whatever. Cheese was also one of the foods for athletes competing in the original Olympic games.

With the rise of Christianity in Western Europe, some of the finest cheeses were produced by the monks in abbeys, and the many French cheeses named for saints attest to the devout faith of the friars who, when they succeeded in producing especially fine cheeses, recognized that much of their success was due to Divine Providence. A cheese produced at the Abbey of Maroilles at Thiérache in northeast France so delighted France's Charles V that he put in a standing order for it. In the twelfth century, the Abbot of Maroilles decreed that the peasants in the surrounding villages should demonstrate their faith by making cheese of all the milk from their cows on June 24th, the day of Saint Jean, and delivering the cured cheeses to their parish priests on Saint Remigius day (October 1st) for transfer to the abbey. Maroilles, a small odoriferous square cheese with a brick-red rind and a soft brown interior, is still the traditional cheese served on Saint Remigius' day in the vineyard country of Champagne.

Best known of the monastery cheeses in the world today are those produced by the Trappist monks. At the time of the French Revolution the Trappists left France, returning from their exile in 1815. They named the inlet where they landed on the Normandy coast "Le Port du Salut," "Port of Salvation," and, when they restored a medieval priory as their abbey, they gave the same name to the cheese they started to make. It was so successful that before long they had opened up more caves within the monastery grounds in which to ripen the cheeses, and, by 1873, Port du Salut, or Port-Salut, cheese was renowned throughout Europe. Today, Trappist orders in many parts of the world make Port du Salut or cheese that is similar in consistency and flavor.

Two other cheeses of Normandy renowned since medieval times are Livarot and Camembert, both soft, aromatic cheeses that are exquisitely delicate at the peak of ripeness (though both can be startlingly and unpleasantly ammonial when they have passed this peak). Camembert was brought to the world's attention by Napoleon. Passing through the region one day at lunchtime, the Little Corsican was served a portion of the cheese and found it so luscious that he jumped up to kiss the cheeks of the waitress who had served it to him.

Despite the fact that Camembert was mentioned in chronicles as early as the twelfth century, it was not until it became world-renowned that a certain Madame Harel asserted that it was her family that had "invented" the cheese, and she was so convincing in her claim that the villagers of Vimoutiers, near which her family's farm lay, erected a statue in her honor. (In fairness to Madame Harel, the Camembert we know today may well have been perfected on her farm, for through the ages, cheese-making has undergone continual changes, the milk of cows has become richer, and techniques have been mastered to bring about more reliable results.)

Across the Channel in England, most cheeses were made on individual farms, though frequently neighbors would "join their milk together" to produce larger cheeses. In fact, it was in many places the custom when a child was born to get out a large "cartwheel" of cheese, cutting out small portions from the center every day until, on the day the child was ready to be christened, the infant could be passed through the center of the cheese for good luck.

Cheshire was the most renowned and the most popular of English cheeses from antiquity on and, as recently as 1954, accounted for more than 49 per cent of all natural cheeses produced in England. Twelfth-century English writers praised the glories of the cheese of Cheshire. During the war between England and Scotland in the 1640s, 300 tons of Cheshire cheese were purchased in a single year for the rations of Cromwell's soldiers fighting in Scotland — a far more generous allotment of cheese than David carried to Saul's fighting men. The most famous of pubs in English history was called "The Olde Cheshire Cheese," a rendezvous for immortal literary figures from Ben Jonson, Shakespeare's contemporary, to Charles Dickens.

Cheshire is a firm, flaky cheese made from whole milk, some of it so pale as to be almost white, some "red" — that is, bright orange-yellow — and some blue, or rather streaked with blue-green veining from spores of *Penicillium glaucum*. The blue Cheshire just happens; it is never deliberately inoculated and so is rare and very special.

Cheddar, the best-known cheese name in all the English-speaking world, is called after a small village in Somerset where cheese is no longer made at all. It gained its fame in the seventeenth century when, thanks to the pooling of milk from individual farmers whose cows pastured on the warm, fertile soil south of the Mendip Hills in Somersetshire, huge cheeses, weighing from twenty to 120 pounds were produced; they were aged from two to five years until the cheese was flaky, sharp, and mellow, as only a fully mature firm cheese can be.

In 1742 Mrs. E. Smith, in her immortal English cookbook, *The Compleat Housewife*, gave this recipe for making Cheddar cheese in one's home:

Take the new milk of twelve cows in the morning, and the evening cream of twelve cows, and put to it three spoonfuls of runnet; and when it is come, break it, and whey it; and when it is well whey'd, break it again, and work into the curd three pounds of fresh butter, and put it in your press, and turn it in the press very often for an hour or more, and change the cloths, and wash them every time you change them; you may put wet cloths at first to them, but towards the last put two or three fine cloths to them; let it lie thirty or forty hours in the press, according to the thickness of the cheese; then take it out, wash it in whey, and lay it in a dry cloth till it is dry; then lay it on your shelf, and turn it often.

A Cheddar weighing 1,100 pounds — a striking thing to behold — was produced as a bridal gift for Queen Victoria. It was made from the milk of 780 cows. Victoria herself never had so much as a wedge of it: the farmers who made it were so proud of their creation that they wanted it put on exhibition, and afterward the Queen permitted them to keep it. The farmers quarreled as to who should have it, the ownership controversy ended in the courts, and the cheese's final disposition remains a mystery.

(Large as Victoria's bridal Cheddar was, it was a dwarf by comparison with a Wisconsin Cheddar produced especially for the 1964-65 New York World's Fair. Weighing over seventeen tons — 34,951 pounds to be exact — the cheese was 6¹/₂ feet wide, 5¹/₂ feet high, and 14¹/₂ feet long. A crew of twenty men worked in round-the-clock shifts for 43 hours to produce it, using 367,000 pounds of milk. Altogether, this represented the daily milk production of 16,000 cows. The cheese was so huge that a special trailer truck with glass sides, appropriately called a "Cheesemobile," was built to transport it to the Fair. Though free samples were handed out to Fair visitors, there was still enough of the cheese left at the conclusion of the Fair to bring it back to Wisconsin, where it was cut into thousands of two-pound souvenirs "for consumers all over the world to enjoy.")

In 1860, a cattle disease that struck England and Wales caused such a shortage of milk, the English started importing Cheddar cheese from American factories, and even today a very large portion of the Cheddar consumed in England is American-made.

The idea of making cheese in factories had originated in the United States a decade earlier, in 1850, when a Rome, New York, dairy farmer named Jesse Williams urged other dairy farmers to sell their excess milk to him instead of each one making his own cheese. The Erie Canal was in full operation, and wheels of Cheddar from Williams' factory were piled on barges, which carried the cheese to country stores from one end of the state to the other. "Store cheese" and "rat cheese" became the common names for this American factory-made Cheddar, but, derisive as the names may have been in the beginning, the cheese was good, and within fifteen years more than 500 other cheese factories were in operation in the State of New York alone. Today, when most of the cheese purchased in supermarkets is of the bland and rubbery "pasteurized" variety, those who remember the "rat cheese" sold over grocery counters thirty and forty years ago speak of it with nostalgic fondness. People liked it as much as did the little mice who met their deaths in cheese-filled traps, drawn inexorably by its potent fragrance.

Nearly all the cheeses that have originated in the United States have been Cheddar types — with the exceptions of Liederkranz and Poona, a cheese made in New York State that has been compared to the French Pont-l'Evêque.

The original Pineapple Cheese was created in Litchfield, Connecticut, in 1808 by a dairy farmer named Lewis Norton. He hung his cheese curd in a net that created diamond-shaped corrugations on the surface as the cheese drained to firmness. To add to the illusion of a pineapple shape, he served the firm cheese dramatically on a silver platter, with a silver top fashioned to look like pineapple leaves, which could be replaced on the cheese between servings. This cheese might be said to be one of the early manifestations of typical American merchandising, for Pineapple Cheese became an elegant thing to serve in nineteenth-century homes.

As in the production of domestic wines, American cheesemakers tended to copy European types instead of inventing their own cheeses. It is now possible to purchase domestic imitations of such foreign cheeses as Telemi, a soft Rumanian sheep cheese, Italian Fontina, German Kümmelkäse, English Stilton, Norwegian Nøkkelost, or Swedish caraway-seed Bondost, to say nothing of Limburger, Gouda, Brie, and Gorgonzola. Some of these copies compare favorably with the originals; others are sorry substitutes. Although this vast array of cheese varieties is impressive and copying cheese types from other countries is not by any means restricted to American producers, it seems a shame that, with all this inventiveness, Americans have not come up with more truly original cheeses — or at least have not given new names to those cheeses that, like Liederkranz, began as imitations but in reality have their own individual goodness.

Among those cheeses that can claim the distinction of being uniquely American is Brick, a firm, rectangular cheese halfway between mild and sharp in flavor, with an aroma that announces itself as soon as the wrapping is opened and with tiny holes or eyes throughout its jonquil-yellow interior. Brick cheese was invented in the mid-nineteenth century by a dairyman of Dodge County, Wisconsin, who drained the cooked curd of his cheese in a brick-shaped mold with mason's bricks pressed on the top to force out the whey. A natural Brick cheese is heavily salted and cured for at least two months, and it is a fine sandwich item, for it slices easily and will melt to a golden lava when grilled between bread.

Monterey Jack, a product of Monterey County, California, is much softer and more delicate than Cheddar when young, but the older variety is quite firm, sometimes even hard, and, like all firm cheeses as they age, much sharper than its younger brother in flavor.

Other renowned American Cheddars, named usually for the states or counties where they have originated, include Colby and Cooper (both from Vermont); Herkimer County from the county of that name in New York State; Coon, another superb New York State cheese; Colorado Blackie; Wisconsin or Texas Longhorn; and Tillamook (made in Oregon). Although all these cheeses are classified as Cheddars, they differ greatly in flavor, color, and texture. Coon cheese, for example, is so pale as to be almost white and has a tantalizingly sharp aftertaste. Tillamook, especially when salt-free (in demand by those on special diets), has a uniquely aromatic flavor, like a shy relative of Limburger.

American Münster (or Muenster) cheese is also unique, for although it began life as an imitation of a cheese made in Alsace-Lorraine, the cheese by this name that is now a standard item in American markets bears no relation whatever to the European Münster. The latter is a pungent, "smelly" cheese, soft in texture, whereas a fine American Münster is always semisoft and mild in flavor, with a delicious buttery texture.

A new cheese called Le Roi, a natural cheese with Cheddar-like flavor but semisoft in consistency, was brought out within recent years by the Purity Cheese Company in Mayville, Wisconsin. The same company produces a large number of natural firm and semisoft cheeses in "baby" sizes, an innovation that was born during the Depression years when the factory owner, Kenneth Royer, reasoned that more people would buy his fine-quality cheeses if they were available in small sizes. Among more than 100 natural cheese varieties now produced by the company are a superb Stilton (which, if not quite the same as an English Stilton, is nevertheless an exceptionally creamy, piquant "blue"), a "smoky Edam," several low-calorie cheeses, and a delicate dessert cheese called Shepherd Girl. Recently the company was given sole right to produce Bel Paese cheese in the United States, following the exacting specifications of the parent Bel Paese company in Italy.

## CHEESE AROUND THE WORLD

Almost every country of the world has its own local cheeses — the only exceptions are those Asian and African nations whose domesticated livestock herds are so small that they leave little or no milk for cheese-making. Sometimes on my travels I have tasted cheeses so exquisite that I have eagerly asked the names — only to learn that they have no particular names and are simply local cheeses that vary in flavor and consistency according to the farmer or the time of the year. Only those cheeses are placed in the world market that can be produced in sufficient quantity in factories to fill recurring orders from brokers and that pass the rigid standards of inspection maintained by customs officials to prevent transmission of disease.

Even so, Phil Alpert, in his Cheeses of All Nations shop in New York City, carries close to 1,000 varieties of cheese from thirty-nine different nations — and his is only one of dozens of stores that have sprung up like mushrooms in cities in all parts of the United States and that sell nothing but cheese (and cheese accessories).

Mr. Alpert opened his cheese shop in New York in 1925, an era when the country was in the throes of Prohibition and as isolationist in its attitude toward food as in its politics. Yet so successful was this little shop with its exotic cheeses that his business thrived and expanded until today he has five different stores, plus agencies in eight other countries. Most of his business is by mail order, with customers writing for cheese from as far away as Hawaii and Alaska and even from certain foreign countries. He sells an average of some seven tons of cheese a week and promotes a Cheese of the Month Club that has more than 10,000 members. His catalogue, or "encyclopedia" as he chooses to call it, goes out to a mailing list of a quarter of a million customers. He carries more than 350 varieties of cheese from

France alone; among the more esoteric items in his catalogue are a Tuareg cheese made by Berber tribesmen in Africa; Ajocilo, a Corsican cheese from the village that was Napoleon's birthplace; Turunmaa, a Finnish cheese somewhat like Tilsiter; Jalapeño, a creamy white pungent cheese from Mexico; and a cheese made by the Hopi Indians in our own American Southwest.

Recently Mr Alpert opened a five-story Cheese and Wine Restaurant in New York City, with curing cellars deep underground. Two floors are given over to the restaurant, which lists nothing but cheese dishes and their accompaniements on the menu, and two other floors are set aside for cheese tastings and the banquet rooms which are at the disposal of cheese-lovers. In addition to his Cheese of the Month Club, Mr. Alpert has organized an International Cheese Club of America whose members may attend monthly cheese tastings at his new restaurant.

The very first cheese shop in New York City opened back in 1860 when a retired naval officer named F. W. Hearn set up a cheese business adjacent to the Fulton Fish Market. Nine years later he was joined by his son Cornelius and today the grandsons and great-grandsons of Captain Hearn are carrying on the same business, with Cornelius Hearn III now presiding over Cheese Shops International, which has branches in 38 American cities.

The first person to try selling cheese by mail order in the United States was a bright young college student in Monroe, Wisconsin, who, in 1926, sent out fliers praising the virtues of the high-quality cheese produced by Green County dairy farmers. A decade later, the Green County cheese mail-order business started offering customers in all parts of the nation assortments of cheeses attractively packaged for gift-giving. By the 1950s Green County cheeses were being sent to half a million customers, with as many as 25,000 gift assortments mailed out every Christmas.

Gift cheeses are now big business on an international scale. In fact, through the many mail-order services now available, plus the cheese stores and delicatessen shops and the gourmet counter in almost every large department store, cheese in all its glory has become available to the most isolated customers. Today, even on a desert island, it would probably be possible to obtain cheese — as long as the island had regular mail service — which would have been regarded as a pure miracle by poor Ben Gunn of Robert Louis Stevenson's *Treasure Island*. For it was Ben Gunn's wistful comment when young Jim Hawkins asked what his life had been like during ten years alone on the deserted isle, "Many a night I've dreamed of cheese — toasted mostly."

# A glossary

## OF THE
## WORLD'S
## CHEESES

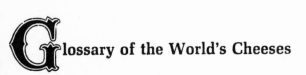

# Glossary of the World's Cheeses

   To list all the varieties of cheese in the world is impossible. Undoubtedly the names of many fine cheeses are missing from the following list, not by intention, but because it is virtually impossible to know of them all. Only natural cheeses have been listed. No attempt has been made to identify or describe the hundreds of kinds of process cheese or cheese food, for such a list would run to encyclopedic length.

   This list will, however, be of help in identifying strange cheeses and should be consulted for clarification when buying cheeses and also when using the recipes and menus that appear on later pages.

ABERDEEN CROWDIE — a fresh, unripened cheese similar to

cottage cheese, made in England and Scotland. It sometimes contains caraway seeds.

ALENTEJO — cheeses produced in a region of this name in Portugal, usually of sheep's and goat's milk blended, sometimes of a mixture of sheep's, goat's, and cow's milk. It is curdled with rennet extracted from a thistle-like plant.

ALLGAÜER — one of several German cheeses produced in the fertile Allgau region just north of Switzerland.

ALTENBURGER — a mellow, semisoft goat's-milk cheese of Germany.

AMERICAN OR AMERICAN CHEDDAR — both the natural and the process Cheddar-type cheese that is factory-made in the United States, ranging from mild to sharp. About 80 per cent of all cheese consumed by Americans is classified as Cheddar.

ANGELOT — see Pont l'Evêque

APPENZELLER — a Swiss cheese made since the days of Charlemagne; the pressed cheese is marinated in cider or white wine before aging. It is moister and creamier than Emmentaler, and much more robust in flavor than Gruyère, with a taste all its own. It is made in plate-shaped fifteen-pound wheels (twelve inches in diameter).

APPETITOST — a Danish cheese made from buttermilk; semisoft, with a nut-like flavor. It sometimes contains caraway.

ARDENNES HERVÉ — a velvet-smooth Belgian dessert cheese.

ASADERO — a white, braided cheese of Mexico, also called "Oaxaco," which melts easily; the name *asadero* means "fit for baking."

ASIAGO — an Italian cheese, the color of cream and sharp-flavored. It is a firm sandwich cheese when young and can be used for grating when older and hard.

AUVERGNE — a blue-veined cow's-milk cheese of France, sometimes called "Bleu d'Auvergne."

AZEITÃO — a very rich, "fat," soft Portuguese cheese made of sheep's milk.


BACKSTEINER — a square or brick-shaped Bavarian cheese, almost as pungent as Limburger but firmer in texture.

BAGNES (or Gomser) — see Raclette.

BANBURY — an English soft cheese.

BANON — a French firm sheep cheese made in foothills of the

46

Alps in summer, sprinkled with brandy, and wrapped in fresh grape leaves.

BARBACENA — a firm white cheese of Brazil.

BARBEREY (or Barberry) — a French cheese similar to Camembert but more pungent. It is sometimes called "Fromage de Troyes."

BATH CHEESE — a delicate-flavored, ripened, soft cream cheese made in the City of Bath, England.

BATTELMATT — a Swiss cheese something like Tilsiter in flavor. It has the same kind of holes as does Emmentaler but is smaller (forty to eighty pounds) and softer.

BAYRISCHER BIERKÄSE — a Bavarian cheese that is usually dunked in beer before eating.

BEAUFORT — a French cheese made in the High Alps. It is round and flat, similar to Gruyère, and is sometimes called "Gruyère de Beaufort."

BEAUGES — a French cheese of the Tomme family (see Tomme).

BEAUMONT — a semisoft French cheese of the same type as Brie and Port du Salut.

BEL LAGO — a semisoft cheese from Switzerland with a delicate but distinctive flavor.

BELLELAY — a cheese made in Switzerland, which is semisoft, buttery, and similar to Gruyère in flavor. Cheeses are wrapped in bark, ripened for a year in moist cellars, and will keep fresh three or four years, becoming more pungent with age. Bellelay was made originally in the Abbey of Bellelay in the Canton of Bern but is now made throughout the Swiss Jura. Sometimes called "Tête de Moine."

BEL PAESE — one of the most popular and best known of Italian cheeses. Creamy-soft and mild in flavor, it is essentially a dessert cheese but may also be used in cooking, in any recipe calling for Mozzarella. A very good American version of Bel Paese is made in Wisconsin.

BERGQUARA — a Swedish cheese something like Gouda that is molded in cylinders. It has been made in Sweden since the eighteenth century.

BERLINER KUHKÄSE — a German soft hand cheese, caraway-seeded.

BERTOLLI — a firm, pale-yellow sheep cheese of Italy, delightfully piquant in flavor.

BIERKÄSE — German cheeses similar to Limburger, semisoft, pungent, smelly. They are often dissolved in beer.

BIFROST — a Norwegian white goat cheese, both natural and process.

BITTO — a hard cheese made in Switzerland and northern Italy and similar to Fontina. It is semifirm and bland, with big eyes when young; the eyes get smaller and the cheese harder and sharper after two years of ripening.

BLEU — any of the French blue- or green-veined cow's-milk cheeses, which are crumbly and sharp.

BLEU D'AUVERGNE — a cow's-milk cheese, ripened in caves. It is a hard cheese.

BLUE — American or English blue-veined cow's-milk cheeses inoculated with *Penicillium roqueforti.*

BLUE DORSET OR BLUE VINNEY — an English aged cheese, chalk-white, with a streak of bright blue running horizontally across the center. It is inoculated with a special mold and is made from partly skimmed cow's milk.

BOLA — a ball-shaped cow's-milk cheese of Portugal, semifirm, crumbly, and yellow.

BONBEL — a semisoft, pale-yellow, bland French cheese. It resembles American Münster in flavor and is excellent with sherry.

BONDANE — a French skimmed- or whole-milk cheese of the Tomme family.

BONDOST (or Bundost) — a Swedish firm cheese, mellow, often flavored with cumin or caraway. A Bondost is also made in Wisconsin.

BOURSIN — a French *triple-crème* cheese, soft, fresh, deliciously delicate.

BRA — a firm Italian cheese made in the Piedmont; the name is also given to a soft, creamy cheese cured in brine.

BRANDKÄSE — a German sour-milk cheese; curd is mixed with butter before being pressed into small bricks, then is ripened in old beer kegs and moistened occasionally with beer.

BRESSE BLEU — a French blue cheese made in the district of Bresse.

BRICK — an American pale-golden, firm cheese, which is named for the brick-shaped molds into which it is pressed; it is also weighted with bricks as it ripens. Its flavor is more pungent than that of Cheddar, but not so strong as that of Limburger; it is semisoft and slices easily. Brick is made mostly in Wisconsin.

BRICOTTA — a Corsican sheep cheese, semisoft and salty; it

is often blended with sugar and rum and formed into small cakes as a dessert.

BRIE — one of the world's great cheeses, often called the "cheese of kings" because so many French monarchs have rated it their favorite. At its best, it is creamy-soft, almost runny, with a smooth yet distinctive flavor and a white, soft crust. It is widely imitated, but true Brie is made only in France.

BRILLAT-SAVARIN — a delightful, delicate, white dessert cheese named after the famed French gourmand.

BRINDZA — a sheep or goat cheese, cousin to the Greek Feta, made throughout the Balkans and Hungary. Some is stored in brine (like Feta), and some is pressed between layers of pine bark, which gives the cheese a resinous flavor. It is used in making the Rumanian dish *mamaliga*.

BROCCIO — a Corsican sheep or goat cheese similar to Bricotta.

CABECOU — see Chabichou.

CABREIRO — a cheese from the Castelo Branco district of Portugal made of mixed ewe and goat cheese in plate shapes. When fresh and young, it is delicate in flavor but becomes very sharp and pungent when aged.

CABRINNETI — a delicate, soft dessert cheese produced in Denmark.

CABRION — a goat's-milk cheese made in the Burgundy district of France, soaked in *eau de vie*, and ripened between layers of grape skins.

CACHAT — a cheese of Provence (France) made with sheep's or goat's milk, soft, creamy, but with an "assertive" flavor. It is sometimes blended with brandy or wine.

CACIOCAVALLO — a cheese made in Italy and throughout the Balkans. Its antecedent was probably a cheese made of mare's milk; a horse's head is still the symbol. A firm, buttery cheese with a light brown exterior and a smoky flavor, it is of the same general type as Provolone. It should be sliced or cubed when young and grated when it is aged and hard. It comes in unusual shapes and may be made of cow's, sheep's or goat's milk or of a mixture. Sometimes it is drawn out in long, thick threads and braided. While ripening, it is rubbed with olive oil and butter and hung from rafters. Despite its smoky flavor, Caciocavallo is rarely smoked.

CAERPHILLY — a creamy-white Welsh or English cheese, mild,

delicate, semisoft to semifirm, and excellent served with, or as a stuffing for, celery. It is said to be Richard Burton's favorite cheese.

CAMEMBERT — one of the world's most renowned cheeses, it has been made in region of Caen, France, since the twelfth century, though Napoleon first brought it world-wide fame and is sometimes credited with having "discovered" it. Cheeses called "Camembert" are made in many countries, including the United States, and although many of them are fine cheeses, they are not the same as the French original. German Camembert, for example, is frequently mixed with pepper, paprika, and caraway to be spread on pumpernickel as a snack or to be eaten with beer. American Camembert more closely resembles the French cheese called "Carré de l'Est." The French Camembert is essentially a dessert cheese and should be soft and delicate in flavor; if shrunken or smelling of ammonia, it is past its prime.

CANESTRATO — a popular Sicilian cheese made of ewe's milk, ripened, then aged. It is bright yellow in color, with a pungent flavor.

CANTAL — a French cheese that has been made for more than 2,000 years and was already world-renowned in Pliny's time. Made in the Haute-Auvergne district of France from cow's milk, it is pressed into the shape of a drum and is rich, savory, semifirm, and golden in color. Its taste resembles no other. Useful both for cooking and for eating plain.

CARRÉ DE L'EST — a cheese sometimes described as a cross between Brie and Camembert, with a "gentle bouquet." Produced in the Champagne district of France, it is always sold in small boxes, the cheese itself wrapped in foil. The crust, too, may be eaten unless it is deep yellow or orange in color.

CASERA OR CASHERA — a salty, crumbly, white goat's-milk cheese made in Greece and Turkey, sharp and firm, and similar in flavor to Fontina. It is soft enough to spread when young, firm and zesty when aged.

CASHKAVALLO (or Caskcaval) — Balkan versions of the cheese known in Italy as "Caciocavallo."

CHABICHOU — a soft goat's-milk cheese of France, smooth and delicious; it comes in the shape of a small ball covered with a blue-green mold. It is excellent with Madeira.

CHANTELLE — a semisoft, ripened French cheese with a pale-golden interior. It is delicious with pears or fresh, ripe pineapple.

CHANTILLY — see Crème Chantilly. There is also an Italian cream cheese of this name, which is as soft as our cream cheese but is ripened and is sometimes flavored with chives.

CHEDDAR — from a Somerset (England) village, where cheese is no longer made at all, this name is used today to cover 80 per cent of all cheese made in the United States, both natural and pasteurized, as well as for spreads and "cheese foods" and for countless cheeses made in nations of the British Commonwealth as well.

CHESHIRE — one of the most famous of English cheeses, made in the City of Chester before the arrival of the first Roman legions. A hard-pressed, firm cheese, which comes in "red," white, and blue varieties.

CHEVRET (or Chevrotins) — a small goat's-milk cheese from the Auvergne and Savoie districts of France; they are chalky-white and delicate. (This name is sometimes spelled "Chevreton".)

CHRISTIAN IX — a caraway-seed Danish cheese, semifirm, which slices easily. Also called King Christian IX.

CLABBER CHEESE — the English name for what we call "pot cheese."

COEUR À LA CRÈME — a delicate, soft, fresh French dessert cheese pressed from curds of naturally soured whole milk and molded in heart-shaped wicker baskets. It is essentially the same as our cream cheese.

COIMBRA — a Portuguese semifirm, salty-sharp cheese (sometimes made from goat's milk) named for the university town where it is made.

COLBY — an American cheese, softer and more open-textured than Cheddar, produced in Vermont. It is white to medium yellow and is good both for cooking and for eating plain.

COLORADO BLACKIE — as the name implies, a natural cheese of Colorado origin, belonging to the Cheddar family. It comes with a black outer wrapping.

COMTÉ — a French cheese similar to Gruyère, ivory yellow, with holes the size of cherries. The rind is usually darker yellow. Repeatedly dressed with salt as it ages, it is usually of very great size and has legendary keeping qualities. It is high in butterfat content and is equally suitable for cooking and eating plain.

COON — a natural Cheddar-type cheese of New York State, well aged, very sharp, piquant, almost white in color, slightly crumbly. It has a characteristic black-cloth covering.

COOPER — a mild Cheddar made in Vermont.

CORNHUSKER — a Nebraska natural aged Cheddar-type cheese but softer than Cheddar.

COTTAGE CHEESE — the simplest form of cheese, made by draining curd of renneted fresh or naturally soured whole or skimmed milk. It is usually seasoned with salt and blended with cream, though some home-made cottage cheese is blended instead with melted butter. (Pot cheese is essentially the same thing but without added salt, cream, or butter.)

COTTENHAM — an English semifirm, double-cream cheese, sometimes veined with blue, that is creamier and richer than Stilton.

COULOMMIERS — a velvety-soft dessert cheese of France, similar to Brie but smaller and with a fresh, delicate flavor. When well ripened, it develops a stronger almond-like flavor. The crust is snowy white, the interior creamy.

CREAM CHEESE — a fresh cheese (American) made from pure cream and whole milk, well drained. It is highly perishable and is never ripened.

CREMA DANICA — a very smooth, soft, *triple-crème* dessert cheese of Denmark. It is superb with fresh black cherries and cognac as dessert.

CRÈME CHANTILLY — although this name is usually given to simple whipped cream in France, it also means a soft, delicate-flavored French dessert cheese.

CRÈME DE GRUYÈRE — a soft, ripened French cheese with the flavor of Gruyère but the consistency of Camembert. It is utterly delicious as a spread for crisp crackers or as a topping for fruit slices.

CREOLE — a soft unripened cheese made in Louisiana of equal parts Cottage cheese and cream.

CROISSANT DEMI-SEL — a French *double-crème* dessert cheese molded in a crescent shape and lightly salt-cured.

DAISY — a mild, firm Cheddar.

DANABLU (or Danish Blue) — the mold-inoculated blue cheese of Denmark, the sharpest of the blues; it is creamy white with a flaky texture.

DANBO — a variety of Danish Samsø, usually square in shape,

mild, smooth, semifiirm, and pale golden in color. It often contains caraway seeds.

DANISH BLUE — see Danablu.

DANISH CRÈME SPECIAL — a *triple-crème* dessert cheese, very delicate, soft, and delicious.

DAUPHIN — a Maroilles-type cheese of France, flavored with tarragon and powdered cloves and pressed in a mold the shape of a half-moon.

DEMI-SEL — a fresh cream cheese of France (Normandy), with 2 per cent salt added.

DEMI-SUISSE — an export version of French Petit-Suisse in individually wrapped portions.

DERBY — an English cheese, close-textured, firm, and of a pale-honey color; it is mild when young, more flaky than Cheddar, more solid than Cheshire. It is often added to salads. When flavored with sage, it has a pale greenish color.

DEVONSHIRE — a soft, unripened English cream cheese made from pure, thick Devonshire cream, drained on straw.

D'OKA — a cheese, similar to Port du Salut, formerly made by Trappist monks in Canada, no longer produced.

DORSET — see Blue Dorset.

DOUBLE-CRÈME — any soft, ripened cheese containing 60 per cent butterfat.

DOUBLE GLOUCESTER — an English firm cheese ripened at least six months, mellow but piquant, and a pale vermilion in color. "Double" indicates a higher butterfat content than that of regular Gloucester.

DUNLOP — a Scottish cheese, flaky, sharp, and firm; it is pale gold, almost white, in color and has a zesty flavor with a sharp aftertaste. It has a higher moisture content than does Cheddar and makes an excellent cocktail cheese.

EDAM — the Dutch "cannon ball" cheese, with a bright red outer rind and a firm, golden interior. It is intended mainly for cutting in wedges or slicing. Several American Edams are now available.

EDELPILZKÄSE — an Austrian blue-veined cheese, high in butterfat, soft when young but both firmer and crumblier when aged.

EDIRNE — a Turkish sheep's-milk cheese, semifirm, white, and very good with or in green salads.

ELBING OR ELBINGER — A German cheese, hard, crumbly, and sharp.

EMMENTALER — the world-renowned, big-holed Swiss cheese that we commonly call "Switzerland Swiss." It is made in wheels that may weigh 175 to 200 pounds and is widely imitated, especially in France, Germany, Denmark, and the United States.

EPOISSES — a cheese of the Burgundy district of France, usually soft but may be semifirm when aged. It is sometimes flavored with black pepper, cloves, or fennel seeds, then soaked in white wine.

ERBO — an Italian cheese sometimes compared to Gorgonzola.

ESROM — a semisoft Danish cheese, both sweet and buttery. The rind may be eaten along with the velvety interior.


FARMER CHEESE — the plain, fresh curd of whole or skimmed milk, finely sieved, sold in brick-shaped segments. In some parts of the United States, the name is given to a cured cheese of mild flavor, firm enough to slice.

FETA — a Greek cheese made of sheep's milk, white and flaky, kept moist by storing in brine. A semisoft cheese, it is excellent as an hors d'oeuvre, especially when accompanied by almond-shaped black Kalamata olives and glasses of Greek retsina wine.

FONDU (or Fondue) — the French word for "melted," used to describe a dish of melted cheese or one of many cheeses that can be melted down after pressing and ripening.

FONTINA — an Italian semisoft cheese that melts easily and has a delicate nutty flavor. It is sometimes made of goat's milk. It is very nice with an amontillado sherry or with mixed sweet and dry vermouth and is as useful in cooking as on the hors d'oeuvres table: It is excellent over polenta or atop casseroles. (There are also a Swiss Fontina and an American cheese of the same name.) When aged, it becomes semifirm with a slightly smoky taste.

FONTINELLA — of the same family as Fontina but firm enough to grate and with a sharper, zestier flavor. An excellent Fontinella is made in Wisconsin.

FORMAGGINI — local Italian cheeses, soft (sometimes fresh, sometimes ripened), and usually eaten dressed with olive oil. The name means literally "small cheeses."

FRIESIAN — a Netherlands cheese similar to Leyden but flavored with cloves or both cumin and cloves (see Leyden).

FROMAGE DE TROYES — see Barberey.

GAISKASLI — a soft, delicately flavored goat's milk cheese made in Germany and Switzerland.

GAMMELOST — a Norwegian flat cheese made with skimmed sour milk. It is brownish with blue-green veins and a crumbly texture. One must have grown up on this cheese to like it.

GARDA — an Italian soft dessert cheese; the crust can be eaten too.

GÉROMÉ — a semisoft, ripened cheese of France, made from whole milk, with a brick-red rind, similar to Alsatian Münster in flavor. Some varieties contain fennel, anise, or cumin seeds.

GERVAISE — a French *double-crème*, soft, ripened cheese, delicate, with a piquant flavor reminiscent of Camembert but blander. It is a variation of Petit-Suisse.

GJETOST (Pronounced "Yet-ost") — a Norwegian cheese made of the whey of goat's milk, brown in color and so sweet it seems more a confection than a cheese. It is usually sliced thin and served on dark Norwegian flat bread.

GLOUCESTER — an English cheese of firm, velvety texture and mild flavor, the best "red" cheese of England. Served usually in chunks with apple juice or cider. Gloucester is lower in butterfat content than is Double Gloucester.

GOMOST — a Norwegian cheese usually made from whole cow's milk but sometimes from goat's milk. It has a buttery consistency.

GORGONZOLA — the blue-veined Italian cheese, named for a village near Milan, the most delicately flavored of all the natural blues. When young it is semisoft, almost creamy, and utterly delightful. It becomes flakier and firmer with age. It is said to have been made in the Po Valley since A.D. 879. (An imitation of Gorgonzola is produced in Wisconsin.)

GOUDA — of Dutch origin, usually larger and richer in butterfat than is Edam. Holland Gouda has a golden rind but the same straw-yellow interior. Baby Gouda has a red rind. The shape is usually round but somewhat flattened on top and bottom; some Goudas are made in a loaf shape. This cheese is creamy when young, becomes firmer when aged. Some aged Goudas are collector's items, piquant and flaky. Gouda is imitated in other countries, including our own.

GOYA — an Argentine cheese, hard, pale gold in color, with a delicately nutty flavor; it is used mostly in grated form.

GRADDOST — a new Danish cheese, semifirm with irregular holes, mild, and sweet.

GRANA — a generic term for Italian cheeses suitable for grating. Parmesan is a *grana*.

GRIS DE LILLE — a variety of Maroilles.

GRUYÈRE — the world-renowned cheese produced in Switzerland. It has smaller holes, a higher butterfat content, and a somewhat softer texture than does Emmentaler. It melts easily, and its smooth, inimitable flavor makes it one of the best of all cheeses for the kitchen. The French also make several fine cheeses that they call "Gruyère" but that are nonetheless imitations of the original.

HABLE CRÈME CHANTILLY — a Swedish soft, ripened dessert cheese made from pasteurized cream; it is rich and delicious.

HAND CHEESE — German and also Pennsylvania Dutch skim-milk, semifirm cheeses, usually molded by hand (though now factory-made in several American states). They are sometimes flavored with caraway and have a pungent flavor.

HARZERKÄSE — a German semisoft, skim-milk cheese sometimes flavored with caraway seeds and quite as "smelly" as Limburger.

HAVARTI — a firm, mild Danish cheese, with both large and small holes, made for 100 years at Havarti, in Denmark's north Zealand.

HERKIMER — a natural Cheddar cheese from Herkimer County, New York, flaky, sharp, and pale yellow, with a dark, cloth rind.

HERRGÅRD — a Swedish yellow cheese, semifirm, halfway between Gouda and Emmentaler in flavor.

HERVÉ — a soft Belgian cheese flavored with tarragon, parsley, and chives; it is similar to Limburger.

HILLERÖD — a Danish firm cheese, at its prime after two or more years of aging. It is as mild as Emmentaler at first taste but with a sharp aftertaste more like that of aged Cheddar.

HOLSTEINER MAGERKÄSE — a cheese of north German origin, made from skim milk and buttermilk; it is semifirm and usually comes in twelve- to fourteen-pound sizes.

HOPFENKÄSE — a German cheese cured between layers of hops, often blended with caraway seeds, milk, or beer. Each cheese weighs about four ounces.

ICELANDIC BANQUET — a delicately flavored, firm cheese

made in Iceland; it melts easily and can be used much as Mozzarella is used for cooking. It also makes a fine cocktail snack.

ILHA — a Cheddar-like cheese made in the Azores.

INCANESTRATO — an Italian or Sicilian cheese whose curd is pressed in wicker baskets, leaving the wicker imprint on the cheese. If made only of ewe's milk, it is called "Pecorino Incanestrato"; it is often, however, made with a mixture of ewe's, goat's and cow's milk. When black pepper is added, it is called "Pepato Incanestrato." A related cheese called "Majocchino" has olive oil added to the curd.

JACK — see Monterey.

JALAPEÑO — a Mexican semisoft cheese that is white and creamy but almost as odoriferous as Limburger.

JARLSBERG — a Norwegian semisoft cheese with large, irregular holes; it is quickly cured by a new process so that, when it is cut, "tears" form in the eyes. It has a flavor something like that of Emmentaler but blander.

JOCKBERG — a Tyrolean mountain cheese made of mixed cow's and goat's milk.

KAISERKÄSE — a mellow, firm, bright-yellow German cheese.

KAJINAK — a cream cheese made from sheep's milk, soft and buttery, sometimes called "Serbian butter," and found throughout the Balkan countries and Turkey.

KASHKAVAL — the Greek or Rumanian version of Caciocavallo but usually made from sheep's or goat's milk. It is creamy when young but firm enough to grate when aged and has a slightly smoky flavor. Kashcavallo, Kachavelj, and Katschkawalj are other variations made in the Balkans and Near Eastern countries.

KEFALOTYRI — a hard, salty Greek cheese made from sheep's or goat's milk and used mostly for grating.

KING CHRISTIAN IX — see Christian IX.

KLÖSTERKÄSE — finger-sized German cheeses, formerly made by monks in German cloisters. They are of a Hartzerkäse type and are served as snacks with beer.

KOCHENKÄSE — a salt-free cheese made in Luxembourg, firm and bland. It is cooked-curd cheese.

KOMIJNIKAAS — a Dutch spiced cheese, containing both cumin and anise seeds.

KÖNIGSKÄSE — a German semisoft cheese similar to Bel Paese.

KOPANISTI — a Greek sheep's-milk cheese, often blue-veined, soft enough to spread but firmer than Feta.

KRÄUTERKÄSE — a Switzerland or German herb-flavored cheese made of skimmed milk. It is similar to Schabzieger or Sapsago.

KUMINOST — a Norwegian cumin-flavored cheese. Kumminost is the Swedish version.

KÜMMELKÄSE — a German cheese flavored with Kümmel and caraway; makes a good snack with beer. A cheese by this name is also made in Wisconsin.


LABNEH — a Syrian sour-milk cheese.

LANCASHIRE — a mild English cheese soft enough to spread like butter when young but firm and crumbly when aged. In grated form, it is used to top the famed Lancashire hot pot and is considered excellent for "toasting."

LE ROI — a new semisoft cheese produced in Wisconsin, piquant flavor, bright yellow color.

LEICESTER — an English firm, flaky cheese, almost russet in color because of the addition of annatto; it tastes something like Cheddar but has a more robust (rather than sharp) flavor.

LEYDEN — a Dutch spiced cheese, with a hard outer crust and a semifirm interior of pale yellow streaked with green (from the cumin seeds added to the curds).

LIEDERKRANZ — one of the most world-renowned of American cheeses, created by Emil Frey, a New York delicatessen man, while trying to produce an imitation of German Schlosskäse Bismark. It is now made in Ohio.

LIMBURGER — of Belgian origin and now made in many countries, including Germany. An excellent Limburger is also made in Wisconsin. This rank-smelling, runny cheese has become a symbol of daring and sophistication. It tastes best with beer.

LIPTAUER — a white, crumbly sheep's-milk cheese made in Germany, Hungary, and Austria; the name is also given to a creamy molded dish garnished with capers and sweet pimiento, a favorite Austrian snack often made with fresh unripened cream cheese.

LIVAROT — a pungent, soft cheese of Normandy made of

partially skimmed cow's milk, similar to Camembert but stronger and smellier.

LONGHORN — an American mild, firm Cheddar named after a breed of cow from whose milk the cheese is made.

LORRAINE — a small, delicate, firm German cheese often containing pistachio or pine nuts.

MAGERKÄSE — a skimmed-milk cheese of Austria, semifirm, sweet, mild, but "thin" (low in butterfat content).

MANCHEGO — one of the finest of Spanish cheeses, a firm cheese made of sheep's milk, creamy-smooth and pale yellow when young, developing a consistency and color much like that of Swiss Emmentaler when older. It is said to have been a favorite of Cervantes. Especially good with a mellow red wine.

MANTECA (or Mantega or Mantecho) — a variation of Provolone, with sweet butter sealed in the very center, shaped like a flask.

MARIBO — a firm Danish cheese, with very small holes. It is mild when young but develops a sharper aftertaste when aged.

MAROILLES — a French cheese made since the seventh century at the Abbey of Maroilles in the Champagne district of France. It is a semifirm, "assertive" cheese with a distinctive taste and aroma. There are a number of French cheeses belonging to the Maroilles family.

MASCARPONE — a sweet, fresh cream cheese of Italy, often with candied fruit in the center; it may be served sprinkled with sugar and rum.

MEL FINO — an Italian cheese halfway between Bel Paese and Gorgonzola, blue-veined and creamy. It is an unusual dessert cheese.

MENORCAN — both a natural and a process cheese produced on the Island of Menorca; semifirm, delicate, but with a distinctive flavor.

MIGNOT — a French cheese similar to Maroilles but smaller.

MINNESOTA BLUE — one of the American natural blue-veined cheeses.

MITZITHRA — a Greek cheese made of the whey left from Feta. It is semisoft, lightly salted, white. A cheese by the same name is made in Turkey of goat's milk. It may be used in the same way as Ricotta.

MONSIEUR FROMAGE — a ripened cream cheese of Normandy, delicate and soft. It comes packaged in five-ounce wooden boxes.

MONT D'OR — a soft, briefly cured goat cheese produced in the Rhône region of France.

MONTEREY (or Monterey Jack) — a California cheese first made in Monterey County, California, about 1892. There are two main types: the softer, pale, semifirm Monterey made of whole milk and a firmer, zestier, more deeply yellow aged Monterey made partially of skimmed milk. The latter is used mostly for grating; both are excellent for cooking.

MONTLÉNIS — a French, firm, blue-veined cheese made of mixed sheep's, cow's, and goat's milk in a region neighboring Roquefort.

MOUNTAIN CHEESE — see Mütschli.

MOZZARELLA — of Italian origin, once made entirely of buffalo's milk but now usually made from partially skimmed cow's milk, though the American imitation of Mozzarella is more often made of whole milk. This cheese is mild, pale, and semisoft; melts easily; and is commonly known as the "pizza cheese." American imitations cannot compare with the Italian original for delicate, sweet flavor.

MÜNSTER (or Muenster) — originated in the Vosges Mountains of Alsace-Lorraine in the seventh century and still made in France. It is a soft, pancake-shaped cheese with a distinctively pungent flavor and odor, best when washed down with a chilled Moselle wine. The American Münster is a completely different cheese; it was first made by German immigrants from the small town of Münster in the Vosges region of Lorraine but over the years has evolved into a mild, semifirm, buttery cheese with small holes, made in wheels or loaves. The American Münster is a fine cooking cheese and, when warmed to room temperature before serving, makes an excellent snack with beer or red wine, especially when accompanied by crisp apples and nuts.

MÜTSCHLI — a semisoft, cream-colored cheese made from the milk of Alpine cows in Switzerland. It is mild and delicious and can be used in making Raclette.

MYCELLA — a Danish blue-veined cheese, less sharp than Danablu, with a pale-cream rather than a snowy-white "complexion."

NEUFCHÂTEL — the French cheese of this name has been made

for centuries in Normandy, a soft creamy cheese with a velvety white crust. (The crust, too, may be eaten when the cheese is young.) The American Neufchâtel is never ripened and is more like our cream cheese but with a lower butterfat content.

NIEHEIMER HOPFENKÄSE — see Hopfenkäse.

NØKKELOST — a Norwegian spiced loaf cheese made from partly skimmed milk.

PAGLIA — a Swiss blue-veined cheese, similar to Gorgonzola.

PAMPASGRASS — an Argentine blue-veined cheese.

PARMA — made in the Italian province of this name, a cross between Parmesan and Provolone in flavor. It is a semifirm to firm cheese that takes more than a year to cure. It is usually served in wedges with red wine.

PARMESAN (or Parmigiano) — one of the best known of all Italian cheeses, used primarily for grating, though, when young and softer, it can also be sliced for eating. Made of whole cow's milk and aged between two and three years, this sharp, pungent hard cheese is a kitchen "must" for soups, pastas, and so forth. The American Parmesan, usually sold already grated in jars, has nothing like the same pungency. Parmesan cheese has been produced in Italy since 1200 and was mentioned by Boccaccio in 1364.

PASTEURIZED PROCESS CHEESE — a blend of two or more kinds of natural cheese, ground in fine particles, then heated together to a temperature of 150° F., cooled, poured into cartons or plastic packages, and hermetically sealed.

PECORINO — firm or hard Italian cheeses made from sheep's milk, the best-known variety of which is Pecorino Romano. They have been produced in southern and central Italy since Roman times, when Pliny listed them as among the best-known cheeses of Italy.

PENNICH — a sheep cheese made in Turkey; the curd is packed into sheep- or lambskin for curing.

PEPATO — a Pecorino-type cheese made in Sicily; the curd is layered with black pepper to give it spicy flavor. Sharp and crumbly, it makes a good cocktail cheese.

PERSILLE DES ARAVIS — a French cheese made from goat's milk, molded into a cylindrical roll, and flavored with parsley.

PETIT SUISSE — a fresh *double-crème* cheese of France, unsalted and made of whole milk with added cream. It is deliciously creamy and delicate but highly perishable. It is superb with strawberries and is sometimes stirred with honey to serve as dessert.

PHILADELPHIA CREAM — the brand name of Kraft's fresh cream cheese.

PINEAPPLE — an American cheese of the Cheddar family molded in pineapple shape.

PIORA — a cheese made in the Italian part of Switzerland, similar to Tilsiter.

PONT-L'ÉVÊQUE — a soft, ripened cheese of Normandy, with a pungent flavor caused by a unique fungoid mold peculiar to that locality. It was already renowned in 1230, when it was called "Angelot." The name was changed in 1600. This cheese is excellent with tawny port.

POONA — an American soft, ripened cheese. It is round and flat with a reddish surface, is sold in two-pound rolls, and is sometimes described as a "mild Limburger."

PORT DU SALUT (or Port-Salut) — the world-renowned semisoft cheese made by Trappist monks of Notre Dame in France since 1816 and now made by Trappist monks in many other countries of the world as well (and in some factories that have nothing to do with the monastic order).

POT CHEESE — fresh curd, unripened and only lightly broken (see Cottage Cheese).

PRÄSTOST OR PRESTOST — a firm Swedish cheese cured with whiskey.

PRIMOST — a Norwegian semifirm, mellow cheese.

PROCESS CHEESE — See Pasteurized Process Cheese.

PROVOLETTI — a small Provolone.

PROVOLONE — an Italian firm cheese with a smoky flavor, molded into various shapes and of all sizes to hang from rafters as it cures. It is usually sliced for eating; also useful for cooking. A cheese by this name made in the United States bears only a slight resemblance to the Italian original.

PULTOST — a Norwegian cheese made of whey and caramelized; it has a sweet flavor.

QUARGEL — an Austrian skimmed milk cheese flavored with cumin.

QUEIJO — the Portuguese word for "cheese," used with the names of towns or provinces for a large variety of cheeses made in Portugal and Brazil.

QUEIJO PRATO — a firm cheese made in Brazil, small-holed, with a smoky flavor.

QUESO — the Spanish word for "cheese" and, like *queijo*, *fromage*, and *käse*, used along with names of regions to designate many varieties of cheese.

QUESO ENCHILADO — an aged firm cheese of Mexico; its rind is covered with hot red chili powder.

QUESO MANCHEGO — see Manchego.

RACLETTE — the name of a popular dish in Switzerland; the cheese used in making it is also sometimes called "Raclette." The word means "scraped": The cheese as it begins to melt is scraped off onto boiled potatoes and served with dill pickles and pickled onions. For recipe see Index.

RAT CHEESE — a popular name for any well-aged natural Cheddar of firm texture.

REBLOCHON — a French cheese produced in the Haute-Savoie region, with a pale-yellow interior, a rind reddish chestnut in color, and a flavor "redolent of Alpine flowers." Of a Port du Salut type, Reblochon can be served as a cocktail cheese but will be better appreciated if washed down with red wine.

REICHKÄSE — a German-Austrian cheese similar to Gouda in texture but hickory-smoked.

RICOTTA — an Italian cheese made from skimmed sheep's buttermilk or the whey left from Pecorino Romano, soft when fresh, becomes hard when aged. The American Ricotta is made from whole or skimmed cow's milk and is much like cottage cheese.

RICOTTA ROMANA — an aged, firm version of Ricotta, hard enough to grate.

RICOTTA SALATA — a version of Ricotta, with more of the liquid drained away, giving it much the same consistency as Feta.

ROBIOLA (or Robiolini) — a soft, ripened cheese of northern Italy, piquant in flavor; it is sometimes blended with oil and freshly ground black pepper when eaten as a supper dish.

ROMADURKÄSE — a soft Bavarian cheese similar to Limburger but with a somewhat less assertive aroma.

ROMANO — an aged, hard cheese grated like Parmesan and used mostly for cooking, though when young the firm granular cheese can be eaten in chunks. Most of the imported Italian cheese of this name is made from sheep's milk (see Pecorino), but some is now made from cow's or goat's milk. The American imitation is made from cow's milk.

63

RONCAL — a cheese produced in the Navarre valley of northern Spain from fresh, whole cow's milk, a firm close-grained cheese with a few small eyes and a sharp flavor.

ROOS — a round sheep's-milk cheese the size of an orange made in Iraq by Kurdish tribes; it is molded by hand and ripened in sheepskin bags for six months.

ROQUEFORT — one of the world's great blue-veined cheeses, the only one of international repute made with sheep's milk. It is often called the "king of cheeses." Roquefort is made of whole ewe's milk during the lambing season, layered with bread moldy with penicillium fungus and ripened in the natural caverns of Roquefort. Roquefort is as useful in the kitchen as on the cocktail table or dessert buffet, well deserving its reputation as a gastronomic jewel.

SAALAND PFARR — a Swedish cheese whose curd is mashed with whiskey before ripening (see Prästost).

SAANEN — a Switzerland cheese said to remain usable for as long as 100 years. Usually the ripening period is five to six years but never less than three years. Saanen is very hard and dry and is used for grating and melting.

SAGE CHEDDAR — a natural American Cheddar flavored with sage before ripening.

SAGE CREAM — an English unripened cream cheese, to which fresh, bruised sage leaves and spinach juice are added, giving it a delicate green color.

SAGE DERBY — an English Derby cheese flavored with sage, for long a traditional Christmas food in Britain.

SAGE LANCASHIRE — a variety of Lancashire (English) containing chopped sage leaves.

SAINGORLON — a new French cow's-milk cheese, very rich, semisoft, ripened, blue-veined, but delicate in flavor. "A knife cuts through its paste as through butter."

SAINT-BENOÎT — a soft French cheese rubbed with charcoal and salt before ripening.

SAINTE-MAURE — a seasonal goat cheese from the Touraine district of France.

ST. IVEL — a soft English cheese inoculated with the same culture that is used for making yogurt; with curing, however, it develops a flavor like that of Camembert.

SAINT-MARCELLIN — a soft goat's-milk cheese made in a village of the same name in the French Alps.

SAINT-NECTAIRE — an aged, firm, sharp goat cheese from the Auvergne district of France.

SAINT-PAULIN — another of the cheeses created by the Trappist monks of Notre Dame in 1816, a variation of Port du Salut. When young it is semisoft and in cold countries will remain that way — but in hot countries it ages to semifirm consistency.

SAMSØ — one of the finest of Danish cheeses, golden, semifirm, with small irregular holes and nut-like, buttery flavor. It is produced on the island of the same name.

SAPSAGO — see Schabzieger.

SARDO — a hard Italian cheese for grating.

SBRINZ — a cheese made in Switzerland, aged and hard, of even texture without any eyes, excellent for grating, and preferable to Parmesan because of its higher fat content and richer flavor. In Switzerland, the firm, not-yet-hard cheese is often cut in very thin slices to eat with bread. Made since ancient times, it is believed to be the cheese Pliny referred to as *caseus helveticus.* (A cheese of the same name made in Argentina is more like Parmesan.)

SCAMORZO (or Scamorze) — a salty, sometimes smoked Italian cheese, soft when young and firm enough to slice when aged. Like Provolone, it is hung in netted bags from rafters to ripen and is rubbed repeatedly with oil.

SCHABZIEGER — a hard cheese of Switzerland, greenish in color because of the addition of powdered clover and sometimes called "green cheese" or "Sapsago." It is made of slightly sour skimmed milk pressed into cones. It has been made exactly the same way since the fifteenth century. (A Sapsago is also made in Wisconsin.)

SCHIMMELKÄSE — a soft German cheese with a white crust, often added to scrambled eggs.

SCHLOSSKÄSE BISMARCK — named after the famous German Prime Minister, this cheese is the one Emil Frey was trying to copy when he created Liederkranz.

SCHMIERKÄSE — the Pennsylvania Dutch give this name to cottage cheese, but in Germany it means a soft, ripened cheese, usually colored bright yellow; it may be flavored with onion.

SELLES-SUR-CHER — a salty, semifirm French goat cheese.

SEPTMONCEL — a French blue-veined Alpine cheese made with a mixture of cow's, goat's, and sheep's milk. It is sometimes called "Jura Bleu."

SERRA DE ESTRELLA — a Portuguese cheese made of ewe's

milk or of a mixture of ewe's and goat's milk, renneted with extract from a thistle-like flower. It is soft or semisoft with irregular eyes and an unusual, piquant flavor.

SLIPCOTE — a soft, fresh, white English cheese, rich as butter and ripened between cabbage leaves only a week or two.

SMOKELET — a small Norwegian smoked cheese.

SOFT JACK — a young Monterey Jack made from whole milk.

SORBAIS — a variety of Maroilles, pungent, bright yellow, with reddish-brown rind.

STILTON — one of the world's great cheeses, subtle, suave, with a lingering aftertaste. This blue-green veined cheese of England must be consumed with bland cream biscuits (crackers) and a glass of mellow old port to be fully appreciated.

STRACCHINO — a generic name for a number of Italian cow's-milk cheeses, of which Gorgonzola is one.

SVECIA — a Swedish cheese, sometimes made with caraway seeds; it is firm and excellent for slicing.

SWISS — The name commonly used in the United States for the big-holed cheese that originated in the Emmantal Valley of Switzerland in the fifteenth century. (In France and England the same cheese is called "Gruyère"; in Switzerland and a number of other European countries it is called "Emmentaler.") Wheels of Switzerland Swiss cheese usually weigh between 160 and 200 pounds; eyes may be as large as an inch in diameter. American natural Swiss is now produced in half a dozen different states, but most of it comes from Wisconsin, where cheese-making immigrants from Switzerland first settled in 1850. A process cheese called "Swiss" is also produced in the United States.

SZEKELEY — a soft Hungarian sheep cheese packed in sheep bladders, which look like fat sausages. It is sometimes smoked.

TAFFELOST — a Norwegian or Danish dessert cheese, semi-soft, creamy white with a red outer rind, which comes in square loaves.

TALEGGIO — an Italian dessert cheese, pale in color, smooth, aromatic, with a rosy-hued crust. It is a member of the Stracchino family.

TELEMI — of Rumanian origin, where it is made of sheep milk. American cheese of same name (made of cow's milk) is semi-soft, much like American Mozzarella.

TIGNARD — a firm, blue-veined goat's-milk cheese made in the Tigne Valley of the Savoie district of France.

TIJUANA — a provocative cheese from Mexico, firm, pale in color, but with a fiery aftertaste because of bits of hot red pepper added to the curd before aging. It is excellent for cocktails and melts evenly and smoothly when used for cooking.

TILLAMOOK — an Oregon Cheddar type, bright yellow, firm, not flaky. The salt-free variety has an indescribably pungent but not sharp flavor.

TILSITER — made originally by Dutch emigrants who settled near Tilsit in Prussia. Several cheeses bearing this name are now made in Germany, Switzerland, Norway, and Denmark, as well as in the United States. Some connoisseurs consider the Swiss and Scandinavian Tilsiters better than the original. Tilsiter is semifirm, with piquant flavor and small, irregular holes.

TOMME — a group of French cheeses made in the Savoie distrist of France, usually of skimmed milk. The Tommes may be flavored with fennel, raisins (dried grapes), or sweet wine.

TOMME DE CHÈVRE — a small cheese made from goat's milk in France.

TOSCANO — an Italian sharp sheep's-milk cheese of the Pecorino family, firm, but soft enough to slice or cut in wedges.

TRAPPISTS — monks who make some of the world's finest cheeses in various countries of the world (see Port du Salut).

TRECCE — a braided Italian semisoft cheese.

TRIPLE-CRÈME — a soft ripened dessert cheese containing more than 75 per cent butterfat.

TRIPLE-CRÈME CHÈVRE — a soft, ripened, fat cheese made from goat's milk. The crust (if white) can be eaten, as well as the creamy interior.

TRONDER — a Norwegian semisoft cheese, mellow, creamy-white color with small irregular holes and a 45 per cent butterfat content.

TUAREG — an unsalted skimmed-milk cheese made by Berber tribes in Africa.

VACHERIN — several quite different cheeses all have this name. Vacherin Fribourg is similar to Bagne; it is semisoft and may be used in Raclette or in baked dishes. Vacherin Mont d'Or is made only in the autumn in both Switzerland and France; a dessert cheese, it is soft and aromatic. It is also good with cocktails, especially if sprinkled with cumin seeds to be served on crackers.

VENDÔME — a soft French cheese made in the former Province of Touraine, ripened in charcoal or sometimes buried in ashes.

VENDÔMIS DE CHÈVRE — a soft, ripened French goat cheese.

VERMONT CHEDDAR — one of the finest of our American aged Cheddars.

VERMONT SAGE — a Vermont Cheddar to which chopped or dried sage has been added before curing.

WARSHAWSKI'S SYR — a semifirm cheese made in Poland from sheep's milk; American Warshawski is made of cow's milk, is pure white and has a wine-like flavor.

WEISSLACKER — a German cheese, soft or semisoft, pungent, and somewhat like Limburger in flavor but much more mild, with a lustrous white crust.

WENSLEYDALE — a superb English cheese, firm, flaky, with a thick rind; the cheese is of a pale, parchment color, with a subtly pungent flavor. It is a favorite with apple pie. Some varieties are inoculated with mold, becoming blue-veined and similar to Stilton when aged. Wensleydale has been made in Yorkshire for a thousand years and was originally produced in medieval abbeys in the region.

WILTSHIRE — an English Cheddar type, very sharp and crumbly.

WISCONSIN LONGHORN — an American Cheddar molded into long cylinder shapes and medium-sharp in flavor. It is excellent for cooking.

YORKSHIRE — an English cheese much like a ripened Neufchâtel when young — soft, bland, and creamy. The same cheese when aged becomes sharp and zesty and is excellent with amontillado sherry.

# HOW TO
## serve
# CHEESE

ow to Serve Cheese

Cheese is one of the most elemental of foods, and the serving of it need not be a ritual. A wedge of good-tasting cheese makes a fine snack at any hour of the day, by itself or along with a crisp apple or pear, washed down with a glass of cold milk or a foaming tankard of beer, a hot cup of coffee or a "dish" of tea — or, best of all, a glass of red wine.

Yet the enjoyment of fine cheeses can be a sensual delight when one is in the mood for gastronomic adventure.

The first step is for you to learn about, say, half a dozen new cheeses. Pick up a box of Bel Paese or a foil-wrapped wedge of Roquefort or a package of Liederkranz. Buy some imported Switzerland Swiss (Emmentaler) and some domestic Swiss at the same time, and compare them at home to see the difference. Offer Port du Salut and Münster on the cheese

71

board or perhaps a soft Gorgonzola and an aged natural Cheddar next time you are having friends in for drinks.

There are many imported and fine domestic cheeses in every supermarket — you need not even go searching for strange markets in the beginning. That is, if you are shy about it or think you haven't the time. One day simply walk into a delicatessen or gourmet shop, and boldly try one or more of the strange cheeses offered there. Chances are, if you look around, that you will find that right in your own shopping district there is a specialty store, a delicatessen, or a farmer's market if not an actual cheese store, that carries a number of unusual and fascinating cheeses. I was surprised (and delighted) to learn one day that an Italian-Greek delicatessen in Mount Kisco, fifteen minutes away from my home town of Pleasantville, New York, carried such cheeses as Feta, Telemi, Fontina and Caciocavallo. Mount Kisco also has its own Cheese Shop, where one may sample any of the exotic cheeses to be seen on the shelves. In fact, almost any delicatessen or cheese-shop manager will let you taste thin samples of any cheese that looks interesting. You need not "buy blind."

The important thing for the amateur *turophile* ("cheese lover") is to keep on trying. Just because a cheese is exotic does not mean that you have to like it. There's no accounting at all for cheese tastes. If the first three you try do not please you, do not be discouraged. The next three may make you ecstatic. Anyway, by this time, you will be intrigued enough by the strange labels, the unsuspected flavors and aromas, to be launched on your adventure — and never again will you be the same.

Always remember there is a cheese for everyone, from the bland, soft kinds as easy on the tongue (and the nostrils) as whipped cream, to the odoriferous varieties that, to the uninitiated, smell frighteningly putrid.

Children at first are suspicious of any but mild, familiar flavors; then, as they grow up, they develop quite willful likes and dislikes. You too, as your taste matures, will begin to be intrigued by cheeses that, in the beginning, you would not have touched (as they say) with a ten-foot pole.

And that will also be the reaction of those you invite to your home.

Nothing is easier — or more dramatic — to serve than cheese.

Let it be the *pièce de résistance*, the climax, the surprise moment of your dinner. All you need to do is buy it — and serve it. No cooking. No fancy sauce. No flaming (nor the worry of having the flame flare briefly then dismally go "phttt"). Set out cheese attractively with or without crackers or biscuits, as the cheese itself demands, and let your guests know something of its fascinating history (if they don't already — and if they do, if they are *that* in the know, they should be impressed by your sophistication at finding such a treasure). You have nothing else to do but supply a suitable fruit and/or a suitable wine (or spirit) and perhaps crackers or bread (depending on the cheese). And without any culinary effort on your part at all, the cheese can make your evening a triumph. Can any host (or hostess) ask for an easier way out?

## GETTING TO KNOW CHEESE

Big cheese-tastings have become quite fashionable; they have even been presented as money-making functions for clubs, and although they always offer opportunities to taste a wide variety of cheeses and can be great fun, if you want to be a connoisseur of cheese yourself, it's best to start out with private cheese-tastings in your own home, either with the family alone or in company with a few appreciative friends. Buy no more than four or five kinds at a time and only in small portions — until you have determined which are your favorites. Some cheeses can be kept fresh in the refrigerator for months; others dry up or become stronger within a matter of weeks (or even days) — but any cheese that is removed several times from the refrigerator and replaced again inevitably loses some of its pristine quality.

For your first home tastings, choose cheeses of a similar nature. For example, one day I bought four blue-veined cheeses — Roquefort, Gorgonzola, Stilton, and Danish Blue (Danablu). One always should taste the blandest cheese first, proceeding to those of more "assertive" flavors and aromas. For my guidance, the cheese man marked the samples by number so that I should know the right tasting order: Gorgonzola first, Stilton second, Roquefort third, Danish Blue fourth. At home I set them out on a table, along with unsalted crackers and a selection of wines. If in doubt, I had been told, always serve red wine with cheese — more often than not, it's the best. But I like to experiment, so I also put out two kinds of sherry, a Rhine wine, some Madeira, and cognac.

It was a revelation to learn how much difference in flavor there was among these four world-famous "blues." Equally surprising was the discovery of why certain wines go better with certain cheeses. A red Burgundy proved to be good with all four of the blues, but the Rhine wine was not right at all, and an amontillado (medium sweet) sherry was better with the cheeses than the very dry cocktail sherry that is my usual preference as a before-dinner drink. Cognac was superb with all of them — at least, to my palate. I find that cognac mates well with almost any cheese. The Madeira was superb with the Gorgonzola and the Stilton, but the Roquefort and Danish Blue were much too sharp for it.

I have since been told by at least one cheese expert that one should never serve Madeira with a blue cheese. Not even cognac should be offered with cheese! Well, I don't agree. For me, experimenting with taste combinations is fun — and if connoisseurs dispute my liking, let the chips fall where they may! After all, the English consider port the best of all drinks to serve with Stilton and a cream sherry almost as good — and both are sweet fortified wines.

On another day, I set out four semifirm cheeses and made much the same sort of experiment. This time I had an utterly delicious young Manchego (a Spanish sheep cheese), a piece of Switzerland Mountain Cheese (Mütschli), a Goya from Argentina, and Icelandic Banquet, a yellow cheese of the same general type as Gouda. Red wine was fine with the Manchego, but the Rhine wine was far better with the Mütschli. (Since then I have learned that a dry white wine complements natural Gruyère and Swiss Emmentaler best too.) The Goya was good with both Madeira and amontillado sherry but not with the dry sherry. The Icelandic Banquet was best with red wine and not with the dry sherry.

Why does it make so much difference? Because both cheese and wine leave aftertastes in the mouth, and, if their flavors do not "marry" well, the aftertastes can lead to family quarrels. One cannot really judge a cheese's excellence if it is consumed with a wine (or other beverage) that fights with it.

A connoisseur of both cheese and wine might disagree violently with the conclusions I have listed above. I have discovered that this subject can arouse passions of controversy, for individual tastes (and the taste buds themselves) vary widely. For this very reason, pairing cheeses and wines and getting varied reactions from those making the experiment can turn into a provocative occasion.

The only way one can learn how Brie differs from Camembert is to taste one right after the other. The same is true of the enormous number of soft and semisoft ripened dessert cheeses. What's the difference between Bel Paese and Port du Salut, between Crema Danica and Gervais or Petit-Suisse? Taste them, on bland crackers, and you will see.

## CHEESE ETIQUETTE

Display good manners to your cheeses if you want them to be on their best behavior.

Always remove cheese from the refrigerator at least an hour before serving, so that the cheese will be at room temperature. The full flavor will not be released when the cheese is cold.

To keep your cheeses happy and healthy between servings, always wrap them carefully in Saran Wrap or a similar plastic-laminated paper that clings tightly to exclude air. A hard cheese like Romano, Parmesan, Kashkaval, or Sapsago does not have to be kept in the refrigerator. It can be hung from hooks on the wall, as the cheese sellers hang it. The semifirm cheeses like Swiss, Cheddar, and Edam ideally should be kept in a dry cellar, safe from rodents, where the temperature is around 50° F. — but who has such a cellar any more? Without such a storage place, the refrigerator is best; the semisoft and soft cheeses must always be kept there.

(The United States Department of Agriculture advises that some cheeses can be frozen, but, inevitably, in the zero temperature of the freezer cheese will dry out and lose much of its flavor. That may be all right for cheeses that are to be used only in cooking or for the run-of-the-mill pasteurized cheeses, but freezing is hardly to be recommended for gourmet cheeses.)

To serve a single big wedge of cheese or an assortment of cheeses, a cheese board is best. Such boards can be found in any dimestore, hardware store, or housewares department and can even be ordered by mail (see Appendix). Most are inexpensive; often they come with matching knives, which fit into slits on the sides of the boards.

A thin-bladed knife is best for cutting semifirm cheeses or blue cheeses. Some people like to use a cheese slicer, but my feeling is that thin slices of cheese are less flavorful than chunks. For Gouda or Edam, a cheese scoop is useful — otherwise, scoop out the cheese with a silver (or stainless steel) butter knife. A butter knife is best too for the semisoft cheeses like Port du Salut and Bel Lago.

Do not place crackers on the cheese board. They belong in a separate serving dish or basket. Semifirm cheeses like Swiss, Cheddar, Tilsiter, and Manchego do not need crackers with them. You will want crackers, however, with the blue cheeses or with those that are soft or semisoft. According to the French, the proper thing to serve with cheese is plain, unbuttered bread — French bread, of course, but personally I find dry bread too much to swallow and not really the cheese's best friend. I prefer crisp thin crackers, and although cheese men insist that the crackers should be as flavorless as possible, I find that certain of the semisoft cheeses are delicious atop thin Norwegian flatbread, sesame-seed crackers, ryebread with caraway, onion-flavored crackers, or toast squares. Such wafers admittedly are not proper for a cheese-tasting, when one is critically analyzing the flavor of a particular cheese, but for service in your home as snacks or afterdinner refreshments, and especially at the cocktail hour, they are fine. The Germans and the Danes both serve their Camembert cheeses on thinly sliced pumpernickel, which makes a very nice flavor combination.

A semisoft cheese is best served on a large plate or small platter. Remove it from its box, and strip off any foil or paper wrapping. If it has a crusted top, that too can be scraped off, if you prefer. Or the crust can be cut away as the cheese is served. The crust on some cheeses may be eaten with the cheese, if it is still soft. Arrange crackers around the cheese on the plate. Stick a butter knife or cheese server in the top. (Save the box and the wrappings for storing the cheese once more, should any be left over.)

The soft cheeses, both the ripened and the fresh (like Crème Chantilly, Petit-Suisse, and Cabrinneti), should be served with very crisp thin crackers (or French bread, if you take a Frenchman's advice) on individual salad or dessert plates, along with individual butter knives for spreading. If the cheese is wrapped in individual wedges, of course each person will have his own wedge. If it comes — as most of them do — in boxes containing from four ounces to eight or ten ounces of a single cheese, the cheese should be removed from its box and wrapper. A fresh crust that is still soft can be eaten with the cheese, but if the crust is dried or moldy, you should cut it away as the cheese is served. (A delicious way to serve Camembert is to scrape off the crust and sprinkle toasted slivered almonds over the cheese.)

Certain of the cheeses that are technically classed as dessert cheeses are also delicious with cocktails — especially the more pungent, like Liederkranz, Port du Salut, Pont-l'Evêque, and even Brie. If you serve such a cheese with cocktails, however, it is well to offer with it a firm or semifirm cheese, perhaps a trio consisting of Liederkranz, plus one of the blue cheeses and a firm cheese like natural Gruyère or Manchego. The soft, rich, delicately flavored dessert cheeses like Crema Danica and Petit-Suisse are not really good cocktail selections. They are not complemented by strong spirits, and their delicacy will be unappreciated.


## WHAT CHEESE TO SERVE WHEN

The three occasions on which it is appropriate to serve an assortment of cheeses are at a cocktail party or buffet, for evening refreshments, and at a big cheese-tasting. Otherwise, it is usually wiser to let a single cheese be the star attraction, accompanied by relishes and dips at cocktail time, by fruit for dessert.

When selecting an assortment of cheeses, choose three or more with distinctly different flavors and textures. The following groups are offered as examples. You can, of course, serve as many as five kinds, if you wish — depending on the number of guests. But keep in mind that the soft and semisoft cheeses are more perishable and that, if you buy too many at a time, those not consumed at your party may end up in the garbage pail, which would be a crime.

# SUGGESTED CHEESE-BOARD ASSORTMENTS

Brie (soft, ripened, delicate, indescribably delicious)
Esrom (Danish semifirm, pale yellow, distinctive flavor)
Kashkaval (firm Balkan sheep cheese, sharp with slight smoky flavor
— Caciocavallo is Italian version)

Reblochon (semisoft, a bit like Port du Salut)
Vermont Aged Cheddar (sharp, firm)
Samsø (semifirm, buttery-smooth, more bland than the Cheddar)

Cantal (French semifirm, drum-shaped, bright yellow)
Gorgonzola
Bel Lago or Weisslacker (semisoft, pale ivory, mild with an interesting
aftertaste)

Crème Chantilly with Chives (a French import, soft, fresh, white
cream cheese with minced chives in curd)
Swiss Emmentaler
Lancashire (English semisoft to semifirm cheese)

Fontina (Italian semifirm to firm zesty cheese — American version
also good)
Danish Blue
Coulommiers (semisoft, pungent French cheese)
Feta (chalky-white, salty sheep cheese)

As the average local cheese store or delicatessen is not likely
to have all these cheeses, you may feel the suggested assortments are impossible to put together. Chin up! These assortments are suggested as samples of cheese "menus." Note that in
each group there is one soft or semisoft cheese, one semifirm
or firm cheese, and a third that is distinctly different from the
other two — either a blue cheese or a semifirm cheese that is
blander (or sharper) than the other semifirm cheese. Using this
pattern, ask your local cheese man to help you select several
quite different types, and, if, alas, it turns out that he does not
know much more than you do about cheese, do a bit of experimenting and ask for small portions there in the store to taste
for yourself.

Or order a selection of cheese by mail. There are now many
firms that fill mail orders. A list can be found in the Appendix
at the back of this book.

## BEER AND CHEESE

As they say in the advertisements, in the American way of life, beer belongs. And cheese belongs with beer.

Surprisingly enough, the cheeses that go best with beer are those that are fairly mild to the palate — like Limburger. At first reading, this statement will probably cause raised eyebrows, if not whistles of surprise. How can Limburger be described as a mild cheese? But Limburger is mild to the palate; only the odor is strong. And it is what happens after the cheese and beverage meet in the mouth that makes the difference.

Liederkranz is another runny-soft cheese that is superb with beer, as are Bierkäse, Romadur, and Weisslacker — all German or German-inspired cheeses. It is not surprising that the best beer cheeses are found in beer-drinking countries. Many Scandinavian cheeses are also excellent with beer — Samsø, King Christian IX, Tilsiter, and the Danish Camembert (which is firmer and blander in flavor than is French Camembert). Edam and Gouda, cheeses of another beer-drinking country (The Netherlands), are also fine choices, as are Switzerland's Emmentaler and pungent Vacherin.

The worst cheeses to serve with beer are the blues. Their flavors are too sharp for beer; they need red wine, cognac, or a brandy-fortified wine like port.

Most people consider that a sharp Cheddar goes well with beer, but others contend that only a mild Cheddar is proper.

In Germany, I discovered that a popular cheese snack with beer is one called *Handkäse mit Musik* — a small, rubbery country cheese about the size of the palm of one's hand, which is dressed with oil, vinegar, and chopped onions. By itself, the "hand cheese" is not noteworthy, but *mit Musik* it makes an interesting beer snack. Harzerkäse, another country cheese, is a favorite with Berliners, who spread the soft cheese on dark bread, above a layer of *Schmalz* (goose fat). I did not have an opportunity to taste it, so I can only pass it on as a suggestion enthusiastically endorsed by steadfast beer drinkers.

Camembert is also served with beer in Germany, the firm German Camembert, but on the same plate will come tiny heaps of spices like black pepper, paprika, and caraway seeds — and sometimes chopped onion too. The spices are blended with the cheese at table and spread on thin slices of black pumpernickel.

Because beer-drinking bouts have a way of going on for hours, becoming more boisterous as palates become wetter, it is well to set out other hearty foods along with the cheese: two or more kinds of bread (rye, pumpernickel, and sesame-seed breads are all good); cold cuts like salami, head cheese, ham, and tongue; and pickles, of course.

## CHEESE AND WINE ANY TIME

The close affinity between cheese and wine makes this twosome as suitable for informal snacking as for gourmet dining. To me the most delightful picnic fare consists of a bottle of red wine, two or three kinds of cheese with appropriate crackers or wafers, and fresh fruit. There is something utterly relaxing about drinking wine and nibbling cheese under the benign warmth of a summer sun. And what other picnic menu is so easy? No refrigeration to worry about, no dishes (except sturdy glass tumblers for the wine — I can't bring myself to drink wine from paper cups), nothing to carry home except the glasses, which are easy to tuck into the glove compartment of the car.

In winter, a bowl of steaming spiced *glögg* or *gluewein* calls naturally for assorted cheeses that can be munched before an open fire, again with fresh fruit piled high in a bowl as the only other necessary refreshment. As almost any cheese goes well with red wine (the basis for hot, spiced wine bowls), you may select your favorites. I would settle for natural Gruyère or a sharp aged Cheddar, plus a mellow, soft cheese like Brie and one of the blues. For the mid-winter fruit bowl, pomegranates are fun, plus big Emperor grapes, ripe bananas, and, of course, crisp red apples. Serve nuts in the shell, too, with nutcrackers. Walnuts, pecans, and even peanuts are suitable.

For summer, chilled white wine like Moselle (served from an ice bucket to give the wine the touch of elegrance it deserves) is superb with Camembert or a mellow, pale Tomme de Raisin, a combination to make one forget the muggiest of heat waves. Or, go Spanish, and offer a huge pitcher of *sangría*, the red-wine punch of Spain, with a choice of Manchego and Sabraes (a blue sheep's-milk cheese of northern Spain cured in fig leaves) or Roquefort.

# HOW MUCH CHEESE TO BUY

If you are like me, you will never be able to walk out of a cheese store with only one kind of cheese under your arm. Invariably, despite the best intentions in the world, I come away with at least five varieties, then wonder when I get home what I am to do with them all. Usually it ends in my giving a party so that all the extra cheese won't be wasted (or go to my waist).

Actually, it is not wise to buy more than you can consume within, say, a month. The soft dessert cheeses, especially, dry up or get strong in a short time, even when refrigerated. Semisoft cheeses last a little longer, and semifirm cheeses will last two months or more if properly wrapped, but even they dry out somewhat in the refrigerator. As a general rule, keep in mind that the firmer the cheese, the longer it will remain fresh — and vice versa.

How much you need for a party will depend, in part, on how many people are coming and also on what else you plan to serve. There is a minimum you must buy for the sake of appearances, for a stingy-looking wedge on a cheese board scares anyone from taking a sample. With some cheeses, a half-pound wedge will look generous enough for a small group, but certain of the firm cheeses are smaller in proportion to weight (because they are more solid), and less than a pound will look skimpy. As the semifirm and firm cheeses keep well for some time, you need not hesitate to buy one and a half to two pounds. What is left over can be served to the family, used in cooking, or brought out for later entertaining.

The soft and semisoft cheeses usually come in packages, so that you must buy the entire package or nothing. If the package is quite small, containing no more than six ounces, you will, for the sake of appearance, have to have a third cheese, and, again for the sake of appearance, the third should be not only somewhat larger but also preferably different in shape and color, to give your cheese board an intriguing look.

For a cocktail party, with a total of twelve guests expected, a total of one and one half pounds of cheese may be ample — that is, if you are serving other things beside cheese. A pound and a half could even be enough for twenty people, depending on what other appetizers you planned to offer. If you are having twenty-five to thirty people, at least two pounds of cheese are necessary. The larger the number of guests, the less cheese per person is necessary.

For evening refreshments, when you are serving only cheese and possibly fruit with drinks, you will obviously need proportionally more cheese per person. Again, you must offer more than your guests are likely to eat. For six people, you will need one and a half pounds altogether. If you are serving coffee or highballs, this amount could be composed of a half-pound wedge of blue cheese, a half-pound of Cheddar or another firm cheese, and an eight-ounce box of Brie. Or, if you plan to offer cognac, port, or cream sherry, as well as coffee, it could include a six-ounce portion of Crema Danica, a half-pound of Stilton, a three-ounce ball of Chabichou, and a half-pound of Wensleydale.

For eight to twelve people, at least two pounds of nothing but cheese become necessary. For more than a dozen guests, two and a half pounds (two ounces per person) are a minimum. For a beer-drinking crowd you would perhaps serve two three-quarter-pound wedges, one of Samsø, another of Kümmelkäse, and two soft or semisoft cheeses, averaging six to eight ounces each, perhaps Limburger and Bel Lago.

For dessert cheese, at the conclusion of a gourmet dinner, one ounce per person is generally enough, though again this amount depends on the type of cheese and how it appears on a plate or platter. You need less of the soft, rich, *double-crème* or *triple-crème* cheeses than of such firm or semifirm cheeses as Stilton, Dunlop, and Gruyère.


## CHEESE AT THE COCKTAIL PARTY

Because the cocktail party remains the favorite means of entertaining for most hostesses, fresh ideas for cocktail appetizers are always in demand. A new cheese or an assortment of cheeses fills this requirement beautifully.

The best type of cheese for cocktails is one with a robust or sharp flavor, preferably semifirm so that it can be cut into wedges or chunks. My favorite is Tijuana, a Mexican cheese that seems mild at first taste; then suddenly you discover it's been spiced with red pepper.

Some other good cocktail cheeses:

Roquefort, Danish Blue. Gorgonzola. or Stilton
Emmentaler (Switzerland) or natural Gruyère
Manchego
Provolone
Kashkaval (or Caciocavallo)
Esrom
Havarti
Edam or Gouda
Tilsiter
Coon, Tillamook, Vermont, or any other aged sharp Cheddar
Dunlop
Icelandic Banquet
Bondost, Christian IX, or any other caraway-seed natural cheese
Port du Salut or Reblochon
Bel Paese
Fontina
Feta
Cheshire
Double Gloucester
Wensleydale

Besides the above cheeses, there are any number of excellent natural-cheese spreads blended with spirits: for example, Cheddar and port, Manchego and Spanish sherry, Cantal and Dubonnet, Nøkkelost and brandy, Kümmelkäse and Kirsch. These spreads come in attractive earthenware crocks generally, as do many "cheese foods." I have tasted some of the latter that are surprisingly good for what they are. In fact, one blue-cheese spread that I was served at a party not long ago was actually better than another natural-cheese spread I tried that bore the label "imported French Roquefort and brandy." On another occasion I had some Danish process cheeses that were creamy-soft and had intriguing flavors. An assortment in individual foil-wrapped wedges of these Buko cheeses included one flavored with clover, pale green in color (like a Sapsago spread); another that was celery-flavored; and still another with caraway seeds.

When you are serving cheese on the cocktail table, what else should be offered along with it? The following sample menus may serve as guides.

# SUGGESTED COCKTAIL MENUS

Tijuana, *Stuffed Edam**
Cherry Tomatoes     Black Italian Olives
Dry-Roasted Cashews
Potted Shrimp, Crackers

Port du Salut, Crackers
Radishes     Macadamia Nuts
Marinated Artichoke Hearts
*Shrimp-Swiss Dip*

Roquefort
Small Whole Beets with Sour-Cream Dip
Mackerel Fillets in White-Wine Marinade
Käsestägen

Esrom Cheese, Bel Paese with Onion Wafers
Shrimp on Buttered Cucumber Slices    Green Olives in Herb Marinade

Tilsiter
Celery with *Blue Cheese Stuffing*     Pickled Mushrooms
Anchovy-Pimiento Canapés

Fontina (or Fontinalli)
Pickled Greek Baby Eggplants     *Pigs in Cheese Blankets*
Corn Chips and California Dip (Sour Cream
and Onion-Soup Mix)

Herkimer County Cheddar
Sweet Gherkins     *Minced Clam Dip*
Olives and Celery

Swiss Emmentaler
Hot Pork Sausages     Cherry Tomatoes
Celery stuffed with
*Cottage Cheese-Caraway Dip*

Feta
Kalamata Olives     Dolmades (Stuffed Vine Leaves)
Red Caviar with Sour-Cream Dip
with Rye Wafers

*Italics indicate recipes to be found in Part Four; see Index.

## CHEESE FOR DESSERT

Certain soft cheeses are specifically designated as "dessert cheeses" because they are too rich and delicate to be appropriate for serving with cocktails or beer. That does not mean that *only* such cheeses are suitable for the dessert course. As a matter of fact, one of the most superb of all cheeses to serve at the end of a fine dinner is green-veined Stilton.

For myself, I prefer dessert cheese served in the living room with coffee and cognac (or liqueurs, port, Madeira, or cream sherry). If half an hour (or more) has elapsed since rising from the table before these treasures are brought out, so much the better. A dessert cheese does not fulfill the same function as does a sweet at the end of the meal. To be fully savored, it should be enjoyed by itself, washed down with the proper spirit, or accompanied by fruit. If cheese is served immediately after a roast and vegetables, the appetite is not sharp enough to appreciate its flavor.

Some of the soft dessert cheeses are very bland and delicate; others are potently aromatic. Which kind you choose will depend on the fruit and/or spirit you plan to serve with it.

A strongly flavored soft cheese like Switzerland's Vacherin or Appenzeller needs a tart fruit like red plums or little green-white Thompson grapes. A very mild, delicate, rich cheese like Crema Danica needs sweeter fruit, perhaps big juicy grapes or sweet Bing cherries.

Here are some other suggested cheese-fruit combinations, any one of which would make a superb dessert to follow the most elegant gourmet dinner:

Stilton with ripe figs or purple plums

Gorgonzola with ripe peaches

Edam or Samsø with honeydew

Crème Chantilly with strawberries

Crème de Gruyère with red-raspberry compote

Camembert with fresh pineapple or grapes

Chabichou with bananas

Provolone with pears or red grapes

Danish Blue with red Delicious apples

85

Roquefort with oranges

Young Parma or Parmesan with apples or cantaloupe

Neufchâtel with quince or guava paste

Feta or any creamy sheep cheese with red Emperor grapes

Taleggio with Queen Anne (white) cherries

Brie with fresh nectarines

Danish Crème Special with peaches or strawberries

Pont-l'Evêque with tart white Thompson grapes

Very likely you will find it easier to set out a bowl of mixed fruit with the cheese board, rather than serving a compote or a single fruit. In this case, the foregoing suggestions may serve as guides to which fruits to arrange in the fruit bowl when certain cheeses are to be offered for dessert.

If fruit is not to be served with the cheese but only the cheese itself with coffee and spirits, it is extremely important to select cheese that will complement, and be complemented by, the spirits you have to offer.

Here again opinions differ sharply on what spirits and what cheeses go best together. The French serve cognac *after* cheese — not with it. They consider it quite barbaric to serve any sweet wine like port or Madeira with cheese at any time. Yet the English regard the sweet fortified wines as perfect with dessert or after-dinner cheeses.

I confess that, whenever someone tells me certain combinations are not "proper," my temperature instantly rises. Perhaps it's the Bohemian in me that rebels at the confining corsetry of etiquette. The only acceptable reason, in my estimation, for not serving a particular wine or other spirit with cheese is that they fight one another gastronomically, but to lay down hard-and-fast rules for what is or is not "proper" is virtually impossible. Even among the wines labeled "dry," there are enormous differences in degree of sweetness.

And, although I agree that a dry red or white wine is best with cheese when the cheese is served *before* the sweet or in the evening as refreshment after dinner, if a cheese is to be served *as* the dessert, a sweeter wine, a brandy, or a fortified wine rests more happily in the mouth.

Boldly I go out on a limb to suggest the following combinations, which I personally have found pleasant as, or following, dessert.

Stilton with port, Madeira, cream (oloroso) sherry, or cognac

Gervais (or Petit-Suisse) with cognac or armagnac (I also like it with Grand-Marnier)

Liederkranz with fine aged bourbon (drunk neat) or beer

Brie with Rémy-Martin cognac, Calvados, or a dry port

Crema Danica with Sorcial Madeira, Cherry Kijafa, or brandy

Natural Gruyère with Harvey's Bristol Cream sherry or a fine Haute Sauternes

Chabichou with Madeira or cognac

Camembert with champagne, cognac, or armagnac

Bel Paese with a Spätlese wine of the Rheingau or a Vouvray

Aged sharp Cheddar with an amontillado (medium sweet) sherry

Bonbel with tawny port

I find a fine cognac excellent with any dessert cheese, though I agree that liqueurs are too cloying to be served with cheese. The fruit brandies, slivovitz, Barack (Hungarian apricot brandy), Kirsch, and Calvados are dry enough to be served with certain dessert cheeses, though I have not been able to try out enough combinations to make any specific suggestions.

Black coffee is best with dessert cheese, but, if you and your guests feel coffee must have cream in it, it becomes a matter of personal choice. Most connoisseurs consider that a deep, dark, bitter coffee, like *espresso* or a *filtre* made with Continental-type dark-roasted coffee sets off the creaminess of cheese most effectively.

## CHEESE-TASTINGS

Big cheese-tastings, at which selections of both cheeses and wines are set out for critical sampling, can be great fun and easy ways to entertain.

One should have ten to a dozen different cheeses to taste, however, along with a sampling of different kinds of wine, as well, and this menu means having at least twenty-five, preferably fifty, guests — or more. A cheese-tasting is an excellent program for a club or other social group. The best way to plan it is to solicit the cooperation of a local cheese merchant and a local wine merchant, each of whom might well offer his products at a discount, as a tasting is an excellent way to promote them.

To have too large a gathering is unwise because then it becomes a melee. Those invited to a cheese-tasting should be people with lively curiosity about food and drink, eager to learn about new gustatory pleasures.

A quick rule of thumb is to allow one-fourth to one-half pound of cheese per person (in inverse proportion to the number of guests) and one-third to one-half bottle of wine per person. Coffee should be prepared for those who ask for it, and bland biscuits are a must to nibble with and between bites of cheese.

Ask the cheese merchant to help you decide on the selection of cheeses for the tasting. The cheeses should all belong to the same general category — cheeses for cocktails, dessert cheeses, cheeses especially good with beer, or mostly semisoft or mostly semifirm-to-firm cheeses. You will need little printed cards to identify the different cheeses and also numbers indicating which cheeses should be tasted first, which second, and so on. The cards are necessary because the bland cheeses should always be sampled first; otherwise your palate is unable to appreciate the more delicate flavors.

If only one type of wine is to be offered, it should be a dry red wine. It's better, though, to have both red and white table wines for comparative tasting. A champagne-tasting could be combined with a cheese-tasting for a gala holiday affair. Or, if most members of your crowd are beer drinkers, have beer with a tasting of appropriate cheeses. With soft dessert cheeses, the French (who produce more cheeses of this type than any other people) insist that only a dry red wine should be offered, but, if a local wine merchant or one of the wine associations is willing to supply a selection of the fortified wines or brandies, it would be fun to see what combinations those attending the tasting find to their liking.

Always the crackers or biscuits served at a tasting should be unsalted and very bland. British water biscuits or cream biscuits are excellent.

Score cards and pencils should be furnished, so that all those present can take home records of the tasting for their own future use.

If there is not a cheese merchant in your locality able or willing to help you plan a tasting, a selection of cheeses for a tasting may be ordered from Cheeses of All Nations (see Appendix), which also will furnish cheese-identification cards already marked and tiny nationality flags to help identify the countries the cheeses come from. This shop will also suggest the best wines to be offered with the particular cheeses. In making your order, specify how many guests you expect and what category of cheese you are most interested in serving. Appropriate crackers will also be sent to you with the order.

# CHEESE IN THE KITCHEN

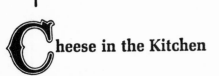

# Cheese in the Kitchen

Such standbys as macaroni and cheese, veal Parmigiana, cheese soufflé, and Welsh rabbit are part of nearly every family's culinary repertoire. Cheese sandwiches go into lunch boxes week after week. In the pages that follow I have tried to collect less known and more unusual cheese recipes and to suggest new ways to prepare the familiar cheese dishes.

Substituting a caraway-seed cheese for American Cheddar can in itself make an old dish seem new. Using imported natural Gruyère in place of pasteurized process Swiss Cheese can make an extraordinary difference in such delights as fondu or hot-cheese appetizer tarts. Spaghetti becomes an exciting entree with three different freshly grated cheeses instead of the usual already-grated Parmesan from a jar. And do discover how perfectly wonderful grated Kashkaval (or Caciocavallo) can be in a macaroni casserole, in place of bland American cheese.

From a practical point of view, cheese is of the utmost importance. Nutritionally it is one of the "perfect" foods, providing the same essential vitamins and minerals as does milk but in condensed form. It is high in calories, but so is steak. In fact, it serves as a protein substitute for meat in meal planning. As an aid to ailing budgets, it is marvelous, for one-fourth to a half-pound of firm cheese (one to one and a half cups grated cheese) will make a macaroni-and-cheese casserole or a soufflé to serve four.

Even those on cholesterol diets may enjoy the firm, well-aged cheeses, for, in the aging process, the fat changes chemically to a formula more easily assimilated. (This was verified as the result of studies made in Switzerland, for Switzerland too has a large number of patients troubled with heart disease.)

For those watching calories, there are many cheeses that are low in fat content, including a number made entirely with skimmed milk. Such low-calorie cheeses can be ordered by mail from several of the cheese firms listed in the Appendix. Those who believe in the low-carbohydrate theory of weight control will be happy to know that virtually all cheeses fall into the category of high-protein, low-carbohydrate content. Again, though, it is the firm, well-aged cheeses that are usually preferable, for they are not nearly so rich in fat as are most of the soft and semisoft cheeses. (Also the weight watchers must face realistically the fact that having cheese for an hors d'oeuvre is like having meat balls and that having cheese for dessert is as hard on one's waistline as is having ice cream or pie.)

If, in reading over the recipes that follow, you hesitate to use certain ones because the cheeses they call for are not available in your market, it is usually quite safe to substitute another cheese of the same general type. Look up the cheese in the Glossary (Part Two). If it is a sharp, semifirm cheese, substitute a sharp Cheddar. If it is a semisoft, pungent cheese, substitute another semisoft cheese. If Ricotta is called for, a Cottage or pot cheese can be used. Provolone may be used in place of Kashkaval. In many recipes a choice of several cheeses is given.

I have deliberately tried to find uses for the more esoteric cheeses for those who, like me, have no sales resistance in the seductive atmosphere of a cheese shop and bring home more cheese than intended. If a cheese purchased solely for eating is there in your refrigerator, slowly drying up, by all means try it in cooking, in place of the more ordinary Cheddar, Parmesan, or cream cheese that recipes call for.

A word about the use of the terms "grated" and "shredded": "grating" means reducing the cheese to very fine particles, and normally grating is possible only with firm or hard cheese. "Shredding" means cutting the cheese, a semisoft or semifirm cheese, into long thin shreds, using the medium holes of a standard grater. The Moulli graters, of course, will automatically shred according to the consistency of the cheese.

Servings have been estimated on the basis of average appetites, and, because I know full well that what is ample for one set of four people will be barely enough for two others, I usually try to estimate the number of servings rather than the number of people the recipe can be expected to satisfy.

For most cooking, I much prefer the natural cheeses because they have more distinctive flavors, but there are some recipes in which process cheeses will probably do as well. In fact, there are times when a process Swiss is actually preferable to a natural Swiss Emmentaler, for the simple reason that the former is not so likely to melt into long thread-like strands — when the cheese is blended with crumbs over the top of a *coquille*, for example.

When one cheese is substituted for another, the results of course will vary. Substituting one blue-veined cheese for another, for example, can make a vast difference, as some blues are much sharper than others. When making a dip, salad mixture, or some other uncooked recipe, it is possible to taste as one goes along, and, if the cheese used is so sharp as to be overpowering, another, blander cheese may be added. This possibility is especially important to keep in mind when using the blue-veined or other mold-inoculated cheeses: Add some cream cheese, shredded Brick, or mild Cheddar to tone down the too-insistent flavor.

# **D**IPS, SPREADS, AND HORS D'OEUVRES

An hors d'oeuvre in the literal sense can be almost any zesty tidbit served before or "outside" a meal, but, as we use the term today, it has come to mean bite-sized appetizers served with cocktails or before dinner, a little more elegant, a little more special, than snacks.

Canapés are pretty, but, for the hostess who does not have professional kitchen help, they can be a headache, tedious to prepare and difficult to keep fresh until the moment of serving. Setting out dips and spreads that guests themselves can put on wafers or crackers is more practical, and in the American social world it has become quite acceptable.

The hostess who prefers to serve canapés and who takes pride in offering tidbits that are exquisitely garnished may make use of many of the following spreads as canapé toppings. A first rule is to use bread, plain, toasted, or fried in butter or olive oil, as the base (never wafers or crackers). Unless the bread is fried, cover each canapé square, triangle, or round thickly with butter. The butter prevents seepage and helps to keep the bread or toast fresh. Spread the cheese mixture over the butter; then add any desired garnish: pimiento strips, capers, sieved egg yolk, caviar, or such minced herbs as parsley, chives, or dill. Place the canapés in a shallow pan, cover tightly with Saran Wrap (or other laminated plastic) and keep chilled until serving time.

Cucumber slices may be used in place of bread as the canapé base, but they too should be thickly buttered. (Or very thin slices of cucumber may be curled atop the canapés, with sieved egg yolk and minced herbs on either side.)

Crocks of ready-to-serve cheese spreads are now available in endless variety: Cheddar with port, Manchego with Spanish sherry, natural Gruyère with chopped pecans, Edam with sauternes — almost any combination that can be dreamed up. Some are made with natural aged cheeses and fine wines; others are simply "cheese foods," blends of process cheese and pasteurized milk with added vegetable gum to keep the mixture soft. There are also special low-fat cheese spreads (made of skimmed milk); process cheeses which are soft enough to spread, in crocks or sausage-like rolls; and powdered mixes that anyone can add to cream cheese or cottage cheese.

Why, with all this variety to choose from, should anyone bother to make his own cheese dips or spreads?

Well, why should anyone bother to cook when there are so many ready-to-heat frozen foods available? The answer is the same.

Besides, dips and spreads can serve as economical uses for old cheeses that are beginning to dry up. See Phil Alpert's recipe for "everlasting cheese," page 115. Mr. Alpert claims to have kept the same crock of cheese (frequently replenished, of course) for as long as eight years!

In Sweden they have been using leftover cheese in much the same way for centuries, but there butter is added to the cheese instead of olive oil, and aquavit or beer instead of brandy or bourbon, plus caraway seeds and a dash of cayenne. The English Potted Cheese is essentially the same, but with Spanish sherry for the spirit and mustard for the spice.

I find that leftover soft dessert cheeses that are beginning to dry up, for example, Camembert or Tal-Fino* or Liederkranz, can often be salvaged by beating in a little Madeira. If the cheese is a bit strong, some plain cream cheese may be beaten in, too (though this trick requires careful judgment — a dessert cheese that has changed with age from soft and delicate to brown and ammonial should be tossed out — nothing can save it). A dip of this kind is nice with sharply flavored vegetable relishes like radishes, cauliflower buds, green-pepper sticks, and crisp celery.

Hot, toasted cheese "dreams" are easy and, especially in cold weather, make a fine accompaniment to chilled drinks. They should be prepared, ready for "toasting," long in advance, then slipped under the broiler just before serving.

*The brand name of a Taleggio made in Italy.

## English Potted Cheese

1 pound Cheshire or Double Gloucester, grated (4 cups)
Dash of cayenne
6 tablespoons softened butter
$\frac{1}{2}$ teaspoon mace
Dash of dry mustard
$\frac{1}{2}$ cup cream sherry

Combine ingredients in the order given, and beat until smooth. Place in a crock or pot, cover with waxed paper pressed over the cheese under the lid. Keep in a cool place (a cellar, if your cellar is cool) or the refrigerator, for at least 24 hours. Makes 2 cups.

POTTED HERB CHEESE: Add $\frac{1}{4}$ cup chopped fresh herbs, bruised in a mortar and pestle. Parsley, sage, thyme, and basil are all good, either alone or in combination.

## Shrimp-Swiss Dip

1 can undiluted frozen shrimp soup
2 tablespoons medium-dry sherry
$1\frac{1}{2}$ cups grated Swiss Emmentaler

Place partially defrosted soup, sherry, and cheese in the top of a double boiler. Heat, stirring occasionally, until smooth. Or place all in a blender, beat until smooth, and heat over hot water just before serving. Serve with chunks of French or Italian bread. This dip can also be served cold as a party spread on rye crackers. Make $1\frac{1}{4}$ cups.

## Bierkäse Dip

$\frac{3}{4}$ pound sharp Cheddar or Coon, grated (3 cups)
2 ounces Roquefort, crumbled

2 tablespoons butter, softened
1 teaspoon grated onion
¹/₄ teaspoon salt
³/₄ cup beer

Combine cheeses and butter and beat by hand or in mixer until smooth (if beating in mixer, add a little beer, about ¹₄ cup). Blend in onion and salt; then slowly beat in remaining beer. Pack into a jar or crock, cover tightly, refrigerate at least 12 hours, then remove to room temperature. Serve this way, or hollow a round loaf of pumpernickel, pile the cheese spread inside, and serve small cubes of pumpernickel (taken from the loaf) with the spread. Makes about 2 cups.

## Cottage Cheese-Caraway Dip

1 cup (¹/₂ pint) creamed cottage cheese
1 teaspoon grated onion
2 teaspoons caraway seeds, crushed

After crushing the caraway seeds with mortar and pestle, combine ingredients, beat in blender until smooth. The flavor will be improved if the dip is prepared at least a day in advance. Mixture is good as a stuffing for celery. Makes 1 cup.

## Swiss-Cream Dip

1 cup (¹/₄ pound) shredded Swiss Emmentaler
¹/₂ cup sour cream
1 teaspoon grated onion
2 tablespoons chopped stuffed olives

Combine ingredients, blend well. Serve as a dip with corn chips. Makes 1 cup.

## Anchovy-Cheese Canapé Spread

2 cups grated domestic Swiss or natural Gruyère
12 anchovy fillets, minced
4 sweet gherkins, minced
2 tablespoons butter, softened

Pound cheese and anchovies to a paste, and work in gherkins and butter until smooth. Serve cold spread on small toast squares, or toast under broiler until cheese melts. Makes enough for 24 one-inch toast squares.

## Coon Cheese Canapé Spread

3/4 cup Coon or any sharp Cheddar, grated or shredded
1 tablespoon Bahamian mustard
1 teaspoon light cream
1 tablespoon horseradish
1/8 teaspoon paprika

Beat all ingredients together until smooth, by hand or in blender. The spread will keep in the refrigerator, but remove it to room temperature 1 hour before serving, to soften it. Spead on toast circles, rye crackers, or cucumber slices. Makes about 1/2 cup.

## Shrimp-Cheese Pâté

1 4-ounce jar tiny Danish shrimp, drained
4 ounces (1/2 cup) soft or semisoft cheese
    like Philadelphia Cream Cheese,
    Crema Danica, or Camembert
Few grains of freshly ground black pepper
1 teaspoon sherry, Medeira, or cognac

Combine all ingredients, beat until very smooth. Serve on toast rounds or cucumber slices, or stuff radishes or celery with the mixture. Makes about 3/4 cup.

# New Orleans Crab Canapé

FORCEMEAT:
2 tablespoons butter
1 small white onion or shallot
1 tablespoon flour
$^1/_2$ cup broth, water, or white wine
$^3/_4$ cup cooked (or $6^1/_2$-ounce can) crabmeat, drained
   and flaked

Melt butter, add onion, and cook over moderate heat until onion is soft. Add flour, stir to blend, cook 1 minute: stir in broth, cooking until smooth. Add crabmeat, simmer 8 to 10 minutes. Remove from fire; cool.

CHEESE TOPPING:
2 tablespoons butter
2 tablespoons flour
4 ounces (1 cup) grated Parmesan
4 ounces (1 cup) grated Swiss or Gruyère
1 loaf white bread
Butter for sautéing

Melt butter, add flour to make a roux, and cook two or three minutes. Add cheeses, blend well. Remove from fire, cool, then form into small firm, round balls.

Cut bread into canapé-sized pieces; sauté in butter. Spread each with the crab mixture; then place a cheese ball over the crab. Just before serving, place in hot oven for 5 minutes until cheese is melted and bubbly. Makes about 50.

# Herring-Cheese Spread

4 ounces Bel Paese or soft Italian Stracchino, cut in small cubes
2 tablespoons sour cream
Dash tabasco or cayenne
2 tablespoons minced fresh or frozen dill
$^1/_4$ teaspoon paprika
6-ounce jar herring marinated in wine, well drained

Place all ingredients in blender, beat until mixture is smooth. Stop machine to stir down occasionally. Makes about 1 cup.

# Liptauer Cheese Mold

8 ounces cream cheese,* softened
2 tablespoons butter, softened
1 minced anchovy
1 teaspoon prepared mustard
1/2 teaspoon crushed caraway seeds
1/4 teaspoon salt
1 tablespoon paprika
Capers, well drained

Cream together cheese and butter; blend in anchovy, mustard, crushed caraway seeds, salt, and half the paprika. Form into a cone shape with the hands, and place in the center of a small plate. With the tip of a table knife, make ridges lengthwise from base to top of the cone forming several wavy indentations. Gently press capers into a pattern from top to bottom. Sprinkle the remaining paprika over the cone. Radishes and black olives may be arranged on the plate as garnish — a very attractive combination both to look at and to taste. Serve with thin slices of pumpernickel. Makes about 1 cup (enough for 12 to 20 people if other cocktail appetizers are served).

*Note: There is also a semisoft Liptauer cheese made in Germany and Austria from sheep's milk. It may be used instead of domestic cream cheese in making the molded cone.

# Easy Cheese Pin-Ups

You should have three or four kinds of firm or semifirm cheese for these pin-ups, as well as a variety of things to spear onto the cheese. Cut cheese into bite-sized cubes, spear with toothpicks; on the other end of each toothpick, press an olive, cocktail onion, a nut, a piece of fruit, or anything that seems appealing. Here are a few examples:

Havarti topped with a tiny sprig of parsley and a pickled cocktail onion.

Roquefort topped with a mandarin orange segment.

Swiss Emmentaler topped with overlapping paper-thin slices of cucumber and a small cooked shrimp.

Fontina topped with a pimiento-stuffed green olive.

Soft Monterey Jack topped with a square of pimiento and a curled anchovy fillet.

Samsø topped with a square of green pepper and black Italian brine-cured olives — or with a cube of honeydew or cantaloupe.

Danish Blue topped with half a large black Ribier grape (seeded).

Edam topped with a seedless white grape.

Caraway-seed King Christian IX topped with a pickled onion.

Caerphilly topped with a walnut half.

Provolone topped with a curl of salami.

Arrange on a platter or in a long, shallow, wooden bowl, so that guests may help themselves. Or place pin-ups in a shallow pan, covered with Saran Wrap until time to serve, but keep at room temperature.

### Cheese Dreams

These "dreams" can be as simple as squares of process American- or Swiss-cheese slices on crackers (cut to fit) — or as fancy as rare imported cheese spread on bread toasted on one side. Cut slices of cheese to fit saltines or toast so that the cheese does not overlap edges. Or place cheese atop evenly cut cubes of French or Italian bread. Place in a preheated broiler 3 or 4 inches from heat just until the cheese melts. Serve at once.

Here are some nice combinations:

Blue cheese on cubes of French or Italian bread

Swiss on pumpernickel or rye

Caraway-seed cheese on rye

Imported Gouda or Edam on rye or pumpernickel

Bel Paese on cubes or thick slices of whole-wheat Italian bread

# Blue Crab Cream

$3/4$ cup cooked fresh or canned crabmeat ($6^1/2$-ounce can)
$1/2$ cup crumbled Roquefort or Gorgonzola
$1/4$ teaspoon cumin
1 teaspoon grated onion
1 teaspoon horseradish
1 tablespoon olive oil
1 tablespoon mayonnaise or sour cream

Drain crabmeat. remove gristle. Place in blender with remaining ingredients; beat until paste-like. Makes $1^1/2$ cups.


# Samsø Cheese Ball

1 pound Samsø or other mild, semifirm cheese, finely shredded
1 cup ($1/2$ pound) butter, softened
1 teaspoon Dijon-style mustard
2 tablespoons Kümmel, Aquavit, or gin
Toasted sesame seeds

Blend cheese and butter together until smooth. Work in mustard and spirits. Shape into one large ball or several small balls. Roll in the sesame seeds, which have been toasted in a moderate (350° F.) oven for 5 minutes until golden. Serve accompanied by radishes. If cheese is served in one large ball, surround it with crisp rye or onion wafers. Makes one 4¹/₂-inch ball or about 18 small balls.


# Provolone-Ham Celery Stuffing

1 cup grated or shredded Provolone
2 tablespoons butter, softened
$1/4$ cup minced ham
Dash Worcestershire sauce

Blend ingredients and pile lightly in celery. Makes enough to fill 15 to 20 cut sections of celery.

# Roquefort Cocktail Balls

$1/4$ pound Roquefort, crumbled (about $3/4$ cup)
1 3-ounce package cream cheese, or $1/4$ cup sour cream
1 teaspoon grated onion
$1/2$ cup crushed almonds or walnuts

Blend together cheeses and work in onion. Form into small balls with fingers; roll each ball in crushed nuts. Chill thoroughly before serving. Makes 10 to 12 small balls.

VARIATIONS:
- Add $1/4$ cup chopped nuts to the mixture instead of rolling in crushed nuts.
- Add $1/4$ cup minced celery and omit nuts.
- Increase Roquefort to 6 ounces, add 2 tablespoons butter and 1 tablespoon dry sherry.
- Add a dash of Worcestershire and/or tabasco to mixture.
- Instead of nuts, roll the cheese balls in minced parsley, minced fresh or frozen dill, or paprika.

# Esrom-Shrimp Canapés

12 ounces ($3/4$ pound) Esrom
1 to 2 tablespoons horseradish, to taste
2 tablespoons butter
6 slices bread
3 medium tomatoes
3 jars tiny Danish shrimp, drained; or
   2 cans tiny California shrimp, drained

Cut the cheese into 12 even slices. Combine horseradish and butter and spread on the slices of bread. Place cheese slices on the bread; cut each sandwich into 4 triangles. Slice tomatoes; then cut part way through each slice, so that tomato slices can be placed upright on the cheese like dancing figures. Arrange overlapping shrimp on either side of the tomato slices. Place canapés in shallow pan, cover tightly with Saran Wrap, and keep in refrigerator until serving time. Makes 24.

## Roquefort-Stuffed Pecans

1/2 pound Roquefort
1/4 cup butter, softened
1 teaspoon grated onion
1 tablespoon minced celery
1/4 teaspoon Worcestershire sauce
Salt and pepper
48 large pecan halves

Mash Roquefort. Add butter, onion, celery, and Worcestershire. Beat until smooth and well blended. Add salt and pepper to taste. Chill. With moistened hands, roll mixture into 24 small balls. Press a pecan half into either side of each cheese ball. Serve within one to 1 1/2 hours after forming. Makes 24.

## Havarti Canapés

3/4 pound Havarti, cut in 6 1/4-inch slices
2 tablespoons sweet butter
6 slices square pumpernickel bread
6 slices cooked bacon, each cut into thirds
24 cocktail onions

Place the slices of cheese over buttered slices of bread. Cut each bread slice into 4 triangles. Place a curl of cooked bacon on each triangle, and with toothpicks fasten cocktail onions to the bacon. Makes 24.

## Cheese-Stuffed Celery

Almost any of the spreads or dips given earlier may be used as stuffings for celery. Especially recommended are Coon Cheese Canapé Spread, Pot Kås, Bierkäse Dip, Shrimp-Cheese Canapé Spread, and Cottage Cheese-Caraway Dip.

# Cheese and Smoked Salmon Canapés

6 slices square rye or pumpernickel bread
Butter
8 ounces (¹₂ pound) Tybo, mild Cheddar, or
    Stracchino, thinly sliced
6 slices smoked salmon
Fresh or frozen dill, minced

Spread bread thickly and evenly with butter. Arrange slices of cheese over bread and cut each sandwich into 6 fingers. Cut the salmon into 36 slivers, arranging a sliver on each bread-and-cheese finger. Sprinkle dill over the salmon. Place canapés in a shallow pan, cover tightly with Saran Wrap, and keep refrigerated until time to serve. Makes 36.

# Stuffed Cantaloupe

1 medium cantaloupe
White or rosé wine
¹₄ pound blue cheese, crumbled
¹₂ pound Ricotta or farmer's cheese
¹₄ cup sour cream or heavy sweet cream
Salt and freshly ground pepper

Cut a slice off the top of the cantaloupe, scoop out the fruit with a melon-ball cutter. Marinate the melon balls in wine until time to serve. In the meantime, blend together cheeses and cream. Season to taste with salt and pepper. Pile the cheese mixture lightly into the cantaloupe shell. If it does not fill the shell, lower the rim of the shell by cutting with knife in jagged edges to form a "basket edge." To eat, spear melon balls with toothpicks, and dip them into the cheese mixture for a very pretty, refreshingly different appetizer. Makes about 1 cup cheese mixture and about 20 melon balls.

### Blue-Cheese Celery Stuffing

1 8-ounce package cream cheese
1 3-ounce package (1/3 cup) any blue cheese, crumbled
1 tablespoon sour cream
2 tablespoons minced fresh or frozen dill
2 tablespoons minced chives, scallions, or shallots
1 teaspoon caraway seeds
Salt
Paprika

Combine all ingredients except paprika, adding salt to taste. Pile lightly in trimmed celery stalks and sprinkle paprika over the top.

### Cheese-Stuffed Pineapple

1 ripe pineapple
1 8-ounce package cream cheese
1/2 cup grated Dunlop or sharp, well-aged Cheddar
1 tablespoon minced chives
1/4 teaspoon dry mustard
1 tablespoon white rum
1/4 teaspoon salt (optional)

Cut off the top of the pineapple far enough down so that a wide rim is formed. Scoop out the fruit and chop it fine. Blend together the cheeses, chives, 1 1/2 cups of the chopped pineapple, mustard, rum, and salt. Pile mixture into pineapple shell. Serve with Triscuits, toast rounds, or squares. Makes about 2 cups.

### Stuffed Cherry Tomatoes

Select large cherry tomatoes, scoop out top of each and pile a little of the same cheese mixture suggested for stuffed mushrooms on top. Or use Camembert, Liederkranz, Crema Danica, or any other semisoft cheese as stuffing. An arrangement of mushrooms and tomatoes, with the same or alternate cheese stuffings, would also be attractive.

## Marinated Swiss Cubes

Cut natural Swiss or Gruyère in cubes and marinate several hours in a spicy garlic-flavored French dressing. Drain well before serving on toothpicks.

## Münster Cheese au Madeira

Cut domestic Münster cheese into cubes and marinate in Madeira wine overnight at room temperature. Serve with toothpicks.

## Radishes au Camembert

Trim radishes, slice off tops, and pile a little Camembert on top of each. Radishes are also delicious with Port du Salut, Brie, Limburger, and any other piquant soft or semisoft cheese.

## Red and Green Cheddar Balls

1/2 pound Cheddar, shredded (2 cups)
4 tablespoons (1/2 stick) butter, softened
2 tablespoons medium sherry or beer
Paprika
Minced parsley

Combine cheese and butter, beat until smooth; gradually beat in sherry or beer. Form into tiny balls. Roll half the balls in paprika and half in parsley. Chill. Serve this way or on round crackers. Makes about 24.

PROVOLONE BALLS: Use 1/2 pound shredded or grated Provolone instead of Cheddar.

TILSITER BALLS: Use 1/2 pound shredded Tilsiter instead of Cheddar. Roll some of the balls in caraway seeds.

# Stuffed Mushrooms

Large mushroom caps, about 24 (1 pound)
$^1/_2$ pound Ricotta or farmer's cheese
1 teaspoon grated onion; or 1 tablespoon minced chives; or
    1 teaspoon crushed instant onion flakes
$^1/_4$ teaspoon salt
$^1/_2$ teaspoon curry powder
Dash paprika

Select medium-to-large mushrooms, and remove stems. Place them in lemon-scented water to whiten. Blend together cheese, onion, salt, and curry powder. Then fill raw mushrooms with the cheese mixture. Dust tops with paprika. This hors d'oeuvre is delicious and very low in calories. Makes 20 to 24.


# Stuffed Edam

1 baby Edam (about 7 ounces)
$^1/_4$ pound (1 stick) butter, softened
1 cup beer
$^1/_2$ teaspoon dry mustard
1 tablespoon grated onion; or $^1/_2$ teaspoon crushed
    caraway seeds (optional)

Slice a 2-inch piece from the top of the Edam, and scoop out the cheese from inside, leaving the red shell intact. Beat the scooped-out cheese with butter and a little of the beer in a blender, slowly adding the remaining beer, the mustard, and the onion or caraway. Pile the mixture into the empty shell. Serve with crackers and stuffed green olives. This dish is best if served within 24 hours. Makes 14 to 16 servings.

STUFFED GOUDA: For a 14-ounce Gouda, use twice as much beer, mustard, and butter. Makes about 30 servings.

## Chutney Cheese

1 8-ounce package cream cheese, softened;
   or 6 ounces Crema Danica or Gervaise
2 to 3 tablespoons milk
$1/2$ cup Major Gray's chutney, chopped fine
$1/2$ cup chopped walnuts
$1/4$ cup chopped pitted dates
2 teaspoons lemon juice

Combine all ingredients, beat to blend. Serve as a dip with saltines or Triscuits. This cheese spread is good with tea or a fruit-wine punch. Makes about $1^2/3$ cups.

## Roquefort-Stuffed Shrimp

18 jumbo shrimp in the shell (about 2 pounds)
1 package (3 ounces) cream cheese
$1/2$ cup crumbled Roquefort
$1/4$ cup mayonnaise
$1/4$ cup minced celery
2 teaspoons grated onion
$1/4$ teaspoon poultry seasoning*
Juice of $1/2$ lemon
Minced parsley or minced fresh dill

Cook shrimp in boiling, salted water until just pink. Drain, shell, and split in halves, lengthwise. Wash, drain thoroughly, and pat dry. Mash cream cheese until soft. Beat in Roquefort, mayonnaise, celery, onion, and poultry seasoning. Gradually beat in lemon juice. Spoon Roquefort mixture evenly over cut surfaces of shrimp, press against cut surfaces of other halves of shrimp. Roll edge of shrimp in parsley or dill. Chill until ready to serve. Serve stuffed shrimp as an appetizer with cherry tomatoes and scallions or celery curls. Makes 18 appetizers.

*Or use a blend of thyme and oregano.

## Cucumber Canapés

1 large or 2 small cucumbers
1 cup (¹/₄ pound) grated firm cheese such as Manchego,
    Swiss Emmentaler, Wisconsin Longhorn, or Provolone
2 tablespoons butter
2 tablespoons minced parsley
1 teaspoon grated onion (optional)

Partially peel cucumber lengthwise; then cut crosswise into ¹/₄-inch slices. In blender, beat together cheese, butter, parsley, and onion. Spread over cucumber slices. If desired, top with thin strips of pimiento, sprinkle lightly with paprika, or press capers on top of each. Makes about 20 canapés.


## Chipped Beef-Cheese Rolls

¹/₂ pound blue cheese (Roquefort, Gorgonzola, Danish,
    or Wisconsin Blue)
6 ounces Crema Danica, Camembert, or cream cheese
2 tablespoons beer or dry sherry
1 4-ounce package dried beef

Cream cheeses together until soft, beating in beer or sherry. Lay out slices of the dried beef, spread some cheese mixture on each slice, then roll up. Chill until firm. Cut in bite-sized portions with a sharp, thin-bladed knife. Serve on crackers or toast rounds. Makes about 40.

VARIATIONS: Substitute thinly sliced ham, olive-and-pimiento loaf, or any other similar luncheon meat for dried beef.


## Radish-Camembert Canapés

Cut either pumpernickel or white bread into circles with a biscuit cutter. Butter each thickly, spread with Camembert, and top with very thin overlapping slices of radish. Cover with Saran Wrap until time to serve, but keep at room temperature

## Hot Cheese Balls

1¼ cups (4 ounces) grated Swiss Emmentaler
1 tablespoon flour
¼ teaspoon salt
½ teaspoon Worcestershire sauce
3 egg whites
Fine breadcrumbs or cornflake crumbs
Oil for frying

Here is a good way to use dried-up bits of cheese, for a drier, older piece of Swiss cheese grates better and melts more readily. Combine the grated cheese with flour, salt, and Worcestershire, blending well. Beat the egg whites until foamy, forming soft not stiff peaks. Add a little of the egg white at a time to the cheese mixture, until you have a paste that can be formed with the fingers into balls about 1 inch in diameter. (You may not need all the egg white; if too much is added, the mixture will become too liquid to handle easily.) Roll the cheese balls in the crumbs until they are thoroughly coated. Chill (or freeze for later frying). When ready to serve,* heat fat or oil to 375° F. in a deep-fat fryer or a deep, heavy kettle or skillet to depth of 1½ to 2 inches; add the cheese balls, and fry one minute if chilled, 1½ minutes if frozen, or until crisply brown. Drain on paper towels; serve while still warm. Makes 12 to 14 cheese balls.

*Note: The cheese balls may be fried ahead of time and reheated, but the flavor is better if they are cooked shortly before serving.

## Carozza Mozzarella (Fried Mozzarella Appetizers)

Cut 3-inch rounds of bread, using biscuit cutter. Place a small slice of Mozzarella cut to fit on each of half the bread rounds, cover with the remaining rounds. Press firmly together. Dip each in flour, then in beaten egg thinned with milk (2 tablespoons for 1 beaten egg). Fry as for grilled cheese sandwiches in a mixture of olive oil and butter. Serve hot. These appetizers should be fried just before serving, but they can be dipped in flour and egg in advance.

# Toasted Cheshire Savories

3 ounces Cheshire, grated
2 egg yolks
1/4 cup fine dry crumbs
6 tablespoons softened butter
1/2 teaspoon dry mustard
Salt and pepper
4 slices bread, trimmed, cut into triangles

Combine cheese, egg yolks, crumbs, butter and seasoning. Beat to a paste and spread over triangles of toast. Place under the broiler until the cheese is melted. Makes 16 triangles, enough to serve 4.

# Italian Cheese Croutons

3 tablespoons olive oil
1/2 teaspoon salt
1/4 teaspoon paprika
3 cups slightly stale 3/4- to 1-inch-square bread cubes
1/3 cup grated Parmesan, Romano, Caciocavallo or Asiago;
  or 1/2 cup shredded firm cheese like Fontina or Fontinella

Heat oil with salt and paprika, add bread, stir until bread cubes are soaked with oil on all sides. Remove from skillet, transfer to pan, sprinkle cheese over top, place in 350° F. (moderate) oven for ten minutes, shaking pan once or twice, until bread has absorbed fat and cheese and is golden. Makes approximately 40 croutons.

# Pastry Dreams

Roll out pie crust, using mix or your favorite recipe. Cut into squares the size of saltines. Bake in preheated 450° F. oven until golden, about 15 minutes. Place cheese squares (any kind that melts easily) over pastry, and, if you like, place a walnut or pecan in center of each spread. Just before serving, return to oven, or place under broiler until cheese melts. Serve hot. (This is a good way to use up scraps of pie crust dough leftover when making pie.)

## Phil Alpert's Everlasting Cheese

2 cups grated or shredded leftover cheese (almost any kind)
2 tablespoons olive oil (preferably Spanish)
2 tablespoons bourbon or cognac
2 to 4 tablespoons cream cheese or butter

Combine ingredients and beat until smooth. Age at least two days before serving. Continue to add more leftover cheese as needed and, if mixture becomes too firm, a little more bourbon or cognac. This mixture will keep in refrigerator indefinitely and improves vastly with age. Makes 1 cup cheese spread. Remove from refrigerator at least one hour before serving.

## Pot Kås (Swedish Potted Cheese)

1$^1$/$_2$ to 2 cups leftover cheese (any kind)
2 tablespoons butter, softened
Dash cayenne pepper
1 teaspoon caraway seeds
1 to 2 tablespoons aquavit, beer, or ale
2 tablespoons minced pimiento (optional)

Beat together by hand or in blender all ingredients until smooth. Age in a covered jar or crock, in a cool place, at least two days. Bring to room temperature before serving. Makes about 1 cup.

## Minced Clam Dip

1 7-ounce can minced clams, well drained
1 8-ounce package cream cheese; or 4 ounces ($^1$/$_2$ cup) any
   soft or semisoft mild cheese, plus 1 or 2 tablespoons
   sour cream
$^1$/$_2$ teaspoon paprika

Combine ingredients, beat to blend well. Serve with crisp wafers. Makes $^3$/$_4$ to 1 cup.

BLUE CLAM DIP: Use 3-ounce package cream cheese and 4 ounces (1 cup crumbled) any blue cheese, instead of eight-ounce package cream cheese.

# ZESTY CHEESE PASTRIES

Crisp cheese sticks, plain or peppered with cayenne, make superb appetizers with almost any drinks, from tomato juice to martinis. They are also excellent accompaniments to soup. Pigs in Cheese Blankets — cocktail frankfurters or Vienna sausages rolled in a cream-cheese pastry, then baked until the pastry is golden — are delightful for any cocktail party. Danish Blue Chips — pastry made with Danish blue cheese and caraway seeds, then cut into rounds with a biscuit cutter and baked until flaky-crisp — will be much more provocative to thirst than would ordinary caraway wafers.

As the making of all cheese pastries requires basically the same techniques, this section also includes several recipes for what are really luncheon dishes — Quiche Lorraine and Swiss Flan, for example. These two also may be served as hors d'oeuvres if cut into small wedges rather than the usual luncheon-sized servings.

Cheese pastries are as old as Western civilization, the first on record having been made in Greece during its Golden Age. *Tiropeta*, literally "cheese cakes," the Greeks called them (and still do to this day), but most of the Greek *tiropeta* are zesty, piquant cheese pastries more suitable for appetizers than for desserts. It is interesting to see how similar some of these very old Greek pastries are to others that are native to Switzerland, France, and even Russia.

For example, while I was dining one day not long ago at the Swiss Châlet, one of the finest Swiss restaurants in New York City, the owner, Conrad Egli, gave me his recipe for little hot cheese tarts which he calls *ramequins*. He always uses puff paste to make these tarts, he explained, because puff paste makes a crisper and flakier crust for what is essentially a custard mixture. Later I came across a recipe for *tiropeta* in a Greek cookbook that called for *phyllo* pastry — the very thin, crisp pastry that the Greeks were making hundreds of years before puff paste was invented.

The cheeses used to fill the little tarts of these two countries are, of course, quite different. In Greece. Feta and Kashkaval are used; in Switzerland, a blend of natural Gruyère and Emmentaler.

116

Another well-known Swiss cheese pie is called *flan*. The pastry for this pie is sometimes closer to a rich biscuit dough, but in other versions a short pastry may be used. The word *flan* means different things in different countries: In Spain it is plain caramel custard, in France a fruit tart in pastry, in Switzerland a cheese custard in pastry. And sometimes Swiss Flan is made with onions and cheese in custard!

### Swiss Flan

PASTRY:
1 cup biscuit mix
3 tablespoons butter
$^1/_4$ cup light cream

To make pastry, chop butter into the biscuit mix, work in cream, and roll out on lightly floured board; or press into a 9-inch pie pan, fluting the edges. Chill while preparing filling.

FILLING:
1 large onion, sliced or chopped
2 tablespoons butter
2 eggs, beaten
2 cups ($^1/_2$ pound) shredded natural Gruyère
$^1/_4$ teaspoon salt

Cook onion in butter until golden; cool slightly. Add eggs, cheese, and salt. Pour this mixture into pastry, and bake in oven preheated to 425° F. (very hot) for 15 minutes; then reduce heat to 350° F. (moderate), and continue baking 25 to 30 minutes or until a knife inserted in the center comes out clean. Serve warm as a luncheon entree to 4 to 6 persons, or cut into small wedges for appetizers. Makes 10 to 12 appetizers.

VARIATIONS: Instead of this pastry, regular pie crust may be used. Or make pastry of 1 cup flour, 1 teaspoon baking powder, $^1/_4$ teaspoon salt, $^1/_3$ cup butter, and 1 beaten egg. Do not attempt to roll out this butter-rich pastry; press it with your fingers into pie pan, fluting the edges.

# Käsestangen (Cheese Twists)

1 cup sifted all-purpose flour
$1/2$ teaspoon salt
Freshly ground black pepper
4 tablespoons ($1/2$ stick) butter
1 cup grated sharp Cheddar, Coon, or Swiss Emmentaler
1 to 2 tablespoons milk

Combine flour, salt, and pepper; cut in butter until particles are size of peas; then work in the cheese and enough milk to form a dough. Chill dough until it is easy to work; then roll it out to $1/8$-inch thickness on a lightly floured board. Cut into "fingers" $1/2$-inch wide; then twist each and place on an ungreased baking sheet. Bake in an oven preheated to 400° F. (hot) until golden, about 12 minutes. Serve hot or cold. These twists can be stored in a tightly covered container for a week or more or can be frozen. Makes about 3 dozen.

TABASCO-CHEESE BALLS: Add a dash of tabasco or cayenne to the flour with salt and pepper; omit milk, and use 1 teaspoon Worcestershire sauce and 1 tablespoon water. Instead of rolling out dough, form it into 1-inch balls, chill thoroughly, then bake in oven preheated to 450° F. (very hot) until golden, about 10 minutes.

CARAWAY-CHEESE TWISTS: Add 2 tablespoons caraway seeds to sifted flour in either Käsestangen recipes.

# Extra-Crisp Käsestangen

This version is a little more difficult to make than the first, but it is much crisper and lighter. These twists are excellent as accompaniments to clear soups, as well as for cocktail appetizers.

2 cups sifted all-purpose flour
$1/2$ teaspoon salt
2 tablespoons vegetable shortening
$1/2$ pound (2 sticks or 1 cup) cold, firm butter
6 tablespoons ice water
1 to $1^1/2$ cups shredded or grated sharp Cheddar or Cheshire

Combine flour and salt, cut in shortening, work with fingers to blend well, then cut in one stick (1 2 cup) of the butter until mixture is in pieces the size of peas. Add the ice water 1 tablespoon at a time, and blend to form a firm dough. Roll out one-half at a time; dot each roll of pastry with butter, and spread the cheese evenly over each. Fold each in thirds, let stand 10 minutes, then roll out again. Again fold each in thirds, and this time chill it in the refrigerator for 10 minutes. Roll out a third time, this time over waxed paper to prevent sticking. The pastry should be about $1/4$ inch thick — thicker than for pies. Cut it into strips $1/2$ inch by 2 inches, twist, then chill 15 minutes. Bake in an oven preheated to 425° F. until crisp and golden, about 15 minutes. Makes about 60.

CURRIED CHEESE TWISTS: Add 1 teaspoon curry powder to the flour.

## Danish Blue Chips

1 cup Danish Blue, crumbled
$1/2$ cup butter
2 cups sifted all-purpose flour
1 beaten egg
Caraway seeds

Make pastry dough by blending together the cheese, butter, and flour. Knead until smooth, chill; then roll out between sheets of waxed paper to $1/4$-inch thick. Cut into rounds with a biscuit cutter, or into fingers $1/2$ inch wide, and twist as for Käsestangen. Brush tops of circles with beaten egg, and sprinkle with caraway seeds. Bake in an oven preheated to 425° F. (very hot) about 10 minutes until golden and crisp. Makes about 4 dozen.

DANISH BLUE WHIRLS: Divide pastry into two parts, rolling each out into a rectangle $1/4$ inch thick. Sprinkle one rectangle with chopped walnuts, the other with chopped black olives. Pat filling with fingers into the pastry. Roll up as for cookie whirligigs, chill both rolls until firm, then cut in slices $1/4$ inch thick. Bake on an ungreased baking sheet in an oven preheated to 425° F. (very hot) for about 15 minutes. Makes about 3 dozen.

119

## Rags and Tatters

1 cup sifted flour
Dash of cayenne pepper
$^1/_2$ stick (4 tablespoons) butter
5 tablespoons grated Parmesan
$^1/_4$ cup grated Cheddar
1 egg, well beaten
Anchovy paste
About 2 tablespoons milk

Combine flour and cayenne; work in butter and cheeses, then 2 tablespoons egg. Knead to make a smooth dough. Chill; then roll out on a lightly floured board to $^1$ ʀ inch thick. Cut in half. Spread anchovy paste very thinly on one half; then brush with beaten egg. Cover with remaining pastry, and press together. Cut with scissors into small, odd shapes. Brush the tops with milk. Bake on an ungreased baking sheet in an oven heated to 450° F. (very hot) until golden. Serve hot. Makes about 30.

## Quiche Lorraine

Puff Paste; or pie dough for 9-inch pastry shell
6 slices bacon
1 cup ($^1/_4$ pound) shredded Swiss Emmentaler or
    Gruyère; or $^1/_2$ cup each
$^1/_2$ cup grated Parmesan
2 cups light cream or dairy half-and-half
2 eggs, well beaten
1 teaspoon salt
Pinch of white pepper or cayenne (optional)

Line a pie pan with pastry, fluting the rim above the edge of pan. Cook bacon until crisp; drain on paper; break into small pieces. Combine remaining ingredients, add bacon and pour into pastry shell. Bake in an oven preheated to 425° F. (very hot) for 10 minutes; then lower heat to 325° F. (moderate) for 30 minutes or until a knife inserted in the center comes out clean.* makes 4 to 6 servings as entree or 10 appetizer servings.

*Note: For crisper pastry, whether using Puff Paste or regular pie dough, freeze the pastry before adding filling.

# Danish Cheese Tarts

PASTRY:
1$^1$ $_2$ cups dry pumpernickel crumbs*
$^1$ $_3$ cup butter, melted
1 egg

Blend crumbs, butter, and egg. Press the crumb mixture firmly against bottom and sides of 6 individual baking dishes (pie pans, casseroles, or shirred-egg ramekins). Bake in a moderate oven (350° F.) for 15 minutes. Cool before filling.

*Note: To make the crumbs, dry the thinly sliced squares of dark whole-grain bread in the oven. Then whirl in an electric blender, or put through a food grinder.

FILLING:
8 strips bacon; or $^1$/$_2$ cup diced ham
1 onion, chopped ($^3$/$_4$ cup)
1$^1$/$_2$ cups Tybo, Havarti, Esrom, Samsø, or Danish Blue
   ( or a mixture of Danish Blue and one of the others)
5 eggs, lightly beaten
2 cups light cream
$^1$/$_4$ teaspoon nutmeg
$^1$/$_4$ teaspoon pepper

Cook bacon until crisp; drain and crumble. (Or brown ham cubes lightly in a little bacon fat or butter.) In the same pan, lightly cook chopped onion; drain. Divide bacon or ham and onion into prepared dishes, spreading evenly. Add 1 cup of cheese cut in small cubes. Blend 5 beaten eggs with cream and seasonings, and strain custard over bacon and onions. Shred or crumble remaining cheese, sprinkle over top. Bake the tarts in a moderate oven (350° F.) for about 20 minutes until the custard is set. A knife inserted near (not at) the center should come out clean. Makes 6 tarts.

# Piroshki

CREAM CHEESE PASTRY:
1 3-ounce package cream cheese, cut in small pieces
1 tablespoon grated sharp Cheddar
1¹/₂ cups sifted all-purpose flour
¹/₂ teaspoon salt

Work cheeses into flour and salt until a well-blended dough is formed. Chill overnight. Roll out on a lightly floured board a little at a time, forming 4-inch squares or rectangles 3 x 6 inches. Place a spoonful of filling on each, roll up, seal the edges. Bake in oven preheated to 400° F. for 15 minutes until crisp and brown. Piroshki should be served hot, but they are also good cold (at room temperature). Makes 8 to 10.

FISH FILLING:
¹/₂ cup cooked white-fleshed fish or tuna,
    drained and flaked
Salt and pepper
1 hard-cooked egg, chopped
1 tablespoon sour cream

Blend ingredients, season to taste.

SHRIMP FILLING:
1 cup cooked or canned medium shrimp, minced
1 teaspoon grated onion
¹/₄ teaspoon dry mustard
1 teaspoon oil
Salt and pepper

Beat ingredients together until well blended.

CABBAGE FILLING:
1 cup shredded cabbage
1 tablespoon shortening or margarine
¹/₂ teaspoon salt
Pepper
2 tablespoons sour cream
Pinch of ginger

Cook the cabbage in the shortening until just soft. Add remaining ingredients. Place in pastry so that edges can be completely sealed.

PIGS IN CHEESE BLANKETS: Roll out Cream Cheese Pastry and cut into rectangles 2 x 4 inches each. Place a cocktail frankfurther inside each, roll pastry around it, and place it overlapped side down on baking sheet. Bake in a hot oven (400° F.) until pastry is golden, 20 to 25 minutes. Pigs can be rolled up ready to bake in advance and placed in the oven just before guests are due or even after they have arrived. The timer should be set to make sure the Pigs come out of the oven in time. Makes 10 to 12. (Double pastry recipe to make 20 to 24.)

### Petits Chaussons (French Cheese Pastries)

2 packages pie-crust mix; or your own favorite pastry
  recipe for 2 2-crust pies
2 cups (¹/₂ pound) firm or semifirm cheese*
  grated or crumbled
¹/₄ pound (1 stick) butter, softened
2 tablespoons minced scallions
1 egg, well beaten

Prepare pie-crust mix as directed on package; roll out a little at a time, and cut into 2¹/₂-inch squares. Shred or crumble the cheese and add softened butter, scallions, and the beaten egg; beat to blend well. In each pastry square, place 1 teaspoon filling; moisten the edges, cover with a second square of pastry; seal by pressing the edges with a fork. Bake in an oven preheated to 425° F. for 12 to 15 minutes. Makes about 40.

*Note: Almost any cheese can be used. Especially recommended are any blue-veined cheese, Provolone, Gruyère, Emmentaler, or a crumbly goat cheese.

# Ramequins au Swiss Châlet (Individual Cheese Tarts)

PUFF PASTE:
2 cups sifted all-purpose flour
$^1/_2$ teaspoon salt
2 tablespoons vegetable shortening
$^1/_2$ pound (2 sticks or 1 cup) cold, firm butter
6 tablespoons ice water

Place flour, salt, shortening, and half the butter in a mixing bowl; chop until butter and shortening are as fine as peas. Add 1 tablespoon water at a time until a stiff dough can be formed with the fingers. Press out on a lightly floured board. Place the remaining butter over the dough in tiny little pieces. Fold dough in thirds, and let stand 10 minutes; roll out again, rolling away from you. Fold in thirds again, place in refrigerator for 10 minutes (wrapped in waxed paper), then repeat. Repeat the process once again, adding more flour to the board and the rolling pin if necessary, but use as little flour as possible. Cut into 10 even portions; roll out one at a time to shape small tart shells, keeping the remaining dough in the refrigerator. As soon as shaped, place each tart shell in the freezer. Chill until frozen. Then place inside muffin cups.

GRUYÈRE FILLING:
2 cups ($^1/_2$ pound) shredded natural Gruyère; or 1 cup
    Gruyère and 1 cup Swiss Emmentaler
1 tablespoon flour
3 eggs, well beaten
1 cup light cream, dairy half-and-half, or milk
$^1/_4$ teaspoon salt

Toss the cheese with the flour; then add eggs and cream and salt. Divide filling among the frozen tart shells in muffin cups. Return to the freezer while preheating oven to 450° F. (to be crisp, the pastry must be very cold when placed in a hot oven). When the tarts have been placed in the oven, reduce the heat to 400° F. Bake 20 minutes or until the filling is puffed and golden, the pastry crisp and flaky. Makes 10.

SHORT-CUT FLAN: Buy frozen patty shells, defrost enough to divide each shell in half, then roll out to make 10 to 12 individual tart shells. Refreeze pastry while mixing filling.

## Tiropeta (Greek Cheese Pie)

FILLING:
2 tablespoons butter
2 tablespoons flour
1 cup milk
3 eggs, beaten
$^{1}/_{2}$ pound Feta, crumbled (2 cups)
$^{1}/_{4}$ pound Kashkaval, grated (1 cup)

To make filling, melt butter, stir in flour, then slowly stir in milk. Cool slightly, add beaten eggs and the two kinds of cheese.

PASTRY:
$^{1}/_{2}$ pound phyllo pastry (or make Puff Paste as in
    preceding recipe for Ramequins)
About $^{1}/_{2}$ pound melted butter

If phyllo pastry is used, place ten layers in the bottom of 9 x 15 x 2-inch pan (cut sheets to fit pan), brushing each layer with melted butter. Spoon the cheese filling over them; then add 6 to 8 additional layers of pastry, brushing each with melted butter. If puff paste is used, omit melted butter, divide the dough in half, and roll out each half to fit pan; place the filling over the bottom crust, then add upper crust. Chill a half-hour before baking. Whichever pastry is used, bake the "pie" in a preheated 375° F. (hot) oven for 30 minutes or until pastry is golden and crisp. Cool slightly; then cut into squares. The dish should be served warm. Makes approximately 16 servings.

# Bourekakia (Greek Appetizer Pastries)

$^1/_2$ pound phyllo pastry; or 1 package pie-crust mix;
    or pastry for a 2-crust pie
$^1/_2$ pound (2 cups) Feta, crumbled
1 cup Ricotta or farmer's cheese
2 eggs, beaten
Minced parsley or freshly ground black pepper (optional)
About $^1/_4$ pound melted butter

Phyllo pastry can be obtained at Greek groceries or delicatessens. If there are none in your locality, make pie crust in the usual way, rolling as thin as possible. Cut into 3-inch squares. Beat together the two kinds of cheese, blend in the beaten eggs, and add the parsley or pepper. If you are using phyllo pastry, first soften the pastry sheets by covering with a dampened towel; then, cut them into 3-inch squares; brush each square of pastry with melted butter; place a spoonful of cheese mixture in the center. Fold into a triangle, pressing the edges together. (Do the same with pie crust, but it is not necessary to brush with melted butter.) Brush melted butter generously over the outsides of the pastry squares, top and bottom. Bake* in an oven preheated to 400° F. for 10 to 15 minutes until golden and crisp. Serve hot. Makes 40 to 50 small appetizer pastries.

*Note: Technically, Bourekakia should be *fried* pastries, but baking them is much easier. Sometimes this recipe is called *Tiropetakia* in Greek cookbooks, and as far as I can tell the only difference is that Bourekakia may occasionally be filled with other things than a cheese mixture.

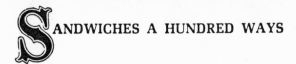

# SANDWICHES A HUNDRED WAYS

The number of possible cheese sandwiches an inventive kitchen artist can dream up is beyond count. To start with, one needs only two pieces of bread and a slice of cheese, and, considering that there are about a thousand kinds of cheese in existence, a thousand different cheese sandwiches are immediately possible. Now consider the different kinds of bread: white sandwich loaf, white French bread, pumpernickel, rye, cracked wheat, caraway bread, egg bread, limpa, protein bread, oatmeal bread, raisin bread, English muffins — and how many more?

With this simple combination of bread and cheese, you can go on to grilled-cheese sandwiches, French-fried cheese sandwiches and baked or broiled open-faced sandwiches.

Now start putting with the cheese a second filling ingredient: ham, sliced onion, green pepper, sliced tomatoes, shrimp, crabmeat, slices of avocado, lettuce, or bacon. Add a relish or sauce (for example, mayonnaise, Tartar sauce or Russian dressing), and the possible variations multiply rapidly.

Hamburgers and hot dogs are basically sandwiches, for they are meat encased in buns, and each has a cheese variation (cheeseburgers and cheese-stuffed hot dogs).

According to the original definition, originating with the hasty meal between bread consumed by the Earl of Sandwich at his gaming tables, an "open-faced sandwich" is a contradiction in terms. But such is progress. A sandwich now can be a small meal piled upon a single piece of bread and eaten with a knife and fork — like the world renowned *smørrebrød* of the Danes. Or it can be a towering triple-decker or a massive Hero. The Earl would be amazed to know what concoctions have been created in his name.

# Grilled-Cheese Sandwich

Place a slice of cheese between two slices of white bread; spread butter (or margarine) on the *outside* of bread; place sandwich in heavy skillet or griddle, and brown on each side. Cut in half before serving.

Any of the following cheeses may be used:

American
Swiss (American)
Swiss Emmentaler
Natural Gruyère
Brick
Provolone
Caraway-seed cheese like Bondost. Kümmelkäse, or King Christian IX
Danbo
Samsø
Fontina or Fontinella
Monterey Jack
Gorgonzola
Cheshire
Gloucester
Edam
Gouda
Mozzarella
Havarti
Bel Paese
Tijuana

In fact, any firm or semifirm cheese that can be sliced will do.

GRILLED SWISS CHEESE SANDWICH: Brown in olive oil rather than in butter — a surprisingly good flavor combination.

GRILLED DANISH BLUE CHEESE SANDWICH: Use cracked-wheat or rye bread.

GRILLED BACON-AND-CHEESE SANDWICH: First fry bacon; then place cooked bacon on sliced cheese for the sandwich. Grill in bacon fat instead of butter.

GRILLED HAM-AND-SWISS CHEESE SANDWICH: Add slices of ham to slices of Swiss Cheese between bread slices.

GRILLED CHEESE-AND-AVOCADO SANDWICH: Place slices of avocado over slices of Monterey Jack or mild Cheddar.

GRILLED CHEESE-AND-TOMATO SANDWICH: Simply add tomato slices.

GRILLED ONION CHEESE SANDWICH: Add slices of onion, and use Cheddar, Swiss, or Provolone.

And so on and on.

## Cheese-Spread Sandwiches

Any of the cheese spreads in the hors d'oeuvres chapter can be used for a sandwich filling.
Here are some additional ideas:
- Combine Phil Alpert's Everlasting Cheese with cottage cheese and crumbled cooked bacon.
- Make egg salad (for sandwich filling), adding bits of diced firm or semifirm cheese (almost any kind — both blue cheese and Provolone are especially good).
- Use Blue Crab Cream as a filling with sliced tomatoes between slices of toasted cheese bread.
- Spread Anchovy-Cheese Canapé Spread between thinly sliced pumpernickel, with radishes and black olives on the side.

## Hot Roquefort-Nut Open Sandwich

Butter slices of toast, and cover each with a slice of Roquefort cheese. Dust cheese with cayenne pepper. Place 5 inches from broiler for 5 or 6 minutes until cheese starts to melt, then sprinkle with slivered almonds until almonds start to brown. Serve at once.

# French-Toast Cheese Sandwiches

2 slices cheese (any sliceable variety)
4 slices white bread
1 egg, beaten
2 tablespoons milk
Dash salt
3 to 4 tablespoons shortening or bacon fat

Place each slice of cheese between two slices bread. Dip sandwich into mixture of beaten egg, milk, and salt. Fry as for French toast in hot shortening or bacon fat, turning to brown on both sides. Makes 2 sandwiches.


# Croque-Monsieur

Croque-Monsieur is virtually the same as French-Toast Cheese Sandwiches, but with ham added and a French name to make it seem more exotic.

$3/4$ cup grated Swiss Emmentaler or natural Gruyère
2 tablespoons heavy cream or softened butter
8 slices white bread
4 slices ham
2 eggs, beaten
$1^1/_2$ teaspoons salt
4 tablespoons milk
6 tablespoons butter or margarine

Combine cheese and cream (or softened butter), beat until smooth, then spread on 4 slices of bread. Top with ham and remaining slices of bread. Beat eggs, salt, and milk together, dip each sandwich in the egg mixture, and fry in butter or margarine until crisply golden on each side. Makes 4 sandwiches. Or each sandwich can be cut in 4 pieces to make 16 appetizers.

# Cheese Western Sandwich

1 tablespoon oil
1 small onion, chopped
2 tablespoons chopped green pepper
1/4 cup minced ham
2 eggs
1/2 teaspoon salt
1/2 cup shredded Longhorn, Jack, or mild Cheddar
Dash of cayenne pepper
4 slices buttered toast

In the oil sauté the onion, green pepper, and ham until lightly browned. Beat eggs, add salt, cheese, and cayenne. Add to the onion mixture, scramble quickly. Serve between toast slices with catsup or chili sauce on the side. Makes 2 sandwiches.

# Grilled Olive-Cheese Sandwiches

1 cup grated American or Swiss process cheese
1/4 cup chopped ripe or green olives
2 tablespoons chopped pimiento
1 teaspoon dry English mustard;
   or 2 teaspoons prepared mustard
1 teaspoon grated onion
12 slices white bread
1 stick (1/2 cup) butter or margarine, softened

Combine cheese, olives, pimiento, mustard, and onion. Spread over 6 slices of bread, cover with remaining bread slices. Spread outsides of sandwiches with softened butter. Cook in skillet, electric grill, or waffle iron until crisp and golden-brown on each side. Makes 6 sandwiches.

## Souffléed Cheese Toast

$1/2$ cup mayonnaise
1 teaspoon prepared mustard
Dash of salt
$1^1 {}_3$ cups shredded Swiss, Provolone, American, or
    any semifirm cheese
2 egg whites, beaten stiff
12 slices white bread, lightly toasted

Combine mayonnaise, mustard, salt, and cheese. Fold in egg whites. Spread over toast. Place toast on baking sheet 3 inches from broiler until mixture puffs and is golden. Serve immediately. Makes 12 servings.

## Smørrebrød

The following recipes for smørrebrød I picked up during a visit to Denmark. In the vast kitchens of Scandinavian Airlines in Copenhagen, I was given a demonstration of how these and other smørrebrød combinations are prepared for passengers on overseas flights. It was there I first learned the importance of spreading bread thickly with butter for the purpose of keeping the bread fresh and how, if the ingredients (other than cheese) are kept in an upright or at least tilted position, they will stay fresh longer. After the smørrebrød have been put together, they are placed in pans, covered tightly with Saran Wrap, and kept refrigerated until time to serve.

The combination of Danish Blue cheese with a fresh, raw egg yolk I learned about at the famous Oskar Davidson restaurant, renowned for its menu list of more than 400 kinds of open-faced sandwiches. The sandwiches vary from simple combinations like cheese and egg to elaborate concoctions that are filling luncheon entrees in themselves. All smørrebrød are meant to be eaten with knife and fork.

132

DANISH BLUE SMØRREBRØD: Trim bread slices, removing crusts, to make square shapes; spread thickly with butter. Place a thin slice of Danish Blue cheese on each slice of buttered bread. Cut tomatoes into moderately thick, horizontal slices, then remove center from each tomato slice, so that a hollow ring is left. Place one ring on each slice of bread and cheese. Inside each tomato ring, gently place a raw egg yolk. Serve as an open-faced sandwich, passing the pepper grinder. This recipe makes a superb luncheon dish. The egg yolk functions as a sauce that harmonizes beautifully with the zesty Danish Blue cheese, and the bit of tomato adds just the right balance. Radishes are good with this sandwich.

SAMSØ SMØRREBRØD: For each serving, thickly butter one slice of white bread. Cover it to the edges with two overlapping slices of Samsø. Over the cheese arrange thin slices of cucumber twisted into dancing shapes, so that they will stand upright. Place dots of mayonnaise (to which fresh minced dill has been added) on either side of the cucumber curls.

HAVARTI SMØRREBRØD: For each serving, thickly butter a slice of white or pumpernickel bread, place two slices of Havarti cheese on the bread and in the center place a spoonful of black-currant jam.

HAM AND BRIE SMØRREBRØD: For each serving, thickly butter a slice of white bread. Lay on the bread a thin slice of boiled (or Danish canned) ham, curling the meat under at one side so that it does not lie flat on the bread. Under the curled-up meat place a curl of head lettuce or a spring of watercress. Place a slice of Danish Brie on the ham (the Danish Brie is firmer than the French and can be sliced more easily); cut cheese slice partway through, so that it can be fanned out. Place a radish rose at the center of the fan. Garnish with a dab of mustard blended with sour cream.

CAMEMBERT SMØRREBRØD: Spread rye bread with butter, then with soft Camembert. Over the Camembert arrange slices of raw mushrooms and well-drained capers. Sprinkle with caraway seeds. Serve as open sandwiches accompanied by cherry tomatoes.

CAMEMBERT-PUMPERNICKEL SMØRREBRØD: Spread soft ripe Camembert on thin slices of dark pumpernickel bread, and top with thinly sliced Bermuda or Spanish onions. This combination is excellent either as an open-faced or as a regular sandwich with beer.

SHRIMP AND CAVIAR SMØRREBRØD: For each sandwich, thickly butter a slice of white bread. Over the butter spread soft Crema Danica or Philadelphia cream cheese. Around the edge arrange tiny Danish shrimp. In the center place a mound of caviar. Between the shrimp and the caviar, place a circle of sieved egg yolk. On top of the caviar place a "dancing figure" of tomato (a tomato slice cut partly through, with the resulting "legs" bent to either side). This sandwich is an expensive piece of frippery but very, very pretty — and delectable to eat. It calls for a shot of aquavit followed by Danish Tüborg beer.


### Danish Ambassador

12 slices white or pumpernickel bread
1 stick (¼ pound or ½ cup) butter
1 tablespoon horseradish
6 slices Esrom
12 slices bacon, cooked and drained
Mayonnaise (optional)
Radishes

Spread half the bread slices with a mixture of butter and horseradish. Top with slices of cheese and then with hot, crisp bacon and remaining bread. Add mayonnaise, if desired. Serve accompanied by crisp radishes. Makes 6 sandwiches.

# Roquefort-Tomato-Bacon Club Sandwich

¹₄ cup (1 ounce) Roquefort. Danish Blue. Gorgonzola,
   or Wisconsin Blue
¹₄ cup (about) cream cheese.
   Crema Danica. or other bland dessert cheese
1 teaspoon horseradish
1 teaspoon instant minced onion
Dash of Worcestershire sauce
16 slices white bread
3 medium tomatoes, sliced
Salt and pepper
8 slices bacon, cooked
Lettuce
Mayonnaise

Blend together the two kinds of cheese, horseradish, onion, and Worcestershire sauce. If the mixture is too stiff, thin it with a little sour cream or mayonnaise. Spread the mixture over 4 slices of bread. Top each with another slice of bread. Add slices of tomato, cut to fit. Sprinkle them with salt and pepper. Add more bread. Add slices of bacon, lettuce, and mayonnaise, and top with remaining bread. Cut each sandwich in triangles to serve. Makes 4 club sandwiches.


# Pan Bagnet

Cut a loaf of French bread lengthwise. Brush the cut sides generously with olive oil. Arrange thinly sliced Bermuda or Spanish onions, slices of pimiento and green pepper, and an-chovy fillets on the bread. Add stoned Greek or Italian black olives and a generous amount of grated Parmesan or shredded Gorgonzola, Gruyère, or Italian Stracchino; sprinkle lightly with wine vinegar, and brush with more olive oil. Add the top layer of bread, and press firmly together.

## Tiered Sandwich Specials

Although the following sandwiches call for only one piece of bread each, they are as complicated to eat as is any club sandwich. Each is a meal in itself — serve with knives and forks.

CHICKEN AND BLUE CHEESE TIERED SANDWICH: For each sandwich, toast a piece of rye bread, and butter the toast while it is warm. Place on the toast a thin slice of Wisconsin Blue or Roquefort, and on the cheese place a slice of Boston or head lettuce, with a slice of chicken or turkey on top of that. Next add a "dancing figure" of tomato (the slice cut halfway through, then twisted to stand upright). Thin slices of cucumber should be curled to stand on either side of the tomato. Over all dribble thousand-island dressing.

PROVOLONE-PASTRAMI TIERED SANDWICH: For this one, butter a slice of pumpernickel, add a slice of Provolone, then cover the cheese with overlapping slices of tomato, add a thin slice of pastrami, and top with overlapping slices of avocado. Cover with Danish Blue Cream Dressing (see Index) or a French dressing.

## Farm Toast

8 slices bacon
4 slices white bread
2 apples, cored and sliced
4 slices American cheese

Cook bacon until it has just started to brown; remove, and drain on paper towel. Add bread slices to the hot bacon fat, and cook quickly until lightly browned; remove. Fry apple slices in the bacon fat until tender and lightly browned. Place apple slices on the fried bread; top each with a slice of cheese and then 2 partially cooked bacon slices. Place 3 to 4 inches from broiler in a preheated oven until the cheese is melted and the bacon crisp. Serve hot. Makes 4 servings.

## Trappist Steak Sandwich

4 thin minute steaks
Unseasoned meat tenderizer (optional)
2 tablespoons butter
Salt and pepper
4 slices white or rye bread, toasted
Dijon mustard
4 slices Port du Salut

Sprinkle steaks with meat tenderizer, according to directions on the label. Quickly melt butter in large skillet, and sauté steaks on each side just until lightly browned. Sprinkle with salt and pepper, and place each steak on a slice of toast. Spread steaks generously with mustard, and cover each with a slice of cheese. Broil until bubbling, and serve at once. Especially good garnishes: pickled beets, mixed mustard pickles, and green onions. Makes 4 servings.

## Tortas Compuestas (Mexican Hero Sandwiches)

Hero sandwich buns
Shredded lettuce
Slices of avocado
Slices of ripe tomato
Slices of firm Monterey Jack*
Pickle relish
Spicy-hot barbecue sauce
Garlic mayonnaise

Remove some of the centers from the buns, and pile lettuce, avocado, tomato, cheese, and relish inside. Spoon both barbecue sauce and garlic mayonnaise over the filling (to make garlic mayonnaise, crush 2 or 3 garlic cloves in a bowl; add 1/2 cup mayonnaise, a tablespoon of olive oil, and a few drops of lemon juice; beat to blend well). Serve with beer or cokes.

*Note: For a still spicier sandwich try slices of Tijuana or Queso Enchilado, imported Mexican cheeses, instead of Monterey Jack.

# Monte Cristo Sandwich

12 slices white bread
Mayonnaise
12 slices Swiss Emmentaler or Manchego
6 slices baked ham, 1/8- to 1/4-inch thick
6 slices roast turkey, 1/8- to 1/4-inch thick
3 eggs, slightly beaten
1/4 cup light cream or milk
Dash of salt
4 tablespoons butter
Parsley
Currant jelly

Spread one side of each slice of bread with a thin coating of mayonnaise. Assemble 6 sandwiches, using 2 slices of cheese and 1 slice each of ham and turkey in each. Trim crusts and filling with a sharp knife, making the edges even; cut each sandwich in half. Beat the eggs with the cream and salt. Dip each sandwich into the egg mixture, and sauté in butter on both sides until lightly browned. Place sandwiches on an ungreased baking sheet, and bake in a hot oven (400° F.) for 3 to 5 minutes or until cheese begins to melt. Garnish with parsley, and serve hot with a small dab of currant jelly. Serves 6.

# Toasted Cheese-Herb Bread

1 loaf French bread
3 to 4 tablespoons olive oil
1½ cups Swiss or Provolone, shredded
2 tablespoons minced parsley

Halve French bread lengthwise. Brush cut sides with olive oil. Sprinkle shredded cheese over the bottom half of the bread; then add minced parsley. Add top slice of bread, wrap loosely with foil, and bake in 350° F. oven 5 to 10 minutes until edges are golden and cheese has melted. Cut into 1½-inch pieces and serve hot with soup or salad. Makes about 6 servings.

# Toasted Crab and Olive Wedge Sandwiches

1 round loaf Italian or French bread*
4 tablespoons (¹/₂ stick) butter or margarine
1¹/₂ cups shredded domestic Swiss or Fontina
2 cups crabmeat
¹/₃ cup mayonnaise
¹/₃ cup pimiento-stuffed olives, sliced
1 tablespoon capers ·

Slice bread in half horizontally and cut each half into 6 pie-shaped wedges, cutting down to the bottom crust but not all the way through. Arrange the bread, cut side up, on a baking sheet; spread with butter, and place under the broiler until lightly toasted. Combine the cheese, crabmeat, mayonnaise, olives, and capers, and spread mixture over the lightly toasted bread. Place in a hot oven (400° F). for 10 to 15 minutes, or until heated through and bubbly. Finish cutting apart. Makes 12 wedges; allow 2 to each serving.

*Note: Sourdough French bread, if available, is especially good. Of course, 6 crusty Hero rolls can also be used, split in half and buttered as above, allowing 2 halves for each person.

# Peanut Butter Sandwich Dreams

Spread bread with peanut butter and lay slices of Swiss or mild American cheese on each. Sprinkle chopped peanuts or almonds over the cheese. Place open sandwiches in broiler until cheese melts.

VARIATIONS: Substitute thinly sliced Mozzarella (particularly good), Provolone, or Münster for Swiss or American cheese. For extra zest, spoon a little catsup or chili sauce over the peanut butter before adding cheese.

# Crab-Cheese Open Sandwiches

1 cup crabmeat
2 tablespoons olive oil
1/2 teaspoon powdered cumin (*comino*)
1 tablespoon grated onion
1 tablespoon minced parsley
1 teaspoon lemon juice
Salt to taste
4 slices bread, trimmed
Sliced Bel Lago (Switzerland) or Tilsiter
   (Danish or Norwegian)

Thoroughly drain crabmeat and remove gristle. Place in blender with olive oil, cumin, grated onion, parsley, and lemon juice. Beat until smooth. Season with salt to taste. Spread this *pâté* over 4 slices of white bread. Lay thin slices of the cheese over the crab *pâté*. Place sandwiches under broiler until cheese melts. Makes 4 sandwiches.


# Ham and Roquefort Barbecue Buns

6 hamburger buns
6 ounces (1 1/2 cups crumbled) Roquefort
6 tomato slices
6 small dill pickles, cut into slices lengthwise
6 thick slices of smoked or boiled ham
2 tablespoons prepared horseradish

Split hamburger buns. Spread bottom half of each bun with crumbled Roquefort cheese. Top with a tomato slice, sliced dill pickle, and a ham slice. Spread ham with horseradish. Top with second half of the bun. Wrap sandwiches loosely in foil. Bake in a hot oven (425° F.) 15 to 20 minutes; or 6 inches above gray coals on a grill for 15 to 20 minutes. Unwrap and serve hot with spicy baked beans and raw relishes. Makes 6 servings.

# Cheese-Chili Burgers

1 pound ground beef
1 teaspoon salt
Freshly ground black pepper to taste
1 tablespoon chili powder
6 slices American cheese or Provolone
1 tablespoon olive oil
6 hamburger buns, lightly toasted
1 medium onion, chopped
$1/_2$ green pepper, chopped
Salt and pepper
Dash of Worcestershire sauce
Dash of Tabasco (optional)
$1/_2$ cup chili sauce or barbecue sauce
$1/_2$ cup beer or red wine

Combine beef, 1 teaspoon salt, ground black pepper, and chili powder; blend well. Form into 12 thin patties. Between each of 2 patties, place a slice of cheese, trimmed so that cheese will be completely covered by meat. Press edges of meat patties together to seal. Brown the patties on both sides in the olive oil; remove, and place inside buns. Add the onion and green pepper to the oil, and cook until soft; sprinkle with salt, pepper, Worcestershire, and tabasco. Add chili sauce and beer or wine. Cook sauce until reduced by one-third; then spoon over meat patties in buns. Makes 6 burgers.

# Cheese-Stuffed Hot Dogs

Split frankfurters halfway through, and insert a sliver of cheese — American, Jack, Cheddar, Mozzarella, or any firm or semifirm cheese — in each. Wrap a slice of bacon around each frankfurter, and grill in the broiler or over charcoal until bacon is crisp. If sandwiches are cooked over charcoal, have water ready to douse flares from dripping bacon fat.

# Monterey Grilled Sandwich

1/4 pound Monterey Jack or mild Cheddar, shredded
2 chopped green onions, including tops
1 small tomato, peeled and chopped
2 tablespoons *pignoli* (pine nuts)
8 pitted black olives, chopped
1 small garlic clove, mashed
2 dashes tabasco
1 tablespoon Spanish olive oil
1 teaspoon wine vinegar
1 teaspoon chili powder
4 tablespoons pimiento cheese spread;
   or 1 3-ounce package cream cheese
1 can whole green chilis, drained and chopped (optional)
3 small loaves French bread or Hero buns, split lengthwise

For this recipe, a soft, young Jack cheese is preferable. Combine shredded cheese with all remaining ingredients, except bread, and beat until as creamy as possible. Spread over split bread or buns, and broil 4 inches from heat until cheese melts. This same mixture may be used as a canapé topping — spread on sesame crackers and place under the broiler until the cheese melts. Makes 6 sandwiches.


# Hash-Burger Grill

1 4-ounce wedge Danish Blue
1/4 cup cream or evaporated milk
1 can (1 pound) corned-beef hash
4 slices bread

Mash Danish Blue with cream to make a smooth paste. Open both ends of the can of corned-beef hash, and remove hash in one piece. Cut into four slices. Arrange hash slices on bread, flattening slightly to cover the bread completely. Broil, not too close to the heat, until the hash is hot and crusty. Spread with the Danish Blue mixture, and return to the broiler to melt and brown the topping, about 1 minute. Makes 4 sandwiches.

# Danish Blue and Ham Grill

4 ounces Danish Blue
$1/4$ cup sour cream
4 large slices cooked ham, $1/4$ inch thick
4 slices bread

Mash Danish Blue with sour cream to make a smooth paste. Trim ham to fit bread. Lay meat on bread, and broil until the meat is hot and beginning to brown. Spread with the Danish Blue mixture, and return to broiler to melt and brown the topping, about 1 minute more.

DANISH BLUE AND BOLOGNA: Use thickly sliced bologna instead of ham; remove skin from edge of bologna, place 2 overlapping slices of bologna on each slice of bread, add cheese before placing under broiler.

# Hot Corned Beef and Avocado Sandwich

1 can (1 pound) corned beef
2 tablespoons prepared mustard
3 to 4 tablespoons mayonnaise
2 to 3 tablespoons sour cream
1 tablespoon horseradish
6 slices toast or 3 split buns
1 ripe avocado, sliced
6 slices Swiss, Provolone, or Mozzarella

Chop corned beef, and blend with mustard, mayonnaise, sour cream and horseradish. Spread over toast or toasted buns. Place slices of avocado above the meat mixture. Lay cheese over the avocado. Place under broiler until cheese melts. Let stand a minute before serving. Serves 6.

# Ham and Asparagus Luncheon Sandwiches

12 stalks cooked green or canned white asparagus
2 tablespoons butter
2 tablespoons flour
$^3/_4$ cup asparagus liquid
$^1/_2$ cup light cream or milk
Salt and pepper
$^1/_2$ cup grated Parmesan or Romano
$^1/_2$ cup shredded Smoky cheese or Provolone
6 slices ham
6 slices white or rye toast
2 tablespoons minced chives

Warm the asparagus spears in their liquid; set aside. Melt butter, stir in flour, then add $^3/_4$ cup asparagus liquid and cream or milk. Simmer until smooth; taste for seasoning, adding salt and pepper as needed. Stir in cheeses, cooking until cheese is melted. Place ham slices on toast, then lay asparagus spears across ham, and cover with the hot cheese sauce. Place under broiler until sauce is lightly browned. Sprinkle with chives before serving. Makes 6 open sandwiches.

# PIZZAS AND CHEESE BREADS

It's hard to believe that a quarter-century ago, the word "pizza" was virtually unknown outside the southern half of Italy. Had anyone asked then what it meant, the answer probably would have been a guess that it must be a musical term, probably related to "The Pizzicato Polka." Yet today, pizza is as American as apple pie — and even in a modern French cookbook, picked up in a supermarket in Paris, what should I see in the hors d'oeuvres section but a recipe for Italian pizzas! That was topped by a Vietnamese cookbook in my possession (written in Vietnamese) with a recipe for pizzas in its section on international dishes!

Although this curious snack spawned in southern Italy is not in any sense a sandwich, it would have pleased the Earl whose name is so honored, for it is easy to eat by hand, gulped down between swigs of coke or while watching a football game. This versatility, above everything, is probably the secret of its success.

I must confess that I am not a pizza enthusiast and, had it not been for the disdain of my growing daughter, would probably have never even tried to make one. But I was stung by her remark, "The pizzas you make are horrible — please don't even try again!" How can a cookbook author take such a blow to her pride without at least trying to regain her good reputation?

I can report, after having laboriously made pizza dough "from scratch" that the difference between a properly made pizza and even the ready-to-use mixes is enormous — to say nothing of the huge gap between the latter and the brown-and-serve variety available at frozen-food counters. Even I ate the fruits of my labor with relish. What is more, the possible variations are enormous, with a little imagination in switching cheeses and other ingredients.

One can even make a cheese pizza dough and top it with sliced fresh tomatoes, sprinkling the tomatoes with crumbled Gorgonzola and bacon, for a version whose delectable goodness would come as a revelation to Neapolitans.

Cheese breads run the gamut from crusty home-baked loaves to sesame-seed buns, curious Camembert-flavored biscuits, and a baked "doughnut," flavored with anise, from South America.

Cheese waffles and cheese pancakes are not exactly "breads," yet how else would one classify them? Try cheese waffles sometime as a base for creamed chicken. Or layer cheese pancakes with a tart jelly or sherried tomato marmalade. They make a scrumptious Sunday brunch!

### Pizza Dough

1 envelope active dry yeast
1 cup warm (not hot) water
1 teaspoon salt
2 tablespoons olive oil
3½ cups sifted all-purpose flour
½ teaspoon sugar (optional)

Dissolve yeast in water. Stir in salt and olive oil, and gradually add flour and sugar (if used). Beat until smooth, then turn out dough on lightly floured board, and knead until dough is elastic. Brush top with olive oil, cover lightly, let rise in warm place until doubled. Divide dough in half, roll each into a ball; then, with fingers, press to fit 2 14-inch pizza pans or rectangular baking sheets. making edges thicker and slightly higher than center. Brush with additional olive oil. Add filling as desired. Bake in oven preheated to 450° F. for 20 to 25 minutes or until crust is golden.

# Cheese Pizza

1 recipe Pizza Dough
2 cups your own homemade tomato sauce; or 15-ounce can
   tomato sauce
$1/2$ teaspoon oregano
1 tablespoon minced Italian parsley
1 teaspoon instant minced onion
1 minced garlic clove
2 tablespoons olive oil
3 large tomatoes, peeled and sliced
Salt and pepper
$3/4$ pound Mozzarella, sliced or shredded
$1/2$ cup freshly grated Parmesan or Romano

Prepare pizza dough. Combine tomato sauce, herbs, onion, garlic, and olive oil. Cook 5 minutes to blend flavors. Place sliced tomatoes over the rolled-out pizzas, and sprinkle with salt and pepper from shakers. Place slices of Mozzarella on the tomatoes. Pour sauce over the cheese and tomatoes, add the grated Parmesan or Romano. Bake in oven preheated to 450° for 20 to 25 minutes. Let cool slightly before serving (hot Mozzarella can burn the tongue). Makes 2 pizzas.

MUSHROOM PIZZA: Use 1 pound sliced mushrooms in place of tomatoes, brush pizza dough with olive oil before placing mushrooms on dough, and brush with additional oil before adding cheese and sauce.

SAUSAGE-GRINDER PIZZA: In 1 tablespoon olive oil in a skillet, brown $1/2$ pound Italian sausage cut in small pieces, 1 green pepper cut in strips, 2 canned pimientos cut in strips, and 1 medium onion sliced. Cook until onion is tender, and spoon onions over dough instead of tomatoes. Top each pizza with sauce and $1/2$ cup Parmesan; omit the Mozzarella.

ANCHOVY AND BLACK OLIVE PIZZA: Add 1 can caper-stuffed rolled anchovies (well drained) and 1/2 cup sliced black olives.

ONION PIZZA: For the Pizza filling, slowly cook 4 to 6 large onions (sliced) in 1/4 cup olive oil until very tender, seasoning to taste with salt and pepper. Spoon the onions over the pizza dough, and arrange slivers of pimiento (about 1/4 cup), pitted sliced black olives, and 6 to 8 anchovy fillets over the onion. (Or, instead of the anchovies, place half-slices of tomato in a pattern, and sprinkle them with salt, pepper, and oregano.) Over all, sprinkle 1/2 cup shredded Swiss or Fontina instead of Mozzarella.

### Bacon-Tomato Pizza with Cheese Dough

1 recipe Pizza Dough
1/2 cup shredded sharp natural Cheddar
4 tablespoons olive oil
4 fully ripe tomatoes, sliced
Salt
1/2 teaspoon oregano or thyme or mixture of the two
Canadian bacon, thinly sliced, or precooked regular bacon
2 cups (1/2 pound) crumbled Gorgonzola
2 tablespoons butter

Prepare Pizza Dough, working Cheddar into dough as you knead. Divide dough in half; roll out each half, brush olive oil over each, then place tomato slices as close together as possible on each. Sprinkle the tomatoes with salt from a shaker and with herbs. Over the tomatoes place Canadian bacon. Over the bacon spread Gorgonzola; dot with butter. Bake in oven preheated to 450° F. 20 to 25 minutes. Makes 2 pizzas.

# Sesame Seed-Cheese Rolls

$^1/_4$ cup warm water (110° F. to 115° F.)
1 envelope active dry yeast
1 teaspoon sugar
1 cup lukewarm water
$^1/_4$ cup sugar
2 tablespoons shortening
2 teaspoons salt
1 egg, beaten lightly
$^1/_2$ pound (2 cups) shredded sharp Cheddar
$^1/_3$ cup toasted sesame seeds*
4 to 5 cups sifted all-purpose flour
Beaten egg whites
Toasted sesame seeds for topping

Combine first 3 ingredients, let stand 5 to 10 minutes for yeast to soften. Add 1 cup lukewarm water, $^1/_4$-cup sugar, shortening, and salt. Cool. Add egg, cheese, and $^1/_3$ cup toasted sesame seeds. Gradually stir in $3^1/_2$ cups of the flour. Turn out onto lightly floured board. Gradually knead in the remaining flour to make a pliant, elastic dough. Knead gently 2 to 3 minutes. Place in a large greased bowl. Grease top of dough lightly. Cover. Place in a warm place (80° F. to 85° F.) to rise until doubled in bulk. Punch down dough. Form into a ball. Cover. Let rest 10 minutes, and shape into small assorted rolls in attractive shapes. Place on lightly greased baking sheets. Brush tops with egg whites beaten only until frothy. Sprinkle with sesame seeds. Cover. Place in warm place to rise until doubled in bulk. Bake 20 minutes (or until done) in a preheated hot oven (400° F.). Makes 3 dozen rolls.

*Note: To toast sesame seeds, place in a moderate (350° F.) oven in a shallow pan for 20 to 22 minutes, turning to brown uniformly.

SESAME SEED-CHEESE BREAD: Shape dough into 2 loaves. Place in 2 greased 8 x $4^1/_2$ x 3-inch loaf pans. Cover. Let rise until doubled in bulk. Brush with egg whites, and sprinkle with sesame seeds. Bake 40 to 45 minutes or until browned in a preheated hot oven (400° F.).

# Basic Cheese Bread

Sandwiches made with cheese bread (plain or toasted) are extra wonderful. Use ham, corned beef, cold roast pork, or sliced cold cuts for the filling, with or without lettuce and mayonnaise.

Cheese bread is also excellent toasted; or, to make French toast, dip the slices of cheese bread in an egg-and-milk mixture and fry in hot fat until golden-crisp on each side.

1/4 cup lukewarm water
1 envelope active dry yeast
1 cup milk
1 tablespoon shortening
2 tablespoons sugar
2 teaspoons salt
6 cups sifted all-purpose flour
1/2 pound sharp Cheddar, grated (2 cups)
1 cup lukewarm water
Salad oil

Place 1/4 cup lukewarm water in small bowl, sprinkle yeast over it, and stir until dissolved. In a saucepan, place milk and shortening, heat until shortening is melted; add sugar and salt, stir to dissolve. Cool milk mixture to lukewarm; then pour into large mixing bowl. Add 2 cups flour, and beat with mixing spoon until smooth. Add grated cheese, then the dissolved yeast and the 1 cup lukewarm water, and beat to blend well. Add remaining 4 cups flour all at once, and beat with spoon until smooth. With greased hands, work dough until easy to handle; turn out on counter top that has been sprinkled with flour. Knead dough with fingers, punching and turning over and over, until it is a smooth ball.

Clean out the mixing bowl, wash with soapy water, dry, then rub with shortening. Place ball of dough in bowl and brush the top with salad oil. Cover it with a clean towel, place bowl in a warm place: near the range or a radiator (but not on top of either), or in an unheated oven, placing a large pan of hot water under the bowl containing the dough. Leave there until dough has doubled in bulk.

Remove risen dough from bowl with greased hands, turn out on floured counter again. and again knead and punch. Then divide dough in half. placing in two greased 9 x 5 x 3-inch loaf pans. Cover these pans with a towel or waxed paper, and again place in warm spot until dough has risen to tops of pans. Bake in an oven preheated to 400° F. for 40 minutes or until the top is golden and crusty.

VARIATIONS:
- Instead of grated Cheddar. use 2 cups caraway cheese. domestic or imported.
- Instead of Cheddar. use 2 cups grated Swiss.
- Use 2 cups of a spiced cheese like Leyden. in place of Cheddar.
- Add 1 cup crumbled blue cheese and 1 cup mild Cheddar or Brick instead of the 2 cups shredded Cheddar.

### Corn-Cheese Crisps

1 cup yellow corn meal
$1/2$ cup sifted flour
$1/4$ teaspoon baking soda
Pinch of salt
3 tablespoons corn oil
$1/3$ cup milk
Grated Parmesan
Melted butter or oil, about 2 tablespoons

Sift together corn meal, flour, baking soda, and salt. Slowly beat in oil and milk. Knead until smooth, place on floured board. Break off small pieces, and roll one at a time, paper thin. Place on ungreased baking sheet and sprinkle with cheese. Bake in oven preheated to 350° F. for 8 to 10 minutes or until golden. Remove, and cool on wire racks. If crisps are not to be served at once, store them covered in dry place. Just before serving, brush each with melted butter or oil, and sprinkle with salt. Serve in place of bread with dinner. These crisps are especially good with Mexican or East Indian food and with hearty salads. Makes 20 to 24 crisps.

## Cheese Biscuits

1 cup grated sharp Cheddar
2 cups biscuit mix or your own biscuit recipe
3/4 cup milk

Add cheese to biscuit mix, stir in milk, beat until smooth, then knead until firm enough to roll out on lightly floured board to 1/2-inch thick. Cut into rounds with biscuit cutter. Bake on greased baking sheet in preheated hot oven (400° F.) for 12 to 15 minutes or until golden. Makes 12 to 16 biscuits.

BLUE CHEESE BISCUITS: Use 1/2 cup crumbled blue cheese instead of Cheddar. Serve with butter and orange marmalade.

SWISS CHEESE BISCUITS: Instead of Cheddar, use 1 cup grated domestic Swiss. Serve biscuits with tart currant or beach-plum jelly.

CAMEMBERT BISCUITS: Instead of Cheddar, use two 4-ounce wedges of soft Camembert (with rind removed) and 1/4 cup shredded Swiss. Serve with butter and wild blueberry or lingon-berry jam.

## Cheese Waffles

1 cup biscuit mix
1 egg
2/3 cup milk
2 tablespoons butter, melted
1/4 cup grated or shredded cheese

Place biscuit mix in bowl, and make well in center. Break egg into well; stir to blend. Stir in milk, melted butter, and cheese. Bake in preheated waffle iron until crisply brown. These waffles are excellent topped with creamed chicken. Makes 2 full waffles, enough for 2 people. Double ingredients to serve 4.

## Cheese-Nut Muffins

1 cup grated American, Brick, or Swiss
1 egg
2 cups biscuit mix
1 cup milk
$^1/_4$ cup coarsely chopped walnuts

Add cheese, egg and milk to biscuit mix, and beat to blend (but mixture should be lumpy). Stir in nuts. Spoon into 12 well-greased muffin tins (or line tins with paper liners). Bake at 375° F. for 25 minutes. Makes 12 muffins.

## Tilsiter Cheese Rolls

1 envelope active dry yeast
1 cup warm water
$1^1/_2$ teaspoons Lawry's Seasoned Salt or Season-All
1 tablespoon brown sugar
2 tablespoons shortening
$1^1/_2$ ounces Tilsiter,
    shredded or coarsely grated (about $^1/_3$ cup)
3 tablespoons heavy cream or evaporated milk
2 to $2^1/_4$ cups sifted all-purpose flour

Dissolve yeast in warm water; add seasoned salt, sugar, short-ening, cheese and cream; stir until well blended. Add flour to make stiff dough and beat until dough leaves the sides of the bowl clean. Cover, and set in warm place to rise until doubled in bulk, about $1^1/_4$ hours. Grease 12 muffin tins, place a "wal-nut" of dough in each, and let rise for 15 minutes. Preheat oven to 375° F. (moderate) while rolls are rising for second time; bake rolls for 20 minutes or until golden and crusty. Remove from tins immediately, and serve while warm. Makes 12 rolls.

# Jewish Dairy Pancakes

1 cup sour cream
1 cup cottage cheese
1 cup sifted flour
4 egg yolks
$^1/_2$ teaspoon salt
2 tablespoons sugar

Beat together sour cream and cheese; add flour, egg yolks, salt, and sugar; beat until smooth. Chill in refrigerator until time to serve. Bake as with regular pancakes on hot greased griddle or electric skillet set at 400° F. Serve hot topped with additional sour cream and with black-currant or raspberry preserves. Makes 4 servings.

Almost any soup is improved by a little zesty Parmesan sprinkled over each serving. What would French onion soup or Italian minestrone be without it?

What's more, when cheese is added to soup the soup instantly becomes a protein food, which often turns it into a hearty luncheon dish.

Although Parmesan is used on soup more often than is any other cheese, unusual soups can be made with Swiss, Provolone, or Cheddar. The Swedish Egg Soup that follows is particularly delicious, a luncheon dish in itself.

### Swedish Egg Soup

4 slices trimmed white bread
4 tablespoons butter
4 or 8 eggs
4 tablespoons tomato catsup or chili sauce
3 to 4 cups chicken or beef broth, heated to boiling
$^1/_2$ cup grated Parmesan or Romano

Fry the bread in butter until golden, and place in 4 individual casseroles; or spread bread with butter, place a slice of bread in each of 4 individual casseroles, and heat in hot (400° F.) oven until butter is melted and bread lightly browned on edges. Over each slice of bread break 1 or 2 eggs, and dot each with a tablespoon of catsup or chili sauce. Add $^3/_4$ to 1 cup hot broth (depending on size of casserole). Sprinkle grated cheese generously over each. Return casserole to oven for 10 minutes or until the whites of eggs are set and cheese is melted. Makes 4 servings.

## Parmesan Cheese Soup

Here's a good way to use stale French or Italian bread. Cut in $3/4$-inch slices, dip each slice in milk (you will need about $1/2$ cup milk for 4 slices), then place soaked bread in soup dishes and cover each generously with grated Parmesan. Add to each serving 1 cup boiling hot chicken or beef broth.

## Catalonian Lentil Soup

3 or 4 tablespoons Spanish olive oil
2 large onions, chopped
1 large carrot, grated or cut into tiny cubes
1 medium tomato, peeled, chopped
$1/2$ teaspoon marjoram or oregano
2 cups lentils
8 to 10 cups water
$1^1/2$ tablespoons salt or to taste
8 slices French bread cut $1/2$-inch thick
1 cup coarsely grated Swiss Emmentaler or Manchego

Cook onions, carrot, and tomato slowly in the olive oil in a large heavy pot until very soft. Add marjoram, lentils (which need no presoaking), water and salt. Simmer covered over low heat for 2 hours or until lentils are tender. Lightly toast the bread. Place a slice of bread in each large soup plate; sprinkle 2 tablespoons cheese over each serving. Add the lentil soup. Excellent when freshly made, even better when warmed up. Makes 8 servings.

VARIATION: If desired, 2 garlic cloves may be placed in the olive oil with the onion and other vegetables. When garlic is soft and yellow, mash it with the back of a wooden spoon or fork to blend with other vegetables. Add marjoram, lentils, water, and salt and a ham bone. Simmer 2 hours or until lentils are tender. Remove ham bone, cutting away any bits of ham to add to the soup. Place toasted bread and cheese in soup plates, add the lentil soup, as above. Makes 8 servings.

## Swiss-Potato Soup

4 medium potatoes, peeled and diced
2 leeks, chopped
2 tablespoons butter
1 onion, sliced
2 cups chicken broth
1¹ ₂ cups milk, or 1 cup milk and ¹/₂ cup dairy half-and-half
Salt and pepper to taste
¹ ₈ teaspoon grated nutmeg
1 cup shredded domestic Swiss or Swiss Emmentaler
1 tablespoon chopped chives

Cook potatoes in water to cover 5 minutes; drain. Add onions and leeks to butter, sauté 2 or 3 minutes. Add potatoes and chicken broth, cook until potatoes are very soft, then pour soup into blender and beat until puréed. Return to pot, add milk, taste for seasoning; add salt and pepper if needed. Add nutmeg and cheese, and cook over moderate heat, stirring until cheese is melted. Do not allow to boil. Serve garnished with chives. Makes 4 to 6 servings.


## Cheese-Corn Soup

1 15-ounce can cream-style corn
1 teaspoon instant minced onion
2 cups milk
¹/₂ teaspoon salt, or to taste
Dash of freshly ground black pepper or cayenne
2 tablespoons grated or shredded mild cheese
    like Münster or Jack
1 tablespoon minced parsley
1 tablespoon crumbled blue cheese (optional)

Combine all ingredients except blue cheese. Heat, without allowing to boil, stirring until cheese is melted. Sprinkle blue cheese lightly over each serving if desired. Makes 4 servings.

## Lupa Shetgia (Swiss Mountain Soup)

4 slices white bread, lightly toasted
1 cup grated or shredded Swiss Emmentaler
1 quart milk, heated to scalding
Salt and pepper
Whole nutmeg, freshly grated
2 tablespoons butter, melted until lightly brown

In each of 4 soup plates, place a piece of toast. Cover each with about 1/4 cup cheese; then add to each 1 cup steaming hot milk. Cover, let stand a few minutes, then sprinkle each with salt, pepper, and nutmeg and spoon 1/2 tablespoon browned butter over top. This soup is a renowned Swiss supper dish, reminiscent of a dish I knew in my childhood as "cheese milk toast." Makes 4 servings.

## Canadian Cheddar Soup

1 large onion, minced
1 carrot, grated
2 tablespoons butter or margarine
2 tablespoons flour
1/2 teaspoon dry mustard
1 teaspoon paprika
4 cups chicken or beef broth
1 cup homogenized milk
1 cup grated mild Cheddar
Salt, if needed
Minced dill or parsley

Cook onion and carrot in butter until soft, stir in flour, and cook until mixture bubbles. Add mustard and paprika. Slowly add broth, bring to a boil, and simmer 10 minutes. Add milk and cheese, stirring constantly over low heat until cheese is melted (do not allow to boil). Add salt to taste. Serve immediately with a little minced dill or parsley on each serving. Makes 6 servings.

## Käse Bouillon mit Ei (German Cheese Soup with Egg)

8 eggs
2 cups homogenized milk or dairy half-and-half
4 tablespoons grated Münster or other mild cheese
4 tablespoon chopped chives
4 cups bouillon, heated to boiling

Beat together eggs, milk, cheese, and chives. Slowly add a little hot bouillon; then combine with remaining hot bouillon, and serve at once. Makes 4 servings.

## Fresh Tomato Soup

4 or 5 medium-to-large tomatoes, peeled and chopped
2 tablespoons butter
$1/2$ bay leaf
$1/8$ teaspoon thyme
2 whole cloves
2 thin slices onion
2 cups water
1 tablespoon cornstarch
$3/4$ teaspoon salt or to taste
Dash of pepper
4 tablespoons grated Parmesan

Place chopped tomatoes in butter and cook over medium heat until tomatoes are soft; add herbs, cloves, and onion; cook 10 minutes over very low heat. Force through sieve; add a little of the water to cornstarch, stir until smooth, then add remaining water and blend with sieved tomatoes. Stir tomato mixture, and cook until slightly thickened. Add salt and a dash of pepper. Serve hot; top each serving with a tablespoonful of cheese. Makes 4 servings.

# The King's Soup

4 medium onions, thinly sliced
¹/₄ pound (1 stick) butter
Pinch of mace
1 tablespoon cornstarch
¹/₂ cup water
2 cups chicken broth
3 cups milk
Salt to taste
2 egg yolks
¹/₂ cup grated or shredded Gruyère or other mild,
  semifirm cheese
1 tablespoon minced parsley
1 cup croutons

Slowly cook onions in butter without browning. Sprinkle with mace. Dissolve cornstarch in the water, add to onions, and slowly add chicken broth and milk. Simmer mixture gently without allowing to boil. Adjust seasoning. Beat egg yolks until thick, combine with grated cheese, add a little of hot broth, and, just before serving, add egg-cheese mixture to remaining soup, beating briskly with whisk. Serve topped with minced parsley and crisp, brown croutons (fried in a mixture of half butter, half oil). Makes 6 to 8 servings.

## American Potato-Cheese Soup

1 can frozen cream-of-potato soup
3 cups milk
1 beef-bouillon cube
¹/₂ pound (2 cups) processed American
  or Provolone, shredded
1 teaspoon caraway seeds, crushed
2 tablespoons minced ham

Combine soup, milk, and bouillon cube; heat, stirring, until well blended (do not allow to boil). Add cheese and caraway seeds. Serve hot with minced ham over top for garnish. Makes 4 servings.

## Zuppa di Piselli (Italian Split-Pea Soup)

1 pound green or yellow split peas
1 large veal knuckle or ham bone
2 quarts water
2 whole cloves stuck in 1 medium onion
1 bay leaf
1 tomato, peeled and chopped
Salt to taste
$^1/_2$ cup grated Parmesan or Caciocavallo

Soak peas in water to cover 2 hours; then drain. Place bone in 2 quarts water with onion, bay leaf, tomato, and salt, if needed. Simmer 2 hours; skim, and strain. Add peas, and cook slowly 1 hour or until peas are soft and tender. Serve topped with cheese. Makes 4 to 6 servings.


## French Onion Soup

4 to 6 medium onions, sliced
2 tablespoons butter
1 tablespoon flour
6 cups beef broth*or 5$^1/_2$ cups broth and $^1/_2$ cup white wine
Salt and pepper
6 slices toasted French bread
$^1/_4$ cup grated mild American or Gruyère
$^1/_4$ cup grated Parmesan

Gently cook onions in butter until very soft, without browning. Stir in flour, and continue to cook another 5 minutes. Slowly add beef broth or mixture of broth and wine. Simmer uncovered 15 to 20 minutes, seasoning to taste. Place toast in 6 individual casseroles, divide soup among the casseroles, add the two kinds of cheese, and place in broiler 4 inches from heat until cheese is melted and lightly browned. Makes 6 servings.

*Note: Beef broth can be made with bouillon cubes or powdered concentrates.

## New England Seafood Chowder

<sup></sup>1/2 cup diced celery
1 tablespoon minced celery leaves
1 medium onion, chopped
2 tablespoons butter
1 can condensed New England-style clam chowder
1/2 pound shelled, cooked shrimp, chopped;
   or 1 cup cooked or canned crabmeat
11/2 cups milk
1/2 cup grated Vermont or Herkimer cheese
Minced parsley

Gently cook celery, celery leaves, and onion in butter until very tender. Add canned clam chowder, shrimp, and milk; stir and heat, without permitting to boil, until mixture steams. Add cheese, and stir until partially melted. Serve topped with minced parsley and accompanied by chowder or oyster crackers. Makes 4 servings.

VARIATION: Instead of milk, try using 3/4 cup chicken broth, 1/2 cup milk, and 1/4 cup heavy cream. The flavor is more subtle, more European, which is all right even for this New England dish, for it was French sailors shipwrecked on the New England coast who gave us the *chaudière* in the first place.

## Crème Soubise (French Cream of Onion Soup)

1 pound (3 to 4 large) yellow onions
4 tablespoons butter
2 cups chicken broth
1 cup (about) very thin vermicelli, uncooked
2 cups milk
3 egg yolks, beaten
1/4 cup heavy cream
1/2 cup grated Parmesan or Swiss cheese

Slice onions, cook gently in butter until tender, then add chicken broth, and cook slowly 20 minutes. Strain or force mixture through sieve, or purée in blender. Add vermicelli and cook 10 minutes. Lower heat, stir in milk, then add a little hot broth to egg yolks; add egg mixture to soup, and cook over low heat, stirring constantly with a whisk, until thickened. Add cream and cheese. Makes 4 to 6 servings.

### Petite Marmite (French Vegetable Soup)

6 fresh carrots, peeled and sliced
3 leeks, sliced
3 white turnips, peeled and quartered
$2^1/_2$ pounds beef shins
$2^1/_2$ pounds soup bones
$2^1/_2$ pounds chicken wings and necks
3 quarts cold water
3 tablespoons salt
$^1/_2$ teaspoon peppercorns
1 teaspoon mixed herbs such as thyme, bay leaf, marjoram
1 quart shredded cabbage
Grated Parmesan
French bread

Place first 9 ingredients in a large soup kettle. Cover, bring to a boil, reduce heat, and simmer slowly $4^1/_2$ hours. Skim occasionally. Strain; discard chicken pieces; remove meat from bones; and return meat and vegetables to soup. If a great deal of liquid has boiled away, add a cup or two of water. Add herbs and shredded cabbage; cook another 10 minutes. Serve hot with grated Parmesan and crusty French bread. Makes about 12 servings.

## French Cabbage Soup

2 small white onions or 4 shallots, minced
3 tablespoons butter or margarine
1 clove garlic (optional)
4 slices bacon, diced
4 cups shredded cabbage
6 cups vegetable or chicken broth
Salt and pepper to taste
6 thick slices French bread, toasted
1 cup grated Parmesan

Cook onions or shallots in butter until soft. Add whole garlic clove to pan; when golden and soft, mash into the butter, then remove and discard shreds. Add bacon, and cook until lightly browned. Add cabbage and broth; cook gently about 30 minutes until cabbage is tender. (Some prefer the soup to be cooked even longer — a matter of taste. I like the cabbage still to be a little crisp and very delicate in flavor.) Season to taste. Toast bread, and place in soup plates. Spoon soup over the bread, and top with cheese. Makes 8 servings.

The word "fondue" means "melted." and, as all cheese melts to a molten gold with heat, it's no wonder such varied dishes should bear this name. The fondue that Brillat-Savarin made was a blend of eggs, Gruyère, and butter. spiced with a great deal of pepper.

The Fondue Neuchâteloise. which most of us today call simply "Swiss Fondue," is made without any eggs or butter at all, with only a bit of flour or cornstarch to thicken the melting cheese, and with a cup of Neuchâtel wine blended in. The cheese gets thicker and thicker as it bubbles, and those who dip their cubes of bread into the gooey mess will have to twirl their forks dexterously, so that the stringy cheese can be twisted around like wayward strands of spaghetti. At the bottom of the casserole, a rich brown crust is the prize that awaits those who manage not to drop a single cube of bread in the bubbling cauldron of pale-yellow cheese. Either Swiss Emmentaler or natural Gruyère may be used in making Fondue Neuchâteloise.

Another equally famous melted cheese favorite of Switzerland is Raclette, which means literally "scraped," and in this case a semisoft cheese is held in front of a vertical Raclette heater or under a broiler until the surface of the cheese is melted enough to scrape off onto hot boiled potatoes. A special cheese, Bagnes, is generally used for making Raclette, though a young Fontina or Mütschli (Mountain Cheese) can also be used. Raclette, like Fondue, makes a fine dish for an informal supper or after-sports refreshment.

A baked fondue, which was a favorite American supper dish in the early part of this century, is made by soaking bread in a custard mixture of eggs and milk, adding cheese, and baking until firm and golden.

A Welsh rabbit (or "rarebit") as made today is essentially a fondue, but Cheddar is the cheese and beer the liquid. The controversy over its name will probably go on to the end of time. Some aver that it gained the name "rabbit" when a Welsh chieftain ran out of game for his tables and, in the emergency, served his guests "toasted" cheese on bread, explaining that it was

"Welsh rabbit." Others insist doggedly on "rarebit" — a rare bit of gastronomical pleasure. The combinations that bear both names today would astonish the patrons of Ye Olde Cheshire Cheese in London. once Ben Jonson's favorite rendezvous. where Welsh rabbit was a standard item on the menu. Actually. as late as the 1770s. the standard way of preparing Welsh rabbit (as Mrs. Smith spelled the name in *The Art of Cookery made Plain and Easy*) was to toast slices of bread. soak the bread in wine. then cover it with thin slices of cheese — this combination to be "toasted" over a hot fire. It was. in fact. much like what we now call a "grilled open-faced sandwich." At the Cheshire Cheese. the rabbit was prepared with three kinds of cheese. "one old, one medium and one very young." the bread soaked with a mixture of stout and ale. Just when and how Welsh rabbit came to be made more like Swiss Fondue is impossible to determine, but stirring the melted cheese in a chafing dish was the standard American way by the 1860s.

Cheese and eggs combine, as if intended as partners by heaven, for a large number of dishes that are perfect for brunch. lunch, supper — or any time. This list includes soufflés, omelets, fritters, and even vegetarian cheese-nut loaves.

In addition to their gustatory appeal, these cheese-and-egg combinations are wonderful medicine for an aching budget.

### The Cheshire Cheese Rabbit

For each serving, use a wide shallow individual casserole or ramekin. Preheat oven to 400° F. (hot); place a lump of butter, about 1 tablespoon, in each dish; set in oven until butter is melted. Then place a piece of toast in each dish, and moisten toast with a little ale. Over each slice of moistened toast lay 3 slices of cheese: aged Cheddar, white Cheshire, and a young Lancashire — or a similar combination of sharp, bland, and softer young cheese. Sprinkle with mustard. Place ramekins in oven until cheese is completely melted, about 15 minutes. Serve at once.

# Fondue Neuchâteloise (Traditional Swiss Fondue)

1 fresh clove garlic
2 cups dry white wine
1 pound natural Gruyère or Swiss Emmentaler;
   or a combination of the two, shredded (4 cups)
1¹₂ tablespoons flour; or 1 tablespoon cornstarch
3 tablespoons Kirsch or cognac
Grated nutmeg or black pepper
Italian or French bread, cut into 1-inch cubes

You must always use a round casserole, chafing dish, or electric skillet to make this fondue successfully (an oval or square dish for some odd reason does not work so well). Rub casserole with cut garlic clove; discard. Pour in wine, and heat until tiny bubbles begin to form. Toss cheese with flour; then add a handful at a time to the wine, stirring after each addition until cheese is melted, keeping heat low. Add Kirsch (or cognac) and nutmeg (or pepper). To eat, dip cubes of bread in the melted cheese, if possible with long-handled fondue forks, trying to get the bread cube into your mouth without dribbling. When fondue is finished, the brown crust remaining on the bottom is especially prized. Serve with black coffee or tea or the same white wine used in making the fondue. Makes 4 generous servings.


VARIATIONS:
- Instead of Gruyère or Swiss Emmentaler, use ¹/₂ pound Swiss and ¹/₂ pound caraway-seed cheese; instead of Kirsch use Jamaica rum.
- Instead of Kirsch, add dry vermouth, preferably Noilly-Prat.
- Instead of using all natural Gruyère, use one third Gruyère, one third Gorgonzola, and one third Tilsiter.

(Fondue forks and other accessories for making this Swiss dish may be ordered by mail from the Swiss Mart; see Appendix.)

# Brillat-Savarin's Fondue

12 large eggs
½ pound (2 cups) shredded natural Gruyère
¾ pound (3 sticks) butter, softened
Freshly ground pepper
Lightly toasted French bread cut into 1-inch slices

Beat eggs until frothy, add cheese and butter, and place in a chafing dish or round casserole. (If using chafing dish, place it above hot water in lower bowl; if using casserole, place on asbestos mat over very low heat.) Stir mixture constantly until smooth and thickened. Stop only to grind pepper directly over the mixture. When consistency is creamy, spoon fondue over French bread. Serve chilled white wine with fondue. Makes 4 to 6 servings.

# Chili con Queso (Mexican Rabbit)

2 onions, chopped
1 green pepper, chopped
4 tablespoons fat, butter, or oil
1 cup (8-ounce can) kernel corn, drained
4 cups (1 pound) grated mild Cheddar or Jack
1 teaspoon chili powder (or more, to taste)
1 teaspoon salt, or to taste
1 egg, beaten
1 can (10½ ounces) concentrated tomato soup

Cook onions and green pepper in fat until soft; add corn, and cook 1 minute. Add cheese, chili powder, salt, and the beaten egg blended with tomato soup. Cook, stirring constantly, until thick and creamy. Serve on toast or on toasted Mexican tortillas. Makes 6 to 8 servings.

WITH FRESH TOMATOES: Use 4 large peeled, chopped tomatoes, cooking them with the onions and pepper. Stir in 1 tablespoon flour before adding corn and other ingredients; omit soup.

## Croûte au Fromage

Here is another Swiss dish which is served as a specialty at the Châlet Suisse Restaurant in New York City. It resembles the original Welsh rabbit as much as modern Welsh Rabbit resembles Swiss Fondue. The more things change, the more they remain the same, as the French say!

1 to 2 tablespoons butter or margarine
3 slices white bread
2 eggs, beaten
1 cup shredded natural Gruyère or Swiss Emmentaler
1 to 2 tablespoons cream
Salt and pepper
3 slices Canadian bacon (optional)

Butter the slices of bread on each side. Sauté on one side in skillet, and place in baking pan or on baking sheet with sautéed sides up. Combine beaten eggs, cheese, and cream, and sprinkle with salt and pepper. Pile mixture on the three slices of bread. If bacon is to be used (though this dish is also excellent without bacon), place one slice atop the cheese mixture on each bread slice. Toast under broiler, 5 or 6 inches from heat, until puffed and golden. Makes 3 servings. Double all ingredients for 6.

## Baked Rarebit

2 egg yolks
$1/2$ cup heavy cream
2 tablespoons melted butter
$1/2$ teaspoon salt
$1/2$ teaspoon dry mustard
2 cups grated sharp Cheddar or Dunlop
$1/2$ cup ale

Combine egg yolks, cream, butter, salt, and mustard; beat until smooth. Add cheese and ale. Turn into buttered 1-quart baking dish.* Bake at 375° F. for 25 minutes until firm. Serve with toasted English muffins. Makes 4 servings.

*Note: For a Rarebit Soufflé, stir in 2 stiffly-beaten egg whites before placing mixture in casserole.

## Raclette

The following recipe was given to me by Heinz Hofer of the Switzerland Cheese Association. Raclette is a fun dish for informal get-togethers, good for suppers or evening snacks. One may buy a special Raclette stove for making the dish, in which case, prepare according to manufacturer's directions. Or, it can be done just as easily in any broiler, according to Mr. Hofer.

The most important thing is to have heat-resistant plates or individual casseroles for each serving, for the cheese must not be moved to a cold plate after it has melted. (I find the Corning Ware individual casseroles ideal.)

You should select a cheese that melts smoothly and readily: for example, Bagnes (or "Raclette de Bagnes," as it is sometimes called), natural Gruyère, or Mütschli.

Use for each serving:
   1 to 2 ounces (1 6 x 6-inch slice)
      Bagnes, natural Gruyère, or
      Mütschli
   1 boiled potato, cut in half

On each plate put cheese and beside it the pieces of boiled potato. The plate or casserole containing cheese and potato should be approximately 4 inches from the heat. As soon as the cheese is partially melted and soft throughout, remove from the oven, and place this hot plate on a cold service plate (otherwise guests may burn fingers on touching hot plates). The cheese is scraped over and then mashed into the potato; then such relishes as dill pickles and cocktail onions should be passed. It is so utterly simple it sounds like nothing — but try it, you'll find it a delightful dish.


## Rum-Tum-Diddy

1 can (10½ ounces) condensed tomato soup
½ pound package Velveeta quick-melting process cheese
½ teaspoon dry mustard

Combine soup, cheese, and mustard; heat, stirring, until cheese is melted. Serve over toast. Makes 4 servings.

WITH BACON: If desired, crumble cooked bacon over top of each serving, allowing one slice of bacon per serving.

## Fondue aux Tomates

   This Swiss variation of Fondue is strikingly similar to Rum-Tum-Diddy.

8 medium tomatoes
4 tablespoons butter
$^1/_2$ teaspoon salt
1 teaspoon sugar
Pinch of basil
$^1/_4$ teaspoon grated nutmeg
$^1/_2$ pound (2 cups) shredded natural Gruyère or Fontina
1 egg, beaten

Scald tomatoes, and peel off skins. When cool, cut in half, and gently squeeze out seeds and excess juice. Chop squeezed tomatoes; sauté gently in butter; when soft, add salt, sugar, basil, and nutmeg. Start adding cheese a handful at a time, stirring until smooth. Just before serving, quickly stir in beaten egg, beating hard and fast to prevent coagulation of egg white. Serve on toast. Makes 3 or 4 servings.


## Baked Fondue

2 cups milk
2 cups soft bread crumbs
1 teaspoon salt
$^1/_2$ teaspoon dry mustard
Dash of cayenne (optional)
2 cups ($^1/_2$ pound) grated Cheddar, Swiss,
   Fontina, or Mütschli
4 eggs, separated

Heat milk to scalding; add bread crumbs, salt, mustard, cayenne, and cheese. Cool slightly; then beat in egg yolks. Fold in stiffly beaten egg whites. Turn into 1$^1/_2$-quart casserole, bake at 350° F. (moderate oven) for 50 minutes or until firm yet puffy. Makes 4 servings.

# New England Codfish Rabbit

1 cup shredded packaged salt codfish, freshened*
    (or leftover cooked codfish)
1 tablespoon butter
1 tablespoon flour
1/4 teaspoon onion juice; or 1 teaspoon grated onion
1 tablespoon pimiento, minced
1 cup milk
3/4 cup grated sharp cheese
1 egg, beaten

Break up codfish with fork. Melt butter, stir in flour, onion juice, and pimiento. Mix thoroughly. Add milk gradually, then the freshened or cooked fish and cheese. Cook until well blended. Add some of hot mixture to egg; then combine; cook over very low heat 5 minutes longer. Serve at once on toast. Makes 4 servings.

*To "freshen" salt codfish: add water as directed on package. This amounts to reconstituting dehydrated cooked codfish.

# Modern Welsh Rabbit

2 tablespoons butter
3/4 teaspoon salt
1/2 teaspoon dry mustard
Freshly ground black pepper
3 cups shredded sharp Cheddar or
    Double Gloucester
3/4 cup beer or ale
1 egg, well beaten

Melt butter in casserole or chafing dish. Add seasonings, cheese, and beer or ale; stir constantly until cheese is melted and mixture smooth. Just before serving, quickly beat in egg. Serve over toast. Makes 4 servings.

BUCK RABBIT: Top each serving with a poached egg.

# Baked Danish Fondue

4 eggs, separated
1 cup milk
1 teaspoon salt
Pinch of dry mustard
8 slices white bread, cut into cubes
2 cups (1/2 pound) cubed caraway-seed Danbo
1 cup beer (preferably Danish Tuborg)
2 tablespoons butter

Beat egg yolks; add milk, salt, mustard, about 3/4 of the bread cubes, and the cheese. Blend well, and let stand until bread has absorbed liquid. Add beer. Beat egg whites until stiff, fold into cheese mixture; turn into 1 1/2-quart casserole. Toss remaining bread cubes with butter and spread over top. Bake at 325° F. until a knife inserted in the center comes out clean. Serve immediately. Makes 4 to 6 servings.


# Frittata alla Toscana (Omelette Tuscan Style)

1 package frozen artichoke hearts
1/4 cup olive oil
1/4 teaspoon salt
1 clove garlic
6 eggs, beaten until frothy
1/4 cup diced Fontina, Stracchino, or Mozzarella
Salt to taste

Place partially defrosted artichoke hearts, olive oil, salt, and garlic in heavy saucepan. Cover tightly, cook over moderate heat until tender, about 7 minutes. Remove and discard garlic. Chop artichoke hearts, place with 2 tablespoons of oil in skillet, pour in the eggs, turning up to let moist egg run under as omelet firms. When omelet is half-cooked, add cheese and salt, and cook until cheese is partially melted. Turn over omelet like a pancake, let it cook a minute on the other side, then slide it out of pan onto warm plate. Makes 3 or 4 servings.

### Basic Cheese Soufflé

3 tablespoons butter
3 tablespoons flour
1 cup milk
$^{1}/_{2}$ teaspoon salt
Pinch of cayenne (optional)
1 to $1^{1}/_{2}$ cups shredded or grated cheese (see variations)
$^{1}/_{2}$ teaspoon cornstarch
4 to 6 eggs, separated

First make a cream sauce: Melt butter, stir in flour, and cook until mixture bubbles. Slowly stir in milk, add seasonings, cook until smooth and thickened. Toss cheese with cornstarch, and add to cream sauce. (This part can be done in advance.) An hour before the soufflé is to be served, beat the egg yolks until thick and stir into cooled sauce. Beat egg whites until stiff, fold in gently. Preheat oven to 350° F. (moderate). Pour soufflé mixture into buttered $1^{1}/_{2}$-quart soufflé dish or straight-sided casserole. Bake 30 to 35 minutes until soufflé is high, puffed, and golden. Serve immediately. Serves 4.

SWISS SOUFFLÉ: Use 1 to $1^{1}/_{2}$ cups shredded Swiss or natural Gruyère (or a mixture of Gruyère and Swiss Emmentaler) and 6 eggs. Bake in 2-quart soufflé dish or casserole.

BLUE CHEESE SOUFFLÉ: Use 1 cup crumbled Danish Blue or Roquefort and 4 eggs. Omit cayenne.

CHIVE-CHEESE SOUFFLÉ: Use a mild Cheddar and add 2 tablespoons minced chives. Omit cayenne.

BROCCOLI SOUFFLÉ: Cook a 10-ounce package frozen broccoli spears or $^{1}/_{2}$ head broccoli until barely tender. Drain, chop, and measure 1 cup. Add to basic recipe with cheese, using American Münster, Swiss, or mild Cheddar.

PROVOLONE SOUFFLÉ: Use 2 cups grated Provolone.

SOUFFLÉ FLORENTINÉ: Cook 1 package frozen chopped spinach as directed on package. Drain thoroughly. Add to basic recipe with cheese, using shredded Fontina, Stracchino, or half Swiss and half grated Parmesan. Instead of cayenne, add a dash of nutmeg.

CARAWAY CHEESE SOUFFLÉ: Use caraway-seed cheese in basic recipe.

BEER-CHEESE SOUFFLÉ: Use beer for half the liquid in making the sauce, add ¹/₂ teaspoon dry mustard with other seasonings, and use sharp Cheddar. Or use ³/₄ cup beer and ¹/₄ cup cream, and use grated Pecorino Romano instead of Cheddar.

### Tortilla con Queso (Spanish Cheese Omelette)

1 medium onion, chopped
1 large raw potato, finely chopped
4 to 6 tablespoons Spanish olive oil
Salt, about ¹/₂ teaspoon altogether
4 eggs, beaten
¹/₂ cup grated Manchego*
¹/₄ cup chopped ham (optional)

Both onion and potato must be chopped very fine. Add to 4 tablespoons olive oil in 8- to 10-inch omelet pan or Teflon skillet, and cook over low heat (220° F. on thermostatically controlled top burner), chopping vegetables occasionally with spatula and turning over to make sure they do not stick. Sprinkle lightly with salt from shaker. Add about half of the beaten eggs; lift vegetables up so liquid egg can run under. Blend cheese and ham (if used) to remaining egg with ¹/₄ teaspoon salt, and pour this mixture over vegetables, lifting up as before and cutting in several places to allow liquid egg to go to bottom — also so that cheese will be blended with vegetables. When omelet is firm and slightly browned on bottom, place plate over top and invert to slip out omelet. Add additional olive oil to pan and return omelet to pan moist side down. Cook until firm and lightly browned on bottom, then slide out. The dish is hearty, rich, and delicious. Makes 2 to 4 servings.

*Note: I have also used grated Kashkaval and Fontinella in this recipe, and both were excellent.

## Ham and Cheese Rabbit

1/2 cup chopped ham
2 tablespoons butter or margarine
1 small onion, chopped
1/2 green pepper, diced
1 teaspoon prepared mustard
1 10 1/2-ounce can condensed Cheddar-cheese soup
1/4 cup beer, sherry, or milk
1 cup grated Swiss or Brick cheese

Sauté ham in butter until lightly browned; add onion and pepper, cook until soft. Add mustard, condensed soup, and liquid. Stir until smooth and hot. Add cheese, and stir until melted. Serve over baked or boiled potatoes. Makes 4 to 6 servings.

## Swiss Cheese Croquettes

4 tablespoons (1/2 stick) butter
5 tablespoons flour
1 1/2 cups milk
Salt and pepper to taste
2 cups (1/2 pound) natural Gruyère
    or Swiss Emmentaler
3 egg yolks
1 beaten egg
1/4 cup milk
Flour
2 tablespoons each olive oil and butter

Melt 4 tablespoons butter, then stir in 5 tablespoons flour until smooth and bubbling. Slowly add milk, stirring until smooth, and season to taste. Add cheese. Cool slightly. Beat in egg yolks. Spread mixture in buttered shallow pan; cover with waxed paper, chill 2 hours. Then form into croquettes. Dip each croquette into a mixture of 1 beaten egg and 1/4 cup milk; then roll in flour. Fry gently in mixture of oil and butter, turning to brown on all sides. Serve with tomato sauce or stewed tomatoes. Makes 4 servings.

# Italian Parmesan Omelette

3 eggs
¹/₄ teaspoon salt
Freshly ground black pepper
1 tablespoon fine bread crumbs
2 tablespoons grated Parmesan
1 or 2 tablespoons milk or cream
2 tablespoons olive oil

Beat eggs until light, and add salt, pepper, crumbs, cheese, and milk. Heat olive oil in 6-inch skillet or omelet pan. Pour in egg mixture over low heat; as omelet begins to firm, rotate pan slightly; then lift up with spatula to allow moist egg to run under. When firm and golden on bottom but still slightly moist in center, fold over omelet, and slide out onto warm plate. Serve with orange marmalade or currant jelly. Makes 3 servings.

# Huevos Cocidos en Arroz (Eggs Baked in Rice)

1 large onion, chopped
2 tablespoons Spanish olive oil
1 cup uncooked rice
2 cups beef or chicken broth
¹/₂ teaspoon salt
Dash of cayenne
6 eggs
¹/₂ cup grated Manchego or Swiss

Cook onion in olive oil until soft; add rice; then add broth, salt, and cayenne, bringing to a boil. Lower heat, and cook covered until liquid is absorbed; then spoon into casserole. Make 6 indentations in rice; break an egg into each. Sprinkle cheese over top. Bake in oven preheated to 400° F. (hot), until eggs are set, about 15 minutes. Makes 6 servings.

## Greek Eggs and Cheese

2 tablespoons olive oil
4 slices Kashkaval (Caciocavallo) or Provolone
4 eggs
$1/4$ teaspoon salt
Freshly ground pepper
Few drops lemon juice
4 slices toast

Warm olive oil in wide, heavy skillet. Place slices of cheese in oil, and, as cheese begins to soften, break eggs over cheese, taking care yolks do not break. Sprinkle with salt and pepper. Cover pan so that eggs steam, keeping heat low. As soon as egg white is firm, squeeze lemon over eggs; then with spatula lift onto toast. Makes 4 servings.

## Huevos Caracas (Eggs Caracas Style)

2 ounces dried beef, shredded
2 tablespoons butter or oil
$1/2$ cup grated Parmesan
1 cup canned tomatoes
$1/2$ to 1 teaspoon chili powder
3 eggs, beaten

Cook shredded beef in butter until it curls; add cheese, tomatoes, and chili powder; cook about 2 minutes. Add a little hot sauce to the eggs, then combine the two, and cook over very low heat, lifting up mixture as it firms. Serve on toast or toasted tortillas. Makes 2 to 3 servings.

# Scrambled Eggs Manchego

1 shallot, minced
2 tablespoons butter
1 small tomato, peeled and chopped
$1/8$ teaspoon oregano
$1/4$ teaspoon salt
5 or 6 eggs, well beaten
$1/4$ cup cubed Manchego, Swiss, or mild Cheddar
Freshly ground pepper

Sauté the shallot in butter until lightly browned; add tomato, oregano, and salt, and cook over very low heat until soft. Add the eggs and cheese; sprinkle with the pepper and a little additional salt from shaker. Turn over with spatula as egg firms. Makes 3 or 4 servings.

A crust of soft, melted cheese atop a casserole, a hidden treasure of creamy Ricotta under slices of eggplant, or a cheese filling inside roll-ups of veal scaloppine — these touches make any entree special.

Because cheese is a protein food, and rich, not all meats can be combined with it successfully. Cheese is best with veal because veal is delicate in flavor and the two therefore complement each other — as long as a delicate cheese is selected. Never must the cheese dominate the meat.

The best cheese to use with beef is a blue cheese; as beef itself is strong in flavor, it can take on a strongly flavored partner.

The same general rule applies when cheese is used with fish. Use a delicate cheese like Gruyère with a bland fish like sole. With salmon, which is a more pungently flavored fish, a blue-cheese mayonnaise is surprisingly good. Shrimp, because it has a decisive flavor, can take on almost any cheese, and shrimp-cheese pastries are marvelous both as entrees and as appetizers.

The use of cheeses with pastas — macaroni, lasagne, spaghetti, and so on — is treated in the next chapter, for, when a pasta is added, the composition of the dish can be much more complex, as the pasta serves to separate the rich ingredients, acting as a kind of buffer between them.

Only a few cheese-and-vegetable entrees are included here. Others will be found in the chapter "Cheese-Kissed Vegetables." The difference? Those in this chapter are so rich and filling that they deserve to be presented as main dishes, whereas the others may either star by themselves or accompany meat dishes.

# Veal Chops Parmigiana

6 boned veal chops, well trimmed*
2 eggs, slightly beaten
2 tablespoons water
$3/4$ teaspoon salt
$3/4$ cup fine dry crumbs
$1/4$ cup grated Parmesan
$1/2$ teaspoon thyme
3 tablespoons olive oil
3 tablespoons butter
1 clove garlic
2 or 3 tomatoes, peeled and chopped
2 shallots or green onions, minced
$1/2$ cup white wine
2 tablespoons brandy
6 slices Mozzarella or Fontina

Blend eggs, water, and salt in one bowl; in a shallow bowl or pan, combine crumbs, Parmesan, and thyme. Dip the meat first in egg mixture, then in crumb mixture. Chill at least 15 minutes; then brown on each side in mixture of hot olive oil and butter. While sautéeing chops, place whole garlic clove in skillet; when garlic is golden, mash it into the oil with a fork. If you prefer only a delicate garlic flavor, remove and discard shreds. Remove browned chops to large, shallow casserole. Pour off all but 2 tablespoons of oil from the skillet. Add the tomatoes and shallots; cook until soft; then add wine and brandy, and simmer 5 minutes. Pour this mixture over the chops. Bake in 350° F. oven for 25 to 30 minutes. During last 10 minutes place slices of cheese over chops. Serve with plain buttered spaghetti or rice and a simple tossed green salad. Makes 6 servings.

*Note: Instead of chops, individual veal scallopini may be used, but allow 2 scallopini per serving.

# Veal Chops Caprice

Sautéeing the chops in pure olive oil rather than in butter makes a subtly different flavor in this simple but unusual entree.

4 large loin veal chops, well trimmed
1 teaspoon paprika
1/2 teaspoon salt
1 tablespoon flour
2 tablespoons olive oil
4 slices natural Gruyère or Swiss Emmentaler

Combine paprika, salt, and flour, and work into chops. Sauté the chops in olive oil until well browned on each side. Lay in a large shallow casserole with a slice of cheese over each; place in broiler oven 4 inches from heat until cheese is melted and lightly browned. Makes 4 servings.

# Ham and Cheese Roulades

2 cups Mornay Sauce II (see Index)
2 egg yolks
8 thin slices natural Gruyère or Swiss
8 thin slices boiled ham
1/2 cup well-seasoned tomato sauce
2 tablespoons heavy cream

Prepare Mornay Sauce II, but use 2 egg yolks in preference to 1 whole egg. Set half of Mornay Sauce aside. Put a slice of cheese on each slice of ham; then roll up. Pour tomato sauce over bottom of shallow casserole and place ham roulades in the tomato sauce, with overlapped sides down; add cream to remaining Mornay Sauce and pour sauce over ham. Just before serving, complete cooking in preheated 350° F. (moderate) oven for about 15 minutes or until sauce is bubbly and lightly browned. Makes 4 servings.

# Veal Cutlet Tessinoise

1 large veal cutlet, cut $1/4$ inch thick
$1/2$ cup milk
1 teaspoon salt
$1/2$ cup flour
2 eggs, beaten
$3/4$ cup fine dry crumbs
6 tablespoons butter
4 tablespoons oil
2 to 3 large tomatoes, thickly sliced
Salt
$1/4$ teaspoon thyme
4 to 6 slices natural Gruyère
$1/4$ teaspoon basil

Cut the cutlet into serving pieces (4 to 6, depending on size of cutlet). Remove center bone. Pound each piece with mallet or edge of plate to flatten and tenderize. Soak $1/2$ hour in the milk and salt. Remove from milk, dredge with flour, dip in beaten eggs, and roll in crumbs. Chill 15 to 30 minutes. Heat butter and oil until butter is melted and sizzling, sauté the cutlets until browned on each side, and remove to large, shallow casserole or oven-proof platter. In same butter sauté the sliced tomatoes, sprinkling with salt and herbs. Place tomato slices on the veal cutlets. Top each cutlet with a slice of cheese. This step can be taken shortly before dinner is scheduled. Complete in oven at 400° F. until cheese melts, about 15 minutes. Makes 4 to 6 servings.

VEAL CUTLETS VELEZ: Instead of tomatoes, place slices of ham over the cutlets, and top with slices of natural Gruyère, Fontina, or Caerphilly.

# Veal with Cheese-Wine Sauce

8 veal scaloppine
Salt and pepper
Few drops lemon juice
2 tablespoons flour
4 slices bread
2 tablespoons butter
2 tablespoons olive oil
1 clove garlic
1/4 cup dry vermouth or dry sherry
1/4 cup water
1/8 teaspoon salt or to taste
3 egg yolks
2 tablespoons shredded Fontina or Gruyère
Minced chives or parsley

Sprinkle the scaloppine with salt, pepper, and lemon juice. Dust on both sides with flour. Next, fry the bread in the butter and oil until lightly browned; drain on a paper towel, and place on platter. Place whole garlic clove and the scaloppine in same pan; brown garlic while meat cooks, then mash into the oil with fork or back of wooden spoon. Gently sauté the meat until delicately browned on each side, about 15 minutes altogether. Lay 2 overlapping slices of meat on each fried bread slice. Pour off excess oil from pan and discard garlic shreds; to the pan drippings add vermouth, water and 1/8 teaspoon salt; boil up, stirring to loosen browned bits from bottom. Cool slightly; then add this sauce to egg yolks and cheese in top of double boiler, beating constantly with a whisk over hot water until sauce thickens. Pour sauce over veal. Garnish with minced chives or parsley. Serve at once with a simple green salad dressed with olive oil and lemon juice. Makes 4 servings.

# Moussaka (Greek Lamb and Eggplant Casserole)

MEAT SAUCE:
2 lamb patties ($^3/_4$ pound minced lean lamb)
1 tablespoon olive oil
1 large onion, sliced
1 or 2 garlic cloves, minced
1 large tomato, peeled and sliced
$^1/_2$ teaspoon thyme
2 tablespoons parsley
$^1/_2$ teaspoon salt
$^1/_2$ cup dry wine
1 egg, beaten

Crumble meat of lamb patties; cook in olive oil with onion in heavy skillet until most of fat is drawn out; spoon off and discard excess fat. Add garlic, tomato, thyme, parsley, and salt; cook 2 minutes. Add wine, and simmer 5 minutes. Cool slightly. Beat egg, and stir quickly into cooled sauce.

EGGPLANT:
1 small (6-inch) eggplant, cut into $^1/_4$-inch slices but not
   peeled
$^1/_2$ cup flour
$^1/_2$ teaspoon salt
$^1/_4$ to $^1/_2$ cup olive oil
2 medium potatoes, thinly sliced
$^1/_2$ cup grated Kashkaval (Caciocovallo)
$^1/_4$ cup fine, dry crumbs

Separately dust eggplant slices with flour blended with $^1/_2$ teaspoon salt; sauté in olive oil until lightly browned on each side. Parboil sliced potatoes 2 minutes in boiling water; drain. Arrange eggplant, potato slices, meat sauce, and cheese in $1^1/_2$-quart casserole with eggplant and cheese on top. Spread crumbs over cheese, pressing down into eggplant. Bake uncovered at 350° F. 45 minutes to 1 hour until crumbs are browned. Makes 4 servings.

## Saltimbocca all'Abruzzese
### (Veal Scaloppine Filled with Cheese)

12 veal scaloppine, pounded very thin
1 teaspoon leaf sage, crushed
1 teaspoon salt
2 tablespoons flour
1/4 pound Mozzarella or soft Fontina, cut in 12 sticks
2 tablespoons butter
2 tablespoons olive oil
1 clove garlic
1/2 cup dry white wine

Pound into one side of the scaloppine a mixture of crushed sage, salt, and flour. On the inside of each scaloppine, place a stick of the cheese; roll up meat, and fasten each roll with toothpicks. Brown meat rolls in the butter and oil. At the same time, place a garlic clove in the pan; mash garlic with fork when golden; then discard shreds. When meat is browned on all sides, remove to serving dish. To pan drippings, add wine and boil up, stirring to loosen all browned bits from bottom of pan. Pour sauce over meat. Serve with rice or buttered noodles and artichoke hearts. Makes 6 servings.

SALTIMBOCCA WITH HAM: Sometimes both veal and ham are used to make Saltimbocca. Place a thin slice of ham over each slice of veal (cut to fit); then place cheese in center of each roll-up.

### Involtini (Pâté-Stuffed Scaloppine)

Involtini are much like Saltimbocca (which means literally "jump in the mouth") but with slightly different ingredients.

12 individual veal scaloppine (about 2 pounds)
1 teaspoon crushed rosemary
1/2 cup flour
1 teaspoon salt
1/2 cup grated Parmesan
1 4-ounce can pâté de foie gras
4 tablespoons Ricotta, farmer's, or pot cheese

2 tablespoons minced parsley
2 tablespoons olive oil
1 cup Marsala or medium-sweet sherry

Combine rosemary, flour, and salt, and pound mixture into one side of the scaloppine, using the edge of a plate; then pound grated cheese into the meat. On the unseasoned side of each scaloppine, place a teaspoonful of pâté, a teaspoonful of Ricotta, and a little parsley. Roll up, and secure with toothpicks. Brown the roll-ups on all sides in the oil. Add the wine, and simmer 10 minutes or until meat is tender. Serve over a bed of hot, cooked rice, with a salad of tomatoes and watercress. Makes 6 servings.

### Pastel de Carne (Uruguayan Beef Pie)

1¹/₂ pounds chopped chuck
1 medium onion, chopped
2 tablespoons olive oil
¹/₂ cup beef broth
1 cup raisins
2 tablespoons medium sherry
3 hard-cooked eggs, chopped
1 cup grated firm cheese (Gouda or mild Cheddar)
1 teaspoon salt or to taste
1¹/₂ to 2 cups seasoned mashed potatoes;
    or 1 envelope instant mashed potatoes,
    prepared as directed on package
¹/₂ cup fine, dry crumbs
2 tablespoons butter

Simmer onions in oil until soft; add meat, and cook until it loses pink color. Add beef broth, raisins, and sherry. Simmer 5 minutes. Add eggs and ¹/₂ cup of the cheese. Add salt to taste. Turn mixture into wide 2-inch-deep casserole. Spread potatoes over top. Mix remaining cheese with bread crumbs, and spread over potatoes. Dot butter over top. Bake in oven preheated to 350° F. (moderate) for 20 to 25 minutes until top is golden. Makes 4 to 6 servings.

# Italian Meatballs

2 ounces ground salt pork
1 clove garlic
1 large onion, chopped
1 pound ground lean beef or veal
1 cup grated Parmesan or Pecorino Romano
$1/2$ cup fine dry crumbs
1 teaspoon salt
$1/4$ teaspoon crushed fennel
Pinch of allspice or mace
1 egg, beaten
1 to 2 tablespoons olive oil
$1/2$ cup beef bouillon
1 teaspoon lemon juice
$1/2$ cup white wine
2 tablespoons minced Italian parsley

Draw out fat from salt pork in heavy skillet until completely melted; add garlic clove and onion, and cook until onion is soft. Mash garlic into fat with tines of fork; blend crushed garlic with onion. Remove onion and garlic from fat, and add to the ground meat, along with cheese, crumbs, salt, fennel, allspice, and egg. Work together with fingers to blend well; form into 1-inch meatballs. Sauté the meatballs in oil in same skillet until crisply browned on all sides. Drain off oil and fat. Add beef bouillon, lemon juice, and wine to meatballs, and cook until liquid is reduced to half. Add parsley. Serve with cooked linguine and additional Parmesan cheese. Makes 4 servings.

## Broiled Flank Steak with Roquefort

$2^1/2$ - 3 pounds Flank steak
$1/3$ to $1/2$ cup olive oil
1 clove garlic, mashed
1 to 2 tablespoons red wine vinegar
$1/4$ cup (about) crumbled Roquefort
Lemon juice, a few drops

Marinate steak in mixture of olive oil, garlic and vinegar at least ¹/₂ hour. Remove steak from marinade, and broil over charcoal 5 minutes on each side for rare. Shortly before removing from fire, sprinkle crumbled Roquefort over the top; cheese will melt from heat of cooked steak. Slice steak at a 65-degree angle; serve sprinkled with lemon juice. A 2¹/₂-pound steak thinly sliced will make about 6 servings.

## Beef and Tomato Casserole

1¹/₂ pounds ground chuck
2 tablespoons olive oil
1 medium onion, chopped
1 or 2 whole garlic cloves
¹/₂ green pepper, chopped
2 tablespoons minced parsley
1¹/₂ teaspoons salt
¹/₂ teaspoon crushed marjoram
1 egg, beaten
3 or 4 ripe tomatoes, sliced
1 cup Ricotta or cottage cheese
1 cup (about ¹/₄ pound) thinly sliced Swiss,
    Mütschli, or American Münster
2 or 3 medium potatoes, peeled and thinly sliced
¹/₂ cup soft bread crumbs tossed with 1 tablesppon melted butter

In olive oil, sauté onion, garlic, and green pepper until onion is golden and soft. Crush whole garlic cloves with fork; if delicate garlic flavor is preferred, remove and discard shreds. Add parsley, salt, and marjoram, then the meat. Cook until meat loses color. Remove from heat, quickly beat in egg. Arrange meat mixture in layers with sliced tomatoes, cheeses, and potatoes in a 2¹/₂-quart greased or oiled casserole, until all ingredients are used, with sliced cheese on top. Sprinkle bread crumbs over casserole. Bake in 400° F. oven for about one hour or until potatoes are done. Makes 4 to 6 servings.

WITH MACARONI: Omit potatoes, and add 2 cups cooked macaroni (1 8-ounce package). Reduce cooking time to 30 or 40 minutes.

## Baked Ham-Stuffed Endives au Gratin

12 Belgian endives
12 thin slices ham
3 tablespoons butter
3 tablespoons flour
$^3/_4$ cup chicken stock made with powdered concentrate or
    bouillon cube
1 cup milk
$^1/_4$ cup cream
Salt and pepper
Dash of nutmeg
1 cup ($^1/_4$ pound) grated domestic Swiss or imported Gruyère
1 egg, beaten
1 cup fine dry crumbs
2 tablespoons butter, melted

Gently cook the endives in salted water until just tender and still a little crisp. Drain and cool. Enclose a rolled-up slice of ham in each endive, place in a row in buttered shallow casserole. Melt 3 tablespoons butter, stir in flour, then slowly add hot chicken stock. Cook 5 minutes; slowly add milk, cream, and seasonings to taste. Remove from heat; cool slightly. Stir in half the cheese mixed with the beaten egg. Pour over the stuffed endives. Combine remaining cheese with crumbs and melted butter; spread over the top. Bake uncovered at 400° F. for 30 minutes until top is lightly browned and sauce bubbling. Makes 6 servings.

## Fried Chicken Parma

1 3-pound chicken, cut up
Salt
Olive oil
$^1/_2$ cup herb-seasoned fine, dry crumbs
$^1/_2$ cup grated Parma or Parmesan
Lemon wedges

Wash chicken pieces, pat dry, sprinkle lightly with salt from shaker, and brush generously with olive oil. Roll each piece in mixture of crumbs and cheese. Place in oiled shallow roasting pan; bake at 375° F. for 1 hour until crisp and brown, turning once and brushing with additional oil. Serve with lemon wedges, the juice to be sprinkled over the chicken at table. Makes 2 to 4 servings.

### Ganfer Spiessli (Geneva-Style Veal and Cheese Kabobs)

1 pound lean veal, from leg or loin,
    cut in 2 x $1/2$-inch squares
$1/2$ pound (about) natural Gruyère or Swiss,
    cut in 2 x $1/2$-inch squares
Flour
1 egg, beaten
2 tablespoons water
$1/2$ teaspoon salt
Fine dry crumbs
4 tablespoons butter
4 tablespoons olive oil

Arrange pieces of meat and cheese alternately on 4 large poultry skewers (4 inches long), with 3 pieces of meat and 2 of cheese on each skewer. Dust thoroughly with flour, so that all outside surfaces are covered. Combine egg, water, and salt; brush egg over all surfaces of meat and cheese, then roll the skewered mixture in the crumbs, again taking care that all surfaces are well coated. Chill in refrigerator about 1 hour. Then melt butter with olive oil in skillet, brown the breaded kabobs quickly on all sides, and transfer to shallow roasting pan. Finish cooking in oven for 20 to 25 minutes, turning once. If some cheese oozes onto bottom of pan, spoon it over tops of kabobs as sauce. Serve with rice or mashed potatoes and broiled tomatoes. Serves 4.

# Juvedge (Yugoslavian Casserole)

1 pound boned lamb, cut from leg or shoulder
2 to 3 tablespoons olive oil
1 pound lean veal, in cubes
3 medium onions, sliced
4 medium tomatoes, peeled and sliced
2 large potatoes, peeled and sliced
2 teaspoons salt, or to taste
$1/2$ teaspoon dried thyme
$1/2$ teaspoon dried basil
$1/2$ cup uncooked rice
$1/2$ cup shredded Kashkaval (Caciocavallo) or
   grated Provolone

Brush large (3- to 4-quart) casserole with olive oil. Arrange meat and sliced vegetables in layers (keeping aside a few tomato slices), sprinkling salt and herbs over each layer. Spread rice over top, and cover rice with reserved tomato slices. Cover casserole and bake at 350° F. for $1^1/2$ hours. Remove cover, spread cheese over top, and return to oven until cheese is melted. Makes 6 servings.

# Cheese-Stuffed Hamburgers

2 pounds lean ground beef
1 slice bread, crumbled
$1/4$ cup chili sauce
$1^1/2$ teaspoons salt
Black pepper
8 small cubes of Danish Blue,
   sharp natural Cheddar, or Havarti

Blend beef, bread, chili sauce, salt, and black pepper to taste. Divide meat into 8 parts, put a nugget of cheese on each, and pat meat around it to enclose completely. Handle lightly. Grill over charcoal, 5 inches from coals, or in preheated broiler about 5 minutes each side for medium rare. Makes 8 hamburgers.

# Glazed Breast of Chicken

4 whole chicken breasts, boned
1 teaspoon salt
Dash of freshly ground pepper
4 tablespoons butter
$1/2$ cup currant jelly
$1/4$ cup white wine
1 teaspoon lemon juice
$1/2$ cup shredded natural Gruyère or Bel Lago
12 to 16 almonds, blanched

Sprinkle chicken with salt and pepper, sauté quickly in the butter over high heat. Meanwhile, beat together jelly, wine, and lemon juice. When chicken is crisply browned, cover it with jelly mixture, reduce heat, cover pan, and simmer 25 minutes. Remove cover, and sprinkle cheese and almonds over top; place skillet under broiler 5 inches from heat until cheese melts. Serve with parsley rice* and sliced tomatoes and cucumbers. Makes 4 servings.

*Parsley Rice: Cook rice in the usual way; while hot, add butter and a fistful of minced parsley; toss to blend.

# Coquilles St. Jacques au Gratin

1 pound sea scallops
$1/2$ cup dry white wine
6 shallots, minced
$1/4$ pound mushrooms, thinly sliced
$1/2$ teaspoon salt
Dash of pepper
$1/2$ to $3/4$ cup fine, dry bread crumbs
$1/2$ cup shredded Swiss or American Münster

Cut scallops in small pieces. Cook in wine with shallots and mushrooms for 10 minutes. Add salt and pepper. Divide into 4 individual casseroles or ramekins. Combine crumbs and cheese, spread over scallops. Bake in preheated 450° F. oven until crumbs are brown, about 10 minutes. Serve immediately. Serves 4.

## Shrimp Coquilles

1 pound shelled shrimp*
1 3-ounce package cream cheese, softened
2 tablespoons crumbled blue cheese
$1/4$ teaspoon salt
$1/8$ teaspoon pepper
Dash of Tabasco or cayenne
1 tablespoon lemon juice
3 tablespoons milk
Boiling salted water
$1/4$ cup fine bread crumbs
2 tablespoons butter

Beat together the two cheeses, salt, pepper, Tabasco, lemon juice, and milk. Place shrimp in boiling salted water; turn off heat, and let shrimp remain covered in water 5 minutes; then remove and drain. Add shrimp to cheese mixture, divide in four portions, and place in ramekins or individual shallow casseroles. Top with crumbs and dot with butter. Bake in oven preheated to 375° F. for 20 minutes or until cheese is bubbly and crumbs are browned. Serves 4.

*Note: $1^3/4$ pounds shrimp in shells.


## Sole au Gratin

4 fillets of sole
$1/2$ teaspoon salt
$1/2$ teaspoon paprika
$1/2$ cup Spanish olive oil
$1/2$ cup sour cream
$1/2$ cup grated Parmesan or $1/4$ cup shredded domestic Swiss

Add salt and paprika to oil. Dip the fillets in the oil, and leave there 5 to 10 minutes. Remove from oil, and place on foil-lined broiler pan 4 inches from heat. Broil until flesh is firm and lightly browned on *one side only*. Combine sour cream and cheese, and spoon over top of fish. Leave in broiler with reduced heat for 5 minutes longer. Serve with parsley potatoes and Frenched green beans. Makes 4 servings.

## Shrimp-Cheese Pastries

1 package pie-crust mix or pastry made from your own recipe
    for 2-crust pie
$1/2$ cup chopped onion
3 tablespoons butter or margarine
1 cup chopped celery
1 5-ounce can shrimp, drained and minced
$1/2$ cup grated domestic Swiss or crumbled Roquefort or
    Gorgonzola

Prepare pie crust in the usual way; roll out thin. Cut into 8 5-inch squares. Cook onion in butter until soft but not brown; add celery, cook until tender. Add shrimp and cheese, stir to blend. Spoon 2 tablespoons of mixture onto each square of pastry. Fold pastry over in triangles, moisten edges, and press together with tines of fork to seal. Bake in oven preheated to 400° F. until golden and crisp, 20 to 25 minutes. Serve hot with a sauce made by blending 1 teaspoon horseradish into $1/2$ cup sour cream. Serve as a luncheon dish with a molded tomato aspic or fruit salad and hot rolls. Makes 8 pastries.


## Australian Baked Fish and Cheese

$1^1/2$ pounds fillet of whiting or similar fish
1 tablespoon oil
$1/2$ cup grated sharp Cheddar, Cheshire, or Dunlop
$1/2$ teaspoon salt
$1/4$ teaspoon pepper
4 tablespoons chopped shallots or green onions
$1/2$ pound fresh mushrooms; or $4^1/2$-ounce can mushrooms
6 tablespoons white wine
$1^1/2$ teaspoons lemon juice
1 tablespoon minced parsley

Rub oil over shallow baking dish; sprinkle with grated cheese. Place fish fillets on cheese; add salt, pepper, and shallots or onions. Top with mushrooms; pour wine over fillets. Bake in preheated 450° F. oven for 15 minutes or until fish flakes easily. Sprinkle with lemon juice and parsley before serving. Makes 4 servings.

195

# Halibut with Gruyère Sauce

HALIBUT:
2 pounds halibut, cut into 4 steaks
Salt
Lemon juice
4 tablespoons butter
1 jar tiny Danish shrimp

Sprinkle halibut steaks with salt and lemon juice and dot with butter. Bake at 325° F. (low) until fish flakes easily, 20 to 25 minutes. During last 5 minutes, lay tiny shrimp over the top (save liquid from shrimp for the Fish Fumet). Serve topped with the Gruyère Sauce. Makes 4 servings.

FISH FUMET:
When buying the fish, ask your butcher or fish man for some heads and bones to use in making this broth. Combine heads and bones of fish, 2 cups water (including shrimp liquid), a few slices carrot, 1 small onion, a sprig of parsley, 1 bay leaf, 3 whole pepper corns, and $1/2$ teaspoon salt. Boil 20 minutes, strain, and set aside. Add water if necessary to make 2 cups.

GRUYÈRE SAUCE:
2 tablespoons butter
3 tablespoons flour
2 cups Fish Fumet
$1/4$ cup light cream
2 egg yolks
$1/4$ cup grated Gruyère
Salt and pepper

Melt butter, stir in flour, then slowly add the Fumet. Simmer 5 minutes. Add cream (do not allow to boil after cream is added). Beat some of broth into egg yolks; then combine the two. Add cheese and stir until melted. Add salt and pepper as needed. Serve on halibut steaks, garnished with parsley. Makes $2^1/4$ cups.

# Chicken Divan

6 whole chicken breasts, boned; or 1 turkey breast, boned
1 large bunch broccoli (about 2¹/₂ pounds), cooked
1 teaspoon salt
1 cup white wine
4 cups Mornay Sauce II (see Index)*
¹/₂ cup shredded Swiss

Cook broccoli until just tender but still crisp. Poach chicken or turkey breast in salt and wine until fork tender. Remove chicken, and save broth to use in making Mornay Sauce. When cool, cut chicken into slices. Arrange broccoli in bottom of 1 large (3-quart) or 2 medium (1¹/₂-quart) casseroles; place sliced chicken or turkey over broccoli, cover with Mornay Sauce, and top with cheese. Bake uncovered at 350° F. until top is lightly browned, about 30 minutes. (This dish may be prepared in advance, except for the final baking. In that case, if refrigerated, allow an additional 10 minutes to bake.) Makes 8 to 10 servings.

*Note: This means doubling recipe for Mornay Sauce, using broth in which chicken or turkey breast cooked as part of the liquid, adding milk as needed.

# Chili-Avocado Casserole

3 ripe avocados, peeled and cut in half
Salt
3 1-pound cans chili con carne with beans
¹/₂ pound semifirm Monterey Jack, sliced; or mild Cheddar, sliced

Place the avocado halves in a shallow casserole, hollow sides up. Sprinkle with salt from shaker. Heat the chili con carne, spoon into avocado halves. Top with sliced cheese. Bake at 300° F. until cheese melts, 15 to 20 minutes. Serve with hot corn bread. Serves 6.

# Baked Eggplant Parmigiana

1 medium eggplant, thickly sliced
$^1/_4$ cup flour blended with salt and pepper
$^1/_2$ to $^3/_4$ cup olive oil
2 medium onions, chopped
3 medium tomatoes, peeled and chopped; or 1-pound can
    tomatoes
1 clove garlic, minced
$^1/_4$ teaspoon oregano
$^1/_4$ cup minced parsley
Salt and pepper to taste
$^1/_4$ cup Marsala or Madeira
1 cup Ricotta or farmer's cheese
$^1/_2$ cup grated Parmesan
Sliced Mozzarella, about $^1/_4$ pound

Soak eggplant slices in salted water; drain, and pat dry with paper towel. Dust with seasoned flour; then fry in olive oil until lightly browned on each side. Set aside. Add onions and tomatoes to same olive oil with garlic, oregano, and parsley; simmer until thickened and fairly smooth. If smoother sauce is preferred, force through sieve, or beat in blender. Add salt, pepper, and wine to sauce. Pour a third of the sauce over bottom of shallow casserole, place half the eggplant slices on sauce, then a layer of Ricotta and Parmesan, then more eggplant, then more cheese, until all is used. Add remaining tomato sauce. Bake at 350° F. for 40 minutes. Top with slices of Mozzarella and return to oven until cheese is melted. Makes 4 to 6 servings.

# Cold Poached Salmon with Blue Mayonnaise

POACHED SALMON:
6 salmon steaks
Water to cover
1 lemon, sliced
1 onion, sliced
Pickling spices

Place salmon steaks in a large skillet or heavy pot, and add water just to cover, plus lemon, onion, and a cheesecloth bag holding pickling spices. Bring water just to a boil, lower heat, and gently simmer about 20 minutes or until fish flakes easily. Cool in the broth. Then carefully remove to platter and chill. Makes 6 servings.

BLUE MAYONNAISE:
$^1/_4$ cup (1 ounce) crumbled Roquefort or Stilton
1 cup mayonnaise
1 anchovy fillet, minced
1 tablespoon drained pickle relish
1 tablespoon chopped, drained capers
1 tablespoon chopped parsley
1 teaspoon lemon juice
2 tablespoons heavy cream

Beat together all ingredients until sauce is consistency of sour cream. Chill. Spoon over salmon steaks to serve. Garnish with parsley, tomato wedges and cucumber slices. Makes $1^1/_2$ cups sauce.

# Chicken Cutlets Cordon Bleu

4 chicken breasts, boned and halved
Salt and pepper
4 slices natural Gruyère
4 thin slices ham
1 egg, beaten
4 tablespoons flour
3 tablespoons butter
1 tablespoon oil
$1/2$ cup fine, dry crumbs

Pound chicken to flatten, working in salt and pepper sprinkled from shakers. Trim edges. Place 1 slice cheese and 1 slice ham over each half breast of chicken, so that neither cheese nor ham hangs over. Brush edges with beaten egg. Top with remaining half of chicken breast, and pound edges to seal. Roll each in flour; then dip in egg; then in crumbs. Sauté in mixture of butter and oil until well browned. Transfer to casserole or roasting pan, place in oven preheated to 375° F., and bake for 20 to 35 minutes. Makes 4 servings.

VEAL CUTLETS CORDON BLEU: Have 4 individual cutlets cut $1/2$ inch thick with pocket cut through center of each. Insert ham and cheese in center, and seal edges with egg. Dredge flour into outside of meat; then dip meat in beaten egg and crumbs.

# Italian Stuffed Cabbage

1 green cabbage, about 2 pounds
Boiling water
3 tablespoons olive oil
1 garlic clove, minced
1 onion, chopped
1 pound ground lean pork
$1/3$ cup grated Romano or shredded Fontina
1 teaspoon salt
1-pound can peeled tomatoes

200

Parboil whole cabbage in boiling water 10 minutes; drain and cool. In skillet, sauté garlic, onion, and pork in the olive oil, until onion is tender. Remove from heat, add cheese. Pull cabbage leaves apart, without separating from head. Place filling between leaves, and tie cabbage with cord to hold in place. Add salt to tomatoes, place half of tomatoes in deep pot or Dutch oven, place stuffed cabbage over tomatoes, and pour remaining tomatoes over cabbage. Cover tightly and cook over low heat for 1 hour. Serve cabbage on platter. Cut in wedges to serve. Makes 4 to 6 servings.

### Cheese-Stuffed Peppers

6 large green peppers
2 medium onions, chopped
4 tablespoons olive oil
$1^1/_2$ cups uncooked rice
2 tablespoons minced parsley
$^1/_4$ cup pine nuts (pignoli) or diced almonds
4 tablespoons shredded Gruyère or Fontina
2 tablespoons raisins or currants
1 teaspoon salt
$2^1/_4$ cups tomato juice
2 tablespoons grated Parmesan

Remove seeds from peppers; cut a thin slice from bottom of each, so it will stand upright. Blanch with scalding water; drain. Cook onions in 3 tablespoons oil until soft; add rice, stir to glaze, then add parsley, pine nuts, and Fontina or Gruyère, raisins, salt, and $1^1/_4$ cups of the tomato juice. Cook, covered, until all liquid is absorbed. Cool slightly; then stuff peppers with this mixture. Brush outside with about 1 tablespoon olive oil. Place in oiled casserole. Sprinkle Parmesan over top. Pour the remaining tomato juice around the stuffed peppers. Bake in 350° F. oven for 1 hour. Serves 6.

VARIATION: Instead of nuts and raisins, $^1/_2$ cup of any chopped leftover meat or chicken may be used.

# PASTAS, RICE, AND SUCH

Most Americans have the idea that Italian spaghetti should always be served drowned in a crimson sea of tomato sauce. Actually, more spaghetti is consumed in Italy with a simple dressing of cheese and butter (or cheese and olive oil) than in any other way. And to my taste this simpler version is better. There's no need to fuss with making a separate sauce. When the spaghetti has been cooked until tender (or *al dente*, as you like), well drained, and slithered, steaming, into a large serving dish, all one needs to do is smother it with grated or shredded cheese and add a generous amount of butter or oil and whatever herbs may be desired. A good sprinkling of black pepper fresh from the grinder will help, too. Then toss the long slippery strands deftly, just until the cheese melts, and you have a dish fit for royalty.

Parmesan is the most frequently used cheese, but almost any other firm, semfirm, or semisoft cheese may be used. For fun, add two kinds of cheese, or three — or even four.

Pasta with cheese is a very, very old dish. This fact was brought home to me during a recent visit to Spain, when I dined in the small town of Villena in the Southeast. I was urged to try the local *gazpacho*. To my amazement I was served, not the icy-cold soup of puréed garden vegetables that most Americans know as *gazpacho*, but a bowl of what seemed to be squares of pasta in a hot sauce pungent with garlic, onion, and a little tomato and thick with pieces of chicken. What I thought was pasta turned out to be what the people in this region call *torta*, a thin, lightly browned, curled-up cake that looks much like a Mexican *tortilla* but is made of wheat instead of corn. *Tortas* are made, I was told, by crushing the heart of the wheat to a paste, working this paste into a dough with water, then patting the cakes very flat and baking them in an oven until crisp. *Torta*, in other words, was man's first bread, baked originally on hot stones next to the cave man's hearth — and the way to make *torta* is essentially the same as for pasta. Pasta dough is more refined, of course, made of finely milled flour blended with water or egg to a stiff dough and rolled out very thin with a roller instead of patted by hand, but the end result is not dissimilar. It was in this same town of Villena that I saw

202

in the local museum fragments of Bronze Age pottery containing garlic and onion seeds and more crude little cheese molds such as those I had seen earlier in Valencia.

As the tomato was not introduced into Europe until the sixteenth century, when Cortés brought the first sample of this strange Mexican fruit back to Spain, and did not gain popular acceptance in Italy until the mid-seventeenth century, pastas must have been tossed for a good many hundreds of years only with cheese and oil or with pungent garlic-flavored sauces. But we need not pity the Romans for that. Inhale the fresh green fragrance of Pesto Genovese (if you are lucky enough to have some fresh basil growing in your herb garden), or dress your spaghetti in the style beloved by Neapolitans — crush a garlic clove or two in a serving bowl before adding the hot spaghetti, then toss the spaghetti with olive oil, Parmesan, and an egg yolk, and you will learn how well the ancients ate.

### Spaghetti Seven Ways

Have a big pot of water boiling rapidly, with waves like a storm at sea. Add a tablespoonful of salt and a tablespoonful of oil. Then add a pound of thin spaghetti (either No. 8 or No. 9), pushing the strands down into the water. Bring the water back to the boil, stir the spaghetti once or twice to keep the strands free, then boil *partially* covered for 10 minutes. (Do not cover tightly or the water will boil over.) Drain in a colander, rinsing once quickly with *hot* water from the tap to wash away excess starch. Turn the hot spaghetti into a *heated* serving bowl, and *immediately* add ingredients to make the sauce or dressing. Toss quickly and serve at once. In 15 minutes your meal is ready. The amounts in the following sauce recipes are correct for 1 pound of cooked spaghetti. A dozen other pastas can be treated the same way. Use egg noodles, linguine, green noodles, fettucini, wide macaroni, or the "little hats" — in fact, any pasta that can easily be tossed. Makes 4 to 6 servings.

PARMIGIANA: While the spaghetti boils, crush garlic in the serving bowl; then toss away the shreds. Add the drained spaghetti to the same garlic-scented bowl; then add $1^1/_2$ cups freshly grated Parmesan, 2 or 3 tablespoons of pure olive oil, and an egg yolk. Grate black pepper over the spaghetti, toss lightly until the cheese coats every strand, and serve.

REGGIO: Brown 2 garlic cloves and 2 chopped shallots in a little olive oil while the spaghetti boils. When garlic is soft, mash it into the oil with the tines of a fork; then discard shreds. Add ½ cup small parsley sprigs to the hot oil (thus frying the parsley). Add this mixture to the drained, hot spaghetti with 1 to 1½ cups grated Pecorino Romano or Parmesan.

TUSCAN STYLE: While spaghetti cooks, brown ½ pound chicken livers, a chopped pimiento, and a little chopped onion in butter. When onion is soft, stir in a single tablespoon of tomato paste and ¼ cup Marsala, sherry, or Madeira. Add the livers, plus the sauce, to hot, drained spaghetti along with 1 cup shredded Fontina or semifirm Parma. Toss until cheese is melted.

WITH TUNA: Drain contents of 7-ounce can white meat of tuna. Add to hot, drained spaghetti with ¼ cup minced parsley and 1 to 1½ cups grated Parmesan or Romano (or use part Parmesan, part Sapsago).

CON PROSCIUTTO (WITH HAM): In 4 tablespoons butter, sauté 1 cup chopped prosciutto or any lean ham, 1 grated carrot, and 1 small chopped onion. When vegetables are tender, add ½ cup tomato juice, cook until liquid is reduced and thickened. Add this mixture to hot, drained spaghetti with 1 cup shredded Swiss (or half Swiss and half Parmesan).

CLAM-CHEESE SAUCE: Drain 2 7-ounce cans minced clams. Add to hot spaghetti with a 3-ounce package cream cheese, ½ cup shredded Fontina or Emmentaler, and 2 tablespoons minced chives. Toss until cheese melts. (This sauce is also delightful on green noodles or fettucini.)

BUTTER-CHEESE SAUCE: To hot, drained spaghetti, add a ¼-pound stick (8 tablespoons) butter, ½ cup grated Parmesan, and 1 cup shredded Fontina or Stracchino.

# Lasagne di Carnevale (Lasagne with Three Meats)

SAUCE:
1 pound chicken livers
1 pound chopped veal or lean pork
2 tablespoons olive oil
1 tablespoon butter
$1/4$ pound sweet Italian sausage, cut in small pieces
1 or 2 garlic cloves, crushed
1 medium onion, chopped
$1/2$ cup minced parsley
1-pound can peeled Italian plum tomatoes
1 6-ounce can tomato paste
$1^1/2$ cups chicken or beef bouillon
$1/2$ cup dry red or white wine
$1/4$ teaspoon oregano
Salt to taste

Sauté chicken livers and veal or pork in olive oil and butter until well browned. Add sausage and cook until browned on all sides. Press garlic cloves through garlic press; add with onion and parsley to meat. Lower heat, and cook until onion is soft. Drain off excess fat. Add tomatoes, tomato paste, bouillon, wine, oregano, and more salt if needed. Simmer 10 minutes while cooking lasagne.

LASAGNE:
1 pound lasagne
1 cup fine, dry crumbs
1 pound Ricotta
1 cup grated Parmesan or Romano
Sliced Mozzarella, about $1/4$ pound

Cook lasagne in plenty of rapidly boiling salted water until tender; drain well. Arrange lasagne over the bottom and up the sides of a large ($2^1/2$-quart) casserole, which has been rubbed with butter or oil. Pour about $1/4$ of the sauce over the lasagne, and add a layer of crumbs, a layer of Ricotta, and a layer of Parmesan. Add more lasagne, more sauce, more cheese, and so forth, until casserole is full. Reserve some crumbs and some sauce for the top. Place sliced Mozzarella over all. Bake in 350° F. oven for 45 minutes until sauce is bubbling and Mozzarella melted to gold. Makes 6 rich servings.

## Linguine Genovese

PESTO GENOVESE (ITALIAN GREEN SAUCE):
2 cups fresh minced basil leaves
2 or 3 cloves garlic
$^1/_2$ cup chopped parsley
$^1/_2$ teaspoon marjoram
$^3/_4$ cup grated Parmesan
1 tablespoon softened butter
3 tablespoons olive oil

Place some of the basil leaves and the garlic in a mortar; crush to a paste with wooden pestle. Add more basil leaves, some of the parsley, and the marjoram, and crush again. Continue until all herbs are used; then work in the cheese and finally the butter and olive oil. The mixture should be the consistency of thick cream. Add to hot cooked noodles, spaghetti, or any other pasta, with additional cheese, preferably shredded Stracchino, Gorgonzola, or Fontina. Makes 1 cup.

Cook linguine in boiling salted water until tender; drain. While hot, toss with Pesto Genovese, using 1 cup Pesto Genovese for each 1 pound cooked linguine. A pound of cooked linguine makes 4 to 6 servings.

## Spaghetti with Four Cheeses

1 pound thin spaghetti (No. 8)
4 ounces (1 cup) Swiss Emmentaler, shredded
4 ounces young Stracchino or Gorgonzola, in small cubes
$^1/_2$ cup diced Edam or Gouda
4 ounces ($^2/_3$ cup) grated Parmesan
4 tablespoons ($^1/_2$ stick) butter
$^1/_4$ teaspoon salt
Freshly ground black pepper

Cook spaghetti in rapidly boiling salted water until *al dente*, about 10 minutes. Drain. While hot, toss with the four kinds of cheese, butter, salt, and pepper until cheeses are mostly melted. With an interesting antipasto, a green salad, red wine, and fruit, this spaghetti makes a fine and full repast. Makes 4 servings.

## Canneloni Napolitano

1 dozen manicotti (2 packages)
1 pound Ricotta
¹₄ pound Mozzarella, cut in small cubes
¹₄ teaspoon freshly ground black pepper
¹₄ teaspoon salt
1 egg, well beaten
2 tablespoons grated Parmesan or Romano
1 teaspoon sugar
6 tablespoons olive oil or softened butter
2 cups Mornay Sauce II (see Index)
  or your favorite tomato sauce
¹₄ to ¹₂ cup white wine, dry sherry, or Marsala
6 tablespoons Parmesan

Parboil manicotti by dropping one at a time into a kettle of rapidly boiling salted water. Cook 10 minutes; carefully remove from water with slotted spoon. Combine next seven ingredients, and beat to blend well. Stuff this filling into shells with spoon. Brush large shallow casserole with half the oil, or rub with softened butter. Prepare Mornay or spaghetti sauce. Spoon half the sauce over bottom of casserole. Place filled manicotti over sauce. To remaining sauce, add the wine, and spoon over top of manicotti. Sprinkle Parmesan blended with remaining oil or bits of butter over manicotti. Cover casserole with foil; bake at 350° F. for 45 minutes. Remove foil. To brown top, leave in oven an additional 15 minutes. Makes 6 servings.

BAKED LASAGNE NAPOLITANO: Use lasagne instead of manicotti. Cook the noodles as directed on package, and drain. Arrange lasagne in oiled shallow casserole (10 x 10 inches), in layers with filling. Top with cheese and oil or butter, bake as directed.

# Baked Spaghetti and Chicken Livers

2 tablespoons butter
1 tablespoon olive oil
1 clove garlic
$^1/_2$ pound chicken livers
$^1/_2$ pound fresh button mushrooms
1 small onion, minced
1 tomato, peeled and chopped
1 cup chicken broth
$^1/_4$ cup Marsala or Madeira
$^1/_2$ cup dry white wine
$^1/_4$ cup minced parsley
$^1/_4$ teaspoon dried tarragon
$^1/_4$ teaspoon freshly ground pepper
Salt to taste
$^1/_2$ pound spaghetti, cooked and drained
$^1/_2$ cup shredded Fontina or Stracchino
   or crumbled Gorgonzola
$^1/_2$ cup fine crumbs
1 tablespoon butter

To make the sauce, heat 2 tablespoons butter and olive oil together, adding whole garlic clove. When garlic is golden, crush with fork. Discard shreds. Add chicken livers and brown quickly until crisp. Remove. Lower heat, brown mushrooms lightly, then add onion and tomato and cook until soft. Add chicken broth, the Madeira and white wine, parsley, tarragon, pepper, and salt. Simmer 5 minutes. Return chicken livers to sauce. Toss sauce with cooked, drained spaghetti, and arrange in casserole. Spread cheese and crumbs over top, and dot with butter. Bake at 350° F. for about 20 minutes until crumbs are browned (if dinner is delayed, it will be safe to leave the casserole in the oven another $^1/_2$ hour, but turn off heat). Makes 4 servings.

# Linguine Bolognese

1 pound linguine
$^{1}/_{4}$ pound salt pork, cubed
2 tablespoons butter
$^{1}/_{2}$ pound lean veal, finely diced
$^{1}/_{2}$ pound lean pork or ham, cut in small cubes
1 garlic clove
1 small onion, minced
2 tablespoons grated carrot
$^{1}/_{4}$ pound fresh mushrooms, sliced
$^{1}/_{3}$ cup Marsala or medium-sweet sherry
1 can (8 ounces) tomato sauce
2 cups chicken broth
$^{1}/_{4}$ teaspoon crushed rosemary or fennel
Pinch of cinnamon
Salt and pepper
$^{1}/_{4}$ cup heavy cream
1 cup grated Romano

Cook noodles in rapidly boiling salted water until *al dente*, about 10 minutes. Drain; keep hot. Meantime, place salt pork in butter, heat until most of fat is drawn out, then discard remaining pieces of salt pork. Add veal, lean pork (or ham) and garlic, and brown quickly. When garlic is golden, mash with fork into fat, and discard shreds. Remove meat with slotted spoon. Lower heat, cook onion and carrot until soft; add mushrooms and cook until golden. Add wine, tomato sauce, chicken broth, and seasonings. Simmer 20 minutes. Return meat to sauce. Taste for seasoning and adjust as needed. Remove from heat; add heavy cream. Toss hot linguine with sauce and the Romano. Makes 8 servings.

# Macaroni and Cheese

$^1$ ₂ pound (8-ounce package) macaroni
   (elbow, short lengths, or wide macaroni, as preferred)
2 tablespoons butter or margarine
2 tablespoons flour
$^3$ ₄ teaspoon salt
$^1$/₈ teaspoon freshly ground black pepper
2 cups milk
1 to 2 cups ($^1$/₄ to $^1$/₂ pound) cheese,
   cubed, shredded or crumbled*
Buttered bread crumbs (optional)

Cook macaroni in rapidly boiling salted water, using at least 4 quarts water. When tender, drain well. Melt butter, stir in flour and cook until it bubbles. Add salt and pepper; then slowly stir in milk and cook until smooth. Add 1 cup cheese; stir until partially melted. Place macaroni in layers with the cheese sauce; over the top place remaining cheese or bread crumbs tossed with melted butter (using 2 tablespoons butter to $^1$ ₂ cup bread crumbs). Bake uncovered in oven preheated to 400° F. for 20 to 25 minutes or until top is golden and sauce bubbly. Makes 4 servings.

*Note: Amount of cheese used will depend on the cheese (less of a sharper cheese is needed) and on family tastes, as well as on whether this dish is to be the main course (a meat substitute) or to accompany a meat dish. Also, less cheese will be used when adding meat, poultry, or seafood to the casserole, as in one of following variations.

## VARIATIONS:

- *Short-cut Macaroni and Cheese.* Instead of making a sauce, toss the cheese with flour; place cooked macaroni in layers with the floured cheese, dotting each cheese layer with bits of butter; then pour milk over the top, reserving some cheese to place over all. Bake 45 to 50 minutes.

- *Macaroni Cheese Custard.* Omit flour altogether, increase cheese to $3/4$ pound (3 cups), beat 2 eggs, blend eggs with the milk, and pour this mixture over layers of macaroni and cheese, with cheese on top. Bake 30 minutes or until firm in center (test with a silver knife).
- *Ham and Cheese Macaroni.* Use only 1 cup cheese, and add slices of baked ham between layers of macaroni.
- *Tomato and Cheese Macaroni.* Use $1^1/2$ cups cheese, and add slices of tomato between layers. Swiss, mild Cheddar (or Cheddar type), Münster, Fontina. Kashkaval, and Provolone are all good cheeses to combine with tomatoes.
- *Shrimp and Cheese Macaroni.* Use only 1 cup cheese, and add 2 cans (6 ounces each) well-drained shrimp or 1 pound shelled, cooked shrimp. Swiss and Gruyère are best choices with shrimp.
- *Tuna-Cheese Macaroni Casserole.* Add 1 can (7 ounces) white meat of tuna, well drained. Use $3/4$ cup crumbled blue cheese and $3/4$ cup shredded Swiss, processed American, or processed Gruyère.
- *Chicken and Macaroni Casserole.* Use only 1 cup of a mild cheese like Swiss or mild Cheddar, Münster, or Jack, or use 1/2 cup grated Parmesan and 1 cup Swiss. Add sliced cooked chicken (or sliced turkey) between layers — as many slices as you have left over from a roast. Instead of milk, use part chicken broth, part cream.
- *Pork and Macaroni Casserole.* Use only 1 cup cheese, and add sliced leftover roast pork between layers. Sharp Cheddar, Kashkaval, or Fontina may be used.
- *Fish and Macaroni Casserole.* Use only 1 cup of a mild cheese like Swiss, Brick, Jack, or Münster. Add cooked flaked fish, preferably sole, flounder, halibut, whiting, or another delicately flavored fish, to the cream sauce.
- *Italian-style Macaroni and Cheese.* Instead of milk, add your favorite tomato sauce to the casserole, omitting flour; use 2 cups cheese, a mixture of Parmesan and Mozzarella.

# Danish Macaroni and Cheese

1 8-ounce package elbow macaroni, cooked
3 tablespoons flour
2-ounce wedge ($^1\!/_4$ cup) Danish Blue, crumbled
$^1/_2$ cup Danish Samsø or Esrom cheese, cut in small cubes
2 cups milk
$^1/_2$ teaspoon salt
$^1/_2$ cup soft bread crumbs
   tossed with 1 tablespoon melted butter

Layer a buttered $1^1/_2$-quart casserole with about one-third of the cooked, well-drained macaroni, and sprinkle macaroni with 1 tablespoon of the flour. Add a layer of crumbled blue cheese, another layer of macaroni, more flour, then a layer of the cubed Samsø or Esrom. Top with remaining macaroni, sprinkling macaroni with the remaining flour. Heat the milk and salt, and pour over macaroni. Spread buttered crumbs over top. Cover dish; bake at 350° F. for 30 minutes. Uncover and continue baking until crumbs are browned. Makes 4 to 6 servings.

# Chili-Macaroni Casserole

8-ounce package elbow macaroni, cooked
1 can (1 pound) chili con carne with beans
$^1/_4$ cup shredded Jack, Teleme, or any semifirm mild cheese

Mix drained macaroni with chili; arrange in casserole and top with cheese. Bake until cheese is melted, about 25 minutes. Makes 3 or 4 servings.

# Caraway Cheese-Noodle Ring

1 8-ounce package noodles, cooked
1 cup milk, heated to scalding
3 eggs, beaten
$1^1/_2$ cups shredded caraway-seed cheese like King Christian IX
1 teaspoon salt
Dash of black pepper or cayenne

Drain cooked noodles thoroughly. Slowly pour hot milk into eggs, beating with whisk. Add cheese, salt, and pepper. Combine milk-cheese mixture with noodles, spoon evenly into buttered 1-quart ring mold. Bake at 325° F. until firm, about 45 minutes. Unmold. Fill center of ring with buttered mixed vegetables, creamed chicken, or curried shrimp and fish. Makes 6 servings.

### Nudeln Pudding mit Käse (German-Style Noodles with Cheese)

$1/2$ pound noodles, cooked and drained
6 tablespoons butter
4 eggs, beaten
1 cup sour cream
$1/4$ cup grated hard cheese; or $1/2$ cup shredded semifirm cheese like American Münster or German Weisslacker

Toss hot, cooked noodles with butter. Beat eggs with cream and stir in cheese. Fold into noodles. Turn into buttered casserole, and bake in 350° F. oven until firm and golden. Serve as part of a vegetable dinner with Brussels sprouts and baked escalloped tomatoes, or serve with cold baked ham or roast pork. Makes 4 servings.

### Risotto Milanese (Saffron Cheese Rice)

1 cup converted rice
1 tablespoon butter
2 cups chicken broth
$1/4$ teaspoon saffron
$1/2$ teaspoon salt
1 cup shredded Swiss or Parmesan

Place rice and butter in saucepan and stir until butter is melted. Meanwhile, heat chicken broth with saffron and salt; when boiling, pour over rice. Cover, lower heat, and cook until liquid is absorbed, about 20 minutes. Add cheese; fold in without tossing. Serve risotto with broiled or baked fish or cold baked ham. Makes 3 or 4 servings.

## American Spaghetti-Ham Casserole

1 8-ounce package thin spaghetti, cooked
4 large slices baked ham
1 package frozen Fordhook limas. partially defrosted
$^1$ $_4$ pound (1 cup) shredded sharp Cheddar
1 tablespoon instant minced onion
2 cups well-seasoned tomato sauce
$^3$ $_4$ cup fine dry crumbs (herb-seasoned crumbs may be used)
2 tablespoons butter

Arrange cooked spaghetti in buttered 1$^1$ $_2$-quart casserole in layers with ham and limas and cheese, reserving cheese for the top.
(Limas need not be pre-cooked.) Add onion to sauce: pour
sauce over the top (if there is not sauce enough to come to the
top of spaghetti, add dry wine or chicken broth), sprinkle
crumbs and remaining cheese over the sauce, and dot with butter. Bake at 350° F. until top is brown and sauce bubbling,
about 35 minutes. Makes 4 servings.

## Cheese Spoonbread

2 cups milk
1 teaspoon butter or margarine
$^1/_3$ cup yellow corn meal
1$^1/_2$ cups shredded American or Cheddar
3 eggs, beaten
$^1/_4$ teaspoon salt
$^1/_4$ teaspoon paprika

Heat milk to scalding with butter, stir in corn meal, and cook
slowly until thickened, stirring occasionally. Remove from heat,
add cheese; cool slightly. Add some hot mixture to beaten eggs;
then turn eggs into remaining corn meal with seasonings. Pour
into buttered 1$^1/_2$-quart casserole and bake at 300° F. for 1 to
1$^1/_4$ hours or until puffed and firm to touch. Makes 4 servings.

## Polenta (Italian Corn Pudding with Cheese)

Corn meal was known only in the Western Hemisphere until the coming of Columbus and after him the *conquistadores*, yet two European countries have strikingly similar native dishes made with corn meal. One is the *polenta* of Italy, where Fontina is usually placed over the steaming cornmeal mush; the other is *mamaliga*, a Rumanian dish popular throughout southeastern Europe. The cheese used with *mamaliga* is Brindza, a salty-sharp sheep cheese. When cheese is added to our American spoonbread, we are in actuality making an American variation of these European specialties!

1 teaspoon salt
4 cups water
2 cups yellow corn meal
4 tablespoons butter
1 cup shredded Fontina

Add salt to water, bring to a rolling boil, and slowly stir in corn meal; reduce heat, cook slowly until thickened into a smooth mush. This process takes about 30 minutes. Add the butter and cheese, cover pan, and remove from heat, allowing butter and cheese to melt. Serve with a tossed green salad for a simple supper, or serve the Polenta as an accompaniment to roast or grilled meat in place of potatoes. Makes 4 to 6 servings.

MAMALIGA (RUMANIAN CORN PUDDING WITH CHEESE): Prepare cornmeal mush exactly as for Polenta. When mush is cooked, pour into square baking pan and let cool. When cold, cut into slices, brush slices with melted butter on both sides, lay in a baking pan, and sprinkle over the top 1 cup ($^1/_4$ pound) Brindza, crumbled. Heat in oven until cheese is melted and corn meal slices are golden-crisp. This dish is often served with bacon or hot sausages and sometimes with creamed mushrooms. Makes 4 to 6 servings.

## Risi Bisi (Italian Rice and Peas)

1 tablespoon minced salt pork or chopped bacon
1 or 2 tablespoons olive oil
1 small onion, minced
3 tablespoons chopped parsley
1 pound fresh peas, shelled; or 1 package frozen peas
$^1/_4$ cup water
1 cup uncooked converted rice
2 cups water
1 teaspoon salt
$^1/_4$ cup grated Parmesan or shredded Stracchino

Cook salt pork or bacon in olive oil in heavy 2-quart saucepan, with onion and parsley until onion is soft. Remove excess fat. Add fresh peas and $^1/_4$ cup water, and cook covered 5 minutes (frozen peas can be cooked simultaneously with rice). Add rice, 2 cups water, and salt. Bring water to a boil, cover, lower heat, and cook until all water is absorbed. Add cheese, toss lightly. Serve with limas and carrots for a vegetable dinner, or as an accompaniment to grilled lamb or veal chops. Makes 4 servings.

## Rice and Cheese Croquettes

CROQUETTES:
6 tablespoons ($^2/_3$ stick) butter
6 tablespoons flour
2 cups milk
$^1/_2$ teaspoon salt
1 cup shredded sharp Cheddar
2 teaspoons grated onion
$^1/_2$ teaspoon dry mustard
Dash cayenne
2 cups cooked rice
2 cups fine, dry crumbs
1 beaten egg diluted with 2 tablespoons water
Fat for frying

Melt butter, stir in flour, then slowly add milk and salt. Cook until smooth and thickened. Set aside half this sauce. To remaining sauce, add Cheddar, onion, mustard, and cayenne, and stir until cheese is partly melted. Add rice, and blend well. Chill; then shape into 12 croquettes. Roll each in crumbs, then in diluted egg and in crumbs again. Chill once more. To cook, heat fat to a depth of 1 inch until sizzling (375° F.), and fry croquettes until golden on each side. Drain on absorbent paper. Or sauté in a small amount of fat or oil, turning until browned on all sides. Serve with hot Caraway-Cheese Sauce. Makes 12 croquettes.

CARAWAY CHEESE SAUCE: To reserved cream sauce, add $1^1/_2$ cups shredded Danbo or caraway-seed cheese, stir until cheese is melted.

## Risotto with Sausage

$^1/_4$ pound sweet Italian sausage, cut in small pieces
1 small onion, chopped
6 tablespoons butter
$1^1/_2$ cups converted rice
3 cups chicken broth
$^1/_4$ teaspoon saffron
$^1/_2$ teaspoon salt
1 cup grated Parmesan or shredded Gruyère or Stracchino

Sauté sausage and onion in butter until lightly browned. Pour off fat. Add rice, and stir quickly to glaze. Heat broth with saffron and salt; when boiling, add 1 cup at a time to rice, bringing to a boil after each addition. Cover, and cook until liquid is absorbed, about 20 minutes. Add cheese, toss lightly. Makes 4 to 6 servings as an entree.

RISOTTO WITH MUSHROOMS: Instead of sausage, sauté $^1/_2$ pound chopped or sliced fresh mushrooms in butter; add 2 tablespoons chopped parsley, and, instead of 3 cups chicken broth, use 2 cups chicken broth and 1 cup tomato juice.

## Tamale Corn Pudding

2 tablespoons olive oil
1 large onion, chopped
$\frac{1}{2}$ green pepper, seeded and chopped
1 clove garlic, minced
1 large tomato, peeled and chopped
1 cup cream-style corn
$\frac{1}{2}$ cup yellow corn meal
1 cup boiling water
1 teaspoon salt
2 tablespoons chili powder
$\frac{1}{2}$ cup sliced pitted ripe olives
$\frac{1}{2}$ pound soft Monterey Jack or mild Cheddar, cubed

Sauté in olive oil the onion, green pepper, garlic, and tomato until soft; combine with corn, corn meal, boiling water, salt, and chili powder. Blend well. Turn into greased $1\frac{1}{2}$-quart casserole, add olives and cheese, and stir to mix lightly. Bake at 375° F. until firm and lightly browned. Makes 6 to 8 servings.

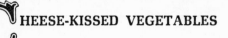

# CHEESE-KISSED VEGETABLES

On almost any vegetable, almost any cheese serves as a lovely, quick, and easy sauce.

I have added Gorgonzola to green beans, German Weisslacker to cabbage, Italian Stracchino to cauliflower, French Crème de Gruyère to broccoli, freshly grated Romano to limas, Norwegian Tilsiter to artichoke hearts — and all were delicious. Simply add the cheese — shredded, in small cubes, or grated — to the hot vegetable in place of butter. It couldn't be simpler! And do try crumbled Roquefort blended with sour cream as a topping for beets — astonishingly good.

Vegetable entrees enriched with cheese star brightly in meatless dinners — and often the kiss of cheese is all that's needed to make a vegetable dish attractive to those children (of all ages) who rebel against fodder in any form.

To start with, here are some very quick tips — the kind of thing one can try at the last moment, risking nothing more than a few shreds of cheese. On succeeding pages, the vegetable recipes become more ambitious and complicated, culminating in real "made dishes," as they were called in old-time "receipt books."

Adding cheese in this way makes a kind of sauce without any bother. In the following section, however, you will find several sauces that are excellent served over vegetables, either by themselves or when the vegetables are used in vegetarian recipes.


### Green Beans au Fromage

Break fresh green beans into 1-inch pieces. Cook in boiling salted water until just tender, about 10 minutes. Drain. Add 1 to 2 tablespoons shredded Swiss, Münster, Roquefort, Stilton, Monterey Jack or Provolone cheese. The cheese melts from the heat of the vegetable. A bit of minced parsley may be added, too, if you like.

## Gingered Cabbage au Fromage

1 medium onion, thinly sliced
1/2 teaspoon green ginger root, minced*
3 tablespoons butter, melted
1 small head cabbage, shredded
3/4 cup water
1/2 teaspoon salt
1/4 cup sour cream
2 ounces (1/2 cup) diced Italian Stracchino, Danish Havarti,
   or German Weisslacker

Sauté onion and minced ginger root in butter until onion is soft. Add shredded cabbage, water, and salt. Cover, and cook over low heat until cabbage is tender, about 5 minutes. Turn off heat, and add sour cream and the diced cheese. Cover pan, and remove from heat; the cheese will melt from the heat of skillet. When cheese has melted, stir to blend evenly throughout cabbage. Serve immediately. Makes about 8 servings.

*Note: Green ginger root is available in Oriental markets; then you can grow your own from a piece of the root in a flowerpot. If not locally available, use 1/4 teaspoon powdered ginger.

## Greek Baked Squash

6 6-inch yellow summer squash or zucchini
4 tablespoons butter
4 tablespoons olive oil
Salt
Ac'cent (monosodium glutamate)
1/2 pound Kashkaval (Caciocavallo) or Provolone, sliced

Cut the squash in half lengthwise. If preferred, scrape off part of outer rind with sharp knife. Gently cook the squash in mixture of butter and olive oil, covered, until softened, about 6 minutes. Remove from skillet and sprinkle generously with salt and Ac'cent. Place in casserole, cut side up. Place thin slices of cheese, cut to fit, over top of squash. Heat under broiler until cheese melts. Serves 6.

## Cheese-Crowned Baked Tomatoes

4 large tomatoes
Salt and pepper
1 cup ($^1/_4$ pound) grated American
2 egg yolks
4 tablespoons heavy cream
$^1/_4$ teaspoon curry powder
$^1/_2$ to $^3/_4$ cup crushed cracker crumbs
3 tablespoons butter

Cut tomatoes in half. Turn upside down and squeeze very gently so that some of seeds and liquid come out. Place in shallow casserole or baking pan cut sides up; sprinkle with salt and pepper. Blend together cheese, egg yolks, cream, curry powder, and salt. Place about 2 tablespoons of this mixture on each tomato half, pressing down into the center with back of spoon. Sprinkle cracker crumbs over top; dot crumbs with butter. Bake tomatoes in 350° F. oven for 15 to 20 minutes. Serve with buttered broccoli and parsley potatoes. Makes 4 servings.


## Danish Blue-Stuffed Squash

4 6-inch zucchini or yellow summer squash
$^1/_2$ cup chopped onion
$^1/_4$ cup butter
4 cups soft bread cubes
4 ounces (1 cup) crumbled Danish Blue, Samsø,
    or mild Cheddar
$^1/_2$ teaspoon oregano

Cut a lengthwise slice from each squash and scoop out pulp, leaving $^1/_4$-inch shell. Scrape off part of zucchini peel, if desired. Chop pulp. Cook onion in butter over moderate heat until golden. Add chopped squash, bread cubes, cheese, and oregano. Pile stuffing mixture into squash shells, arrange on a baking pan with a little water in the pan. Bake in a 350° F. oven 30 minutes until squash is tender and stuffing lightly browned. Makes 4 servings.

## Fritada di Tomate (Mediterranean-Style Baked Tomatoes)

4 large tomatoes, peeled and chopped
1 small onion, chopped
$^1/_2$ cup chopped parsley
2 slices stale white bread
$^1/_2$ teaspoon salt
1 cup grated Romano
2 tablespoons olive oil, preferably Spanish

In a bowl combine tomatoes, onion, parsley, bread, salt, and $^3/_4$ cup cheese. Brush olive oil over sides of shallow 10-inch casserole or 9-inch cake pan. Place tomato mixture in casserole or pan, and top with remaining cheese. Bake uncovered in 350° F. oven for 1 hour. Excellent as a side dish with roast veal. Makes 4 to 6 servings.

## Escalloped Tomatoes with Cheese

Empty a large (1-pound 12-ounce) can peeled tomatoes into a casserole. Stir in $^3/_4$ teaspoon salt, 2 teaspoons sugar, 1 teaspoon Ac'cent (monosodium glutamate), $^1/_4$ teaspoon oregano, (optional) and 1 slice stale white bread, broken into pieces. Spread $^1/_2$ cup grated Parmesan or $^3/_4$ cup shredded Münster or Cheddar or grated Kashkaval over top. Bake uncovered 1 hour at 375° F. or $1^1/_2$ hours at 325° F. Makes 4 to 6 servings.

## Braised Celery with Gorgonzola

Slice celery diagonally into long thin slices, allowing about 1 stalk per serving. Place in saucepan with a few thin slices of onion and a tablespoon of butter; cook gently in the butter a minute or two. For 4 stalks celery, or 2 cups sliced, add $^3/_4$ cup of water and an envelope of chicken-stock concentrate (I use MBT). Cover the pan, and cook until the celery is tender, about 6 minutes. Uncover, bring liquid to a quick boil until reduced to a few tablespoons of liquid, and add a tablespoon of crumbled Gorgonzola. The cheese should be melted by the time the celery is dished up and it makes a superb sauce for the celery.

## Tomatoes Stuffed with Rice and Cheese

8 large tomatoes
2 cups (¹/₂ pound) crumbled Danish Blue
4 cups cooked rice*
4 scallions, chopped (including most of green tops)
6 tablespoons oil
2 tablespoons lemon juice
¹/₄ teaspoon black pepper
Butter

Cut a slice from top of each tomato; then scoop out pulp (leaving ¹/₄-inch shell). Discard seedy portion. Chop remaining pulp, and combine with 1³/₄ cups cheese, the cooked rice, scallions, 6 tablespoons of oil, lemon juice, and black pepper. Stuff tomatoes with mixture, so that rice mounds over top. Place dots of butter and remaining cheese over top. Bake in oven preheated to 400° F. for 20 to 25 minutes. Serve with baked potatoes (start baking 30 minutes before tomatoes are placed in oven) or buttered noodles and green peas. Makes 8 servings.

*For 4 cups cooked rice, you need 1¹/₃ cups uncooked long grain rice or 2 cups packaged precooked rice.

VARIATIONS: Instead of Danish Blue, try Havarti, Esrom, or shredded natural Cheddar.

## Cheese-Topped Potatoes

Bake potatoes as usual. When done, cut a cross in the top of each, insert in each a piece (about 1 tablespoon) cheese and a dab of butter or a spoonful of sour cream. Pass the salt. Blue cheese is very good, and so is Gruyère; or try Münster, Fontina, Caerphilly, or Lancashire.

## Limas with Curried Cheese Sauce

Cook 1 package frozen Fordhook limas as directed; drain. Beat together ¹/₄ cup shredded Swiss cheese, ¹/₂ cup sour cream, and ¹/₄ teaspoon curry powder. Add to hot beans, and heat gently. Makes 3 or 4 servings.

# Onion-Cheese Custard

4 large onions, sliced
1/2 stick butter or margarine
1 teaspoon salt
1 1/2 teaspoons curry powder; or 1 teaspoon cumin
    plus 1/2 teaspoon curry powder
1 cup milk, heated to scalding
3 eggs, slightly beaten
1 cup shredded Fontina, soft Jack, or Münster

Cook onions slowly in butter until tender and golden, about 20 minutes. Add salt and curry powder, blending well. Slowly add hot milk to beaten eggs, beating constantly with whisk. Add cheese to milk-egg mixture; then combine with onions. Pour into buttered 1 1/2-quart casserole. Bake at 325° F. until a knife inserted in center comes out clean. Serve with asparagus or green beans and broiled tomatoes for a delectable meatless supper. Makes 4 servings.


# Danish Vegetables and Cheese Kabobs

MARINADE:
1 cup olive oil
1/3 cup vinegar
Pinches of tarragon and basil
Salt and freshly ground black pepper

KABOBS:
Zuchini, scrubbed and thickly sliced
Whole mushrooms
Cherry tomatoes
Canned white onions
Danish Tybo, Havarti, or Samsø, cut in 1 1/2-inch cubes

Place vegetables in marinade for 30 minutes before grilling. Lift vegetables from marinade, and arrange on skewers alternately with cheese cubes; grill 5 inches from coals until cheese softens and vegetables are glazed. Serve on toasted, crusty French rolls.

# Swiss Vegetable Custard

¹/₂ cup (1 stick) butter*
1¹/₂ cups sliced yellow summer squash (2 small squash)
1¹/₂ cups diagonally sliced fresh broccoli
1 egg
¹/₄ cup milk
1 teaspoon salt
¹/₄ teaspoon dry mustard
Dash of cayenne
¹/₂ cup (2 ounces) shredded Swiss
¹/₄ cup grated Parmesan

In a large skillet melt butter; sauté sliced raw vegetables until they can be pierced with fork. In a mixing bowl beat egg; stir in milk, salt, mustard, cayenne, and Swiss cheese. Place vegetables in 1-quart casserole or baking dish; pour egg mixture over vegetables; sprinkle Parmesan over top. Bake 15 to 20 minutes in oven preheated to 375° F. until cheese is lightly browned and custard firm. Serves 4 to 6.

VARIATIONS: Instead of squash and broccoli, this dish can be made with carrots and green beans, with carrots and celery, or with zucchini and already-cooked limas. Raw vegetables must be sliced ¹/₄-inch thick (cut the broccoli, beans, carrots or celery diagonally, the squash crosswise).

*Note: Reduce butter to ¹/₄ cup, if preferred.

# Blue Cheese Cabbage Skillet

6 slices bacon
5 cups coarsely shredded cabbage
1 tablespoon sugar
¹/₄ cup red or white wine vinegar
³/₄ cup (about 4 ounces) crumbled Wisconsin Blue
Salt and pepper

Fry bacon until crisp; drain on absorbent paper, and crumble. Drain off all but ¹/₄ cup bacon drippings. Add cabbage, and cook over medium heat five minutes. Add sugar, vinegar, cheese, and bacon. Mix well, and cook five minutes, stirring occasionally. Season with salt and pepper to taste. Makes 4 to 6 servings.

# Hot Cauliflower-Roquefort Mousse

$1/2$ large fresh cauliflower, broken into sprigs and cooked;
   or 1 10-ounce package frozen cauliflower, cooked
$1/2$ cup butter or margarine
6 tablespoons flour
$1^1/2$ cups milk
4 eggs, separated
4 ounces Roquefort, crumbled ($1/3$ cup)
$1/2$ teaspoon salt
$1/4$ teaspoon white pepper (optional)
$1/8$ teaspoon crushed thyme
4 egg whites

Drain cooked cauliflower well. Force through a strainer or whirl in a blender. Melt butter; stir in flour, cooking until mixture bubbles. Gradually stir in milk. Cook over low heat, stirring constantly until smooth and thick. Gradually beat sauce into egg yolks. Stir in cooked cauliflower, Roquefort, salt, pepper, and thyme. Cool. Beat egg whites until stiff but not dry. Fold egg whites into Roquefort mixture. Pour into a well-buttered, 2-quart soufflé dish or casserole. Bake in a preheated moderate oven (350° F.) about 45 minutes or until puffed and brown. Serve hot with sliced baked ham and broiled tomato halves. Makes 4 to 6 servings.

# Buñuelos (Spanish Potato-Cheese Balls)

1 to 2 cups mashed potatoes; or 1 envelope instant
   mashed potatoes, prepared as directed on package
$1/2$ cup grated Romano or Parmesan
$1/3$ cup crushed saltines
2 eggs, beaten
Salt to taste
Oil for frying

Combine all ingredients but oil; beat until smooth. Drop by heaping tablespoonfuls into hot oil (375° F.) $1/2$-inch deep, in deep, heavy saucepan. Fry until brown on all sides. Serve hot. Makes 16, or 4 servings.

# Swiss Potato Casserole

3 cups sliced, cooked potatoes
1 cup shredded Swiss Emmentaler
1/2 cup finely chopped green scallions
1/4 cup minced fresh or frozen dill
1 teaspoon salt
1/2 teaspoon monosodium glutamate
1/4 cup chopped dry-roasted or unsalted peanuts
Butter or margarine
1 cup (1/2 pint) sour cream
1/4 cup grated Swiss Emmentaler
1/4 cup fine, dry bread crumbs
1/4 cup butter, melted

In a deep buttered 2-quart baking dish, arrange one layer of sliced potatoes. Combine the shredded cheese, scallions, dill, seasonings, and peanuts. Place a layer of this mixture over the potatoes, dot with butter, and spoon on some of the sour cream. Repeat with additional layers of potatoes, cheese mixture, butter, and cream, ending with potatoes. Combine the grated cheese with crumbs and melted butter, and spread this mixture over top. Bake covered at 375° F. (moderately hot) for 30 minutes, uncover and bake 15 minutes longer. For a meatless dinner, add broiled tomatoes and a green vegetable. Or serve with baked or broiled fish, along with a green salad. Makes 6 servings.

# Cauliflower au Fromage

Break up a small cauliflower into sprigs and cook in tightly covered saucepan with 1 cup water until just tender, about 6 minutes. Drain. To hot cauliflower add about 2 tablespoons Italian Stracchino, or some other semisoft cheese, and a teaspoon of minced fresh or frozen dill or minced parsley. Toss to blend, and serve at once.

## Papas Chorriadas (Colombian-Style Potatoes with Cheese)

6 medium potatoes, cooked
2 tablespoons butter or margarine
1 large onion, sliced
1 large tomato, peeled and chopped
2 tablespoons flour
$1/2$ teaspoon salt
$1^1/2$ cups milk
1 cup ($^1/4$ pound) shredded Queso de Papa,
   domestic Swiss, or mild Cheddar
2 tablespoons heavy cream

This dish is similar to our creamed potatoes but has a far tastier sauce. Cooked potatoes should be cut in cubes and kept warm while making the sauce. Melt butter, cook onion and tomato until soft, then stir in flour and salt. Slowly add milk, and cook until smooth and thickened. Add the cheese, stir until melted, remove from heat, and add cream. Add diced, cooked potatoes to the sauce. Serve hot with cold baked ham and a green vegetable (like Brussels sprouts). Makes 6 to 8 servings.

## Italian Squash Casserole

1 pound zucchini or yellow squash
2 tablespoons olive oil
$1/2$ teaspoon salt
Freshly ground pepper
$^1/4$ cup grated Parmesan or Romano
2 ounces Fontina, sliced or cut in small pieces

Scrape zucchini, cut into $^1/4$-inch slices. Brush casserole with olive oil, and lay sliced zucchini in casserole in layers, sprinkling each layer with salt, pepper, and Parmesan. Cover casserole; bake in oven preheated to 350° F. for 25 minutes. Uncover, place Fontina over top, and return to oven until cheese melts. Makes 4 servings.

## Asparagus in Curry-Cheese Sauce

1 large bunch (2$^{1}/_{2}$ pounds) asparagus
$^{1}/_{4}$ cup butter or margarine
3 chopped scallions or shallots
1 teaspoon curry powder
$^{1}/_{4}$ to $^{1}/_{2}$ teaspoon salt
3 tablespoons flour
1 cup asparagus liquid
$^{1}/_{2}$ cup milk
$^{1}/_{4}$ cup heavy cream
$^{1}/_{3}$ cup grated Sapsago or Caciocavallo or shredded Swiss

Carefully scrub asparagus spears; snap off and discard tough ends. Cook spears covered in salted water just until tender-crisp, about 6 minutes. Remove from liquid, saving 1 cup of liquid for the sauce. Place asparagus in buttered shallow casserole. Separately melt $^{1}/_{4}$ cup butter or margarine in skillet; add scallions or shallots, curry powder, and salt, and cook 1 minute. Stir in flour, then the asparagus liquid and milk. Cook, stirring, until smooth and thickened. Add cream and cheese. Pour this mixture over the asparagus, and bake in oven preheated to 425° F. (very hot) until sauce is lightly browned. Makes 6 servings.

## Cheese-Topped Broiled Tomatoes

Cut tomatoes in thick slices, and lay on foil-lined broiler pan. Sprinkle slices with salt, pepper, oregano, thyme, and monosodium glutamate. Pile a little shredded Swiss (or Münster, Cheddar, or Jack) over the top of each. Broil 4 inches from heat until cheese is melted, about 12 minutes.

## Spinach Timbales

3 pounds fresh spinach, cooked;
   or 4 10-ounce packages frozen chopped spinach, cooked
1 tablespoon grated onion
$^1/_2$ cup (1 stick) butter, melted
4 eggs, well beaten
$^1/_2$ teaspoon garlic powder (optional)
$1^1/_4$ cups Roquefort-Bacon Sauce (see Index)

Drain cooked spinach thoroughly; blend with onion, butter, beaten eggs, and garlic powder. Spoon into 8 well-buttered custard cups. Bake in oven preheated to 375° F. for 20 minutes or until mixture is firm and puffed. While timbales bake, prepare Roquefort-Bacon Sauce. Loosen timbales from custard cups when done, unmold, and serve topped with sauce. The timbales are marvelous as a luncheon entree or served, without the sauce, with broiled chicken and a fruit salad. Makes 8 servings.


## Beets with Roquefort Cream

Parboil fresh beets until tender, cool, then peel off skins; or use canned whole beets. To serve hot, reheat beets in a tablespoon of butter (though they are excellent cold). Beat about a tablespoon of crumbled Roquefort with $^1/_4$ cup sour cream. Spoon over hot or cold beets. Top with minced chives or minced fresh or frozen dill.

# SAUCES AND SALAD DRESSINGS

The two most-used cheese sauces are Mornay, which traditionally is made with Gruyère, and Cheddar. Both start with a basic cream sauce (Bèchamel).

As making a cream sauce is considered a chore by so many women and as they are likely to use a canned condensed cream soup as a shortcut anyway, I have deliberately worked out several quick versions of these two classic sauces, and, although the connoisseur may consider them inferior to the authentic original recipes, I was surprised (and pleased) myself to find that both were very good indeed.

Besides sauces made with cheese, you will find on the following pages other sauces that are frequently used in making cheese dishes: Tomato Sauce, Béchamel, Soubise, and Hollandaise. There are also several cheese butters, which are excellent for serving over hot vegetables or as bases for canapés (on which shrimp or other seafood may be placed).

The salad dressings included in this section are mostly those that are prepared ahead and served over tossed salads. Other salad dressings are given as parts of the recipes in the salad section.

### Béchamel Sauce (Basic Cream Sauce)

2 tablespoons butter
2 tablespoons flour
1/2 teaspoon salt
1/8 teaspoon nutmeg
1 cup milk; or 1/2 cup each milk and cream
1 egg (optional)

Melt butter in heavy pan, stir in flour, and cook until mixture bubbles. Add salt and nutmeg; then slowly add milk. Cook over low heat until smooth and thickened, stirring occasionally. If egg is to be added, beat separately until light, add a little of the hot sauce to egg, then combine the two. Serve over vegetables or croquettes. Makes 1 cup sauce.

## Mornay Sauce I

1 cup Béchamel Sauce made with egg
¹⁄₄ cup grated natural Gruyère or Wisconsin Swiss

Prepare the Béchamel; to hot sauce add the cheese and stir until melted. Makes 1 cup.


## Mornay Sauce II

The great Escoffier gave a choice of Parmesan or Gruyère in his recipe for Mornay Sauce, but I personally much prefer natural Gruyère. He also called for part veal or chicken broth, but the chicken-stock concentrate with milk achieves much the same result. For fast days, vegetable bouillon cubes may be used instead of chicken broth.


2 tablespoons butter
2 tablespoons minced onion
2 tablespoons flour
1³⁄₄ cups milk
2 envelopes chicken-stock concentrate;
    or 2 chicken bouillon cubes
¹⁄₈ teaspoon grated nutmeg
1½ cup shredded natural Gruyère or Swiss
1 egg


Melt butter, gently cook onion until soft, then stir in flour, and cook mixture until it bubbles. Slowly add milk and the chicken-stock concentrate. Cook, stirring, until smooth. Add nutmeg and cheese and stir until cheese is melted. Remove from heat. Stir some of hot sauce into egg; then combine the two. Let heat of sauce cook the egg. Keep warm until needed, or use as called for in recipe. Makes 2 cups.

## Quick Mornay Sauce

1 10$^1$ 2-ounce can condensed cream of chicken soup
$^1$ 3 cup light cream; or $^1$ 4 cup white wine
$^1$ 2 cup shredded Gruyère or Swiss
Dash of nutmeg


Combine condensed soup with cream or wine; cook, stirring, until smooth. Add cheese and nutmeg and cook until cheese is melted. Makes about 1$^1$ 4 cups. When doubled, makes 2$^1$ 2 cups.


## Classic Cheddar Sauce

2 tablespoons butter
2 tablespoons flour
$^1$/$_2$ teaspoon salt
1$^1$/$_2$ cups milk
$^3$/$_4$ to 1 cup grated or shredded aged natural Cheddar
Dash of paprika
$^1$/$_2$ teaspoon dry mustard

Melt butter, stir in flour and salt and cook until flour bubbles. Slowly stir in milk; cook until smooth and thickened. Add cheese, paprika, and mustard, and cook until cheese is melted. Makes about 2 cups.


## Quick Cheddar Sauce

1 can condensed Cheddar-cheese soup
$^1$ 3 cup light cream; or $^1$/$_4$ cup dry white wine
$^1$/$_4$ cup natural Cheddar, shredded
$^1$/$_4$ teaspoon dry mustard

Heat soup with cream or wine and cheese. Add mustard. Stir until cheese is melted. Makes 1$^1$/$_2$ cups.

## Tomato Sauce

1¹/₂ to 2 cups chopped onion
2 minced garlic cloves
¹/₄ cup olive oil; or 4 tablespoons (¹/₂ stick) butter
2 teaspoons salt
6 to 8 tomatoes, peeled and chopped; or 1 large can
   (1 pound 14-ounce) peeled tomatoes
1 6-ounce can tomato paste
1 teaspoon oregano; or blended spaghetti-sauce seasoning
¹/₂ teaspoon sugar
¹/₄ cup minced parsley (optional)

Simmer onion and garlic in oil until soft and golden but not browned. Add salt and tomatoes; cook until tomatoes are very soft, about ¹/₂ hour. Force through sieve or food mill or purée in blender, return to pan, and add tomato paste, oregano, sugar, and any other desired seasonings to taste. Continue cooking over very low heat until thickened to purée consistency. Makes about 2 cups.

TOMATO-CHEESE SAUCE: To finished tomato sauce, add ¹/₄ cup grated Parmesan or ¹/₂ cup shredded American or aged Cheddar. This sauce can be used on baked veal chops, cooked rice, or cooked pastas.

## Ale Sauce

2¹/₂ cups grated sharp cheese such as Dunlop, Cheddar, or
   Havarti
1 tablespoon butter
¹/₂ cup ale
¹/₂ teaspoon Worcestershire sauce
¹/₂ teaspoon salt or to taste
¹/₄ teaspoon dry mustard
Dash cayenne

Combine all ingredients in top of double boiler and stir until smooth. This sauce is delicious over hard-cooked eggs, asparagus, broccoli, or cabbage. Makes about 2¹/₂ cups.

## Sauce Soubise

1 cup sliced onions
2 tablespoons butter
2 tablespoons flour
1/2 cup chicken broth*
1/2 cup rich milk or light cream
Salt and pepper

Simmer onions in butter until tender; stir in flour, slowly add chicken broth, and cook until thickened. Add milk or cream, cook an additional minute or two. Season to taste. Makes 1 cup.

*Note: For a shortcut, make the broth by dissolving 1 envelope or 1 teaspoon chicken-stock concentrate in 1/2 cup water.

SAUCE SOUBISE WITH CHEESE: Add 1/4 cup shredded Gruyère. This sauce is excellent over fish, veal, and chicken or with vegetables such as cauliflower, cabbage, and asparagus. If desired, after sauce has been added, place dish under broiler until top is delicately browned.

## Cheese Hollandaise

1/4 to 1/2 cup shredded or crumbled cheese, well chilled*
1 tablespoon lemon juice
3 egg yolks
1/2 cup (1/4 pound) cold butter
Freshly ground pepper

Place cold cheese, lemon juice, and egg yolks in top of double boiler; beat with whisk constantly until cheese melts. Then add a lump of butter at a time, stirring briskly after each addition, until smooth. Remove from heat, grate pepper over sauce, and stir to blend. Chill. This sauce is excellent over asparagus, cauliflower, artichoke hearts, or broccoli. Makes 1 cup.

*Note: Use 1/4 cup crumbled Danish Blue, 1/4 cup grated Parmesan, or 1/2 cup shredded Swiss, Gruyère, or mild Cheddar.

## Hollandaise (Blender Recipe)

¼ pound butter, melted
2 egg yolks
1 tablespoon lemon juice
¼ teaspoon salt

Take care in melting butter to keep heat low and to remove from heat the moment all butter is melted. Skim off white particles. Place egg yolks in electric blender, beat until thickened, then slowly add the melted butter with beater in motion. When thickened, add lemon juice and salt. Should sauce curdle, remove from blender, place an additional egg yolk in the blender, and add the curdled sauce a little at a time with blender in motion. Makes ¾ cup.

## Hollandaise (Classic Recipe)

3 egg yolks
1 tablespoon cream
¼ pound (½ cup) sweet butter
1 tablespoon lemon juice
Salt to taste

Place egg yolks and cream in top of double boiler over hot water, beat with whisk until slightly thickened, then add a lump of butter at a time, beating to blend into egg yolks after each addition. When all butter has been added, stir in lemon juice and salt. Chill. Makes ¾ cup.

## Gruyère Butter

Beat together in a blender equal quantities (by cup measure) of shredded Gruyère or Swiss and butter until smooth and soft. Very good over hot boiled potatoes, cabbage, or green beans. (Other cheeses that can be turned into butters are Fontina, Stracchino, Samsø, and caraway-seed cheeses.)

# Gorgonzola Butter

Combine 4 tablespoons each softened butter and Gorgonzola. blend until smooth. This is excellent as a canapé spread. to be topped with caviar or small shrimp: or add to hot vegetables as a sauce. Makes 1 2 cup.

# Sapsago Butter

1 4 pound butter. softened
1 cup grated Schabzieger (Sapsago)

Beat butter until creamy: work in cheese. Spread over toast squares for an hors d'oeuvres or use on hot vegetables as a sauce. Makes 1 cup.

PARMESAN BUTTER: Use grated Parmesan instead of Sapsago.

# Roquefort-Bacon Sauce

3 4 cup milk
1 8-ounce package cream cheese
4 strips bacon, cooked and crumbled
3 ounces (3 4 cup) crumbled Roquefort

Stir milk and cream cheese over moderate heat until smooth. Add bacon and Roquefort and stir until Roquefort is melted. Makes 1¹ 4 cups. Excellent over noodles or spinach timbales.

# Roquefort French Dressing

¹/₂ cup olive oil
¹/₄ teaspoon salt
¹/₄ cup vinegar
¹/₄ teaspoon thyme
¹/₄ cup crumbled Roquefort

Blend all ingredients and beat until smooth. Makes 1 cup.

### Danish Blue-Cream Dressing

2 ounces Danish Blue ($^1/_2$ cup crumbled)
$^1/_2$ cup sour cream
1 teaspoon (about) lemon juice

Blend cheese and sour cream well; add lemon juice to taste. Serve as a sauce for artichoke hearts or canned artichoke bottoms, for hot cauliflower, for Brussels sprouts, or for small canned beets. Or use as a salad dressing for chopped raw cabbage.

ROQUEFORT-CREAM DRESSING: Use Roquefort (which is not so sharp in flavor) instead of Danish Blue.

### Parmesan French Dressing

$^1/_2$ cup olive oil
$^1/_2$ teaspoon salt
$^1/_8$ teaspoon freshly ground black pepper
3 tablespoons vinegar
2 tablespoons freshly grated Parmesan

Combine ingredients and beat to blend. Makes $^3/_4$ cup.

SAPSAGO DRESSING: Use grated Sapsago instead of Parmesan.

CHEDDAR DRESSING: Substitute an aged sharp Cheddar for Parmesan.

### Creamy Horseradish Sauce

1 can ($10^1/_2$ ounces) cream of celery soup
$^1/_4$ cup milk
1 3-ounce package cream cheese
1 to 2 tablespoons horseradish, according to taste

Combine soup, milk, and cream cheese in saucepan and stir over moderate heat until smooth. Add horseradish. This sauce is excellent with fish or over boiled beef. Makes $1^1/_2$ cups.

## Edelweiss Salad Dressing

$^1/_4$ cup shredded Swiss Emmentaler
$^1/_2$ cup olive or salad oil
$^1/_4$ cup lemon juice
$^1/_2$ teaspoon salt
1 to 2 teaspoons sugar (optional)
1 chopped hard-cooked egg
1 tablespoon minced chives or dill
2 tablespoons chopped pimiento

Combine ingredients; marinate an hour or so before adding to a green salad. Makes 1$^1/_2$ cups, enough for 6 to 8 cups salad greens.

## Blue Cheese and Bacon Dressing

1 cup olive oil
$^1/_4$ cup wine vinegar
2 tablespoons lemon juice
$^1/_2$ teaspoon salt
$^1/_2$ teaspoon dry mustard
1 teaspoon Worcestershire sauce
$^1/_2$ pound Wisconsin Blue, crumbled
1 quart (about) torn mixed salad greens
3 slices cooked bacon, crumbled

Beat together oil, vinegar, lemon juice, salt, mustard, and Worcestershire. Add about $^1/_4$ pound of cheese, beat until smooth. Crumble in remaining cheese. Add this dressing to salad greens. Add bacon just before serving. Makes 4 to 6 servings.

VARIATION: Chopped hard-cooked eggs are also good in this dressing.

# Wisconsin Blue-Cream Dressing

1 cup sour cream
$^1/_2$ cup mayonnaise
1 to 2 tablespoons grated onion
2 tablespoons vinegar
$^1/_4$ cup crumbled Wisconsin Blue
1 slit garlic clove

Combine sour cream, mayonnaise, onion, vinegar, and cheese. Beat to blend. Rub salad bowl with garlic until garlic is crushed thoroughly; discard shreds. Add salad greens to bowl; then toss with dressing. Makes enough for 6 cups salad greens.

CHEDDAR CREAM DRESSING: Use $^1/_4$ cup grated sharp Cheddar instead of Wisconsin Blue.

Salads tossed with Roquefort dressing are listed on nearly every American restaurant menu, and the world-famous Caesar Salad is, of course, always made with a bit of Parmesan. But besides salads tossed with cheese dressing, there are many in which cheese is an important and zesty ingredient. Chef's salads nearly always are made with slivers of Swiss cheese. Herb-flavored cream-cheese balls often appear as garnishes for fruit salads or are spaced within the shimmering molds of aspics.

Such salads are, obviously, heartier than simple tossed greens, and quite often serve as the main courses of luncheons.

For salads, the natural cheeses are always preferable, because the flavor of the cheese is all-important.

### Caesar Salad

2 or 3 garlic cloves
Olive oil
1 cup small bread cubes
$1/2$ teaspoon fresh garlic salt
2 quarts mixed salad greens
$1/2$ teaspoon dry mustard
Freshly ground black pepper
2 anchovy fillets, diced
1 raw or coddled egg
4 tablespoons olive oil
$1^{1}/_{2}$ tablespoons red wine vinegar
3 tablespoons grated Parmesan

Brown 1 peeled garlic clove in olive oil until golden; remove. Add bread cubes, sauté until golden on all sides; remove, drain on paper. To make garlic salt, place 1 peeled garlic clove in mortar, add as much salt as it will take and crush into a paste. Add croutons and $1/2$ teaspoon of the garlic salt to salad greens, tossing deftly. Add remaining ingredients to salad bowl, using plenty of black pepper. When egg is added, use quick, sure strokes to beat quickly into salad greens. Serve at once. Makes 6 to 8 servings.

## Cheese Caesar

This recipe is not for the authentic Caesar Salad, but it's an interesting variation, as it uses two kinds of cheese.

1 garlic clove, cut in half
$^1/_4$ cup olive oil
2 cups bread cut in small cubes
1 large head romaine lettuce
1 head iceburg lettuce
$^1/_4$ cup grated Parmesan
$^1/_4$ cup crumbled blue cheese
$^1/_2$ cup olive oil
$^3/_4$ teaspoon salt
Freshly ground black pepper
3 or 4 tablespoons lemon juice
1 egg
2 anchovy fillets, minced (optional)

Place garlic in $^1/_4$ cup oil to season, mash slightly with fork. Toast bread cubes in the oven (300° F.), tossing once or twice with fork, until golden. When crisp, place in garlic-scented oil; toss; drain on absorbent paper. Thoroughly soak salad greens in ice water, remove, shake well to drain thoroughly, then chill in covered vegetable crisper lined with paper towel. Shortly before time to serve, shred salad greens, place in large salad bowl along with the two kinds of cheese. Toss salad with the $^1/_2$ cup oil, salt, pepper, and lemon juice; add the raw egg, tossing quickly until greens glisten but no egg can be seen. Add the oil-soaked croutons and toss again. Add anchovies or not as you please. Makes about 6 servings.


## Ensalada Queso (Mexican Cheese Salad)

$^1/_2$ green pepper, cut in slivers
1 pimiento, cut in slivers
$^1$ ₄ cup (about) slivers of Monterey Jack
Few onion slices
4 tablespoons Spanish olive oil
1$^1/_2$ tablespoons red wine vinegar

Salt and pepper
1 or 2 whole garlic cloves
4 to 6 cups salad greens, torn into bite-sized pieces

Combine green pepper, pimiento, cheese, onion, olive oil, vinegar, salt, pepper, and garlic in bowl. Marinate an hour or longer. Remove garlic. Add cheese mixture to salad greens just before serving. Makes 4 servings.

## Switzerland Cheese Salad

$1/2$ cup prepared French or Italian dressing
1 teaspoon prepared mustard
1 medium onion, chopped or thinly sliced
$1/2$ pound (2 cups) shredded or diced Swiss Emmentaler
Salt and pepper to taste

Combine dressing, mustard, and onion; let stand 15 minutes. Add cheese, and salt and pepper to taste if necessary. Serve this way or with added torn crisp lettuce, tossed in a salad bowl. This salad is excellent with cold cuts and fresh ripe tomatoes. Makes 4 servings.

VARIATIONS:
- To the dressing, add a teaspoon of horseradish.
- Add 2 or 3 tablespoons minced parsley.
- Add to the salad a few thinly sliced radishes and $1/2$ cucumber, sliced.
- Make it a potato-cheese salad by adding 2 cups cooked diced potatoes; this recipe will make 6 to 8 servings.
- For an extra hearty salad, add not only potatoes but also slivers of bologna (about $1/4$ pound).
- Add $1/2$ cup minced celery.
- Use salad mixture (omitting lettuce) to stuff scooped-out tomato halves. Serve topped with Roquefort Cream Dressing (see Index).

COMTÉ SALAD: Mix diced Comté (a French cheese) with onion, and omit Emmentaler; use Dijon mustard; dress salad simply with olive oil and vinegar, adding salt to taste.

SALAD VALAIS: Use cubed Bel Lago or Mütschli instead of Emmentaler.

# Chef's Salad

DRESSING:
1/2 cup olive oil
1/2 teaspoon salt
1/2 teaspoon dry mustard
2 tablespoons capers
3 or 4 tablespoons red wine vinegar

Combine all ingredients. Makes 3/4 cup dressing.

SALAD:
1 cup (about) thin slivers cooked ham
1 cup (about) thin slivers cooked breast of chicken
2 cups thin slivers of natural Gruyère, Emmentaler,
   or aged Wisconsin Swiss
6 cups mixed salad greens(escarole, Boston lettuce,
   watercress)
1 ripe avocado, cut into slivers
1/2 cup dressing
Small radishes

Keep ham, chicken, and cheese in plastic bags until ready to serve. Thoroughly soak salad greens, shake to dry, then place in paper-lined vegetable crisper to chill until needed. Slice avocado and marinate in the dressing. At serving time, arrange salad greens in large bowl, place bunches of slivered meat, chicken, and cheese around top, interspersed with radishes and avocado slices removed from the dressing. Add 1/2 cup of the dressing and toss at table. Makes 6 to 8 servings.

VARIATIONS:
- Instead of ham, use slivers of cooked roast pork or beef. Add slivers of green pepper.
- Instead of Swiss cheese, use slivers of Tilsiter.
- Instead of Swiss cheese, crumble Roquefort into the dressing; use slivers of caraway-seed cheese in the salad.
- Add 10 to 12 cooked, shelled shrimp.
- Instead of ham and chicken, use slivers of pastrami and tuna.
- Instead of Swiss, use slivers or small cubes of Provolone.

- Omit chicken, and add quartered hard-cooked eggs, diced celery, and artichoke hearts to the ham and Swiss-cheese slivers; omit avocados.
- Or, make up your own combination!

## Seafood Salad with Roquefort Dressing

1 cup cooked diced lobster meat
1 can (7 ounces) tuna, drained
1 small onion, thinly sliced
$1/4$ cup minced celery
2 tablespoons minced parsley
$3/4$ cup Roquefort French Dressing (see Index)
$1/2$ pound cooked shelled shrimp
Tomato wedges
Stuffed green olives

Combine lobster, tuna, onion, celery, parsley, and $1/2$ cup of the dressing. Toss to blend. Arrange in mound on platter. Garnish with shrimp, tomato wedges (cut just before serving), and olives. Sprinkle with remaining dressing. Makes 4 to 6 luncheon servings.

## Zesty Cheese Cole Slaw

2 cups shredded cabbage
$1/4$ cup any sharp cheese, cut into $1/2$-inch cubes
1 teaspoon grated onion
2 tablespoons mayonnaise
1 teaspoon horseradish
2 tablespoons oil
1 tablespoon vinegar
Salt and pepper to taste

Combine all ingredients. Makes 4 servings.

## Nordic Cheese Salad

2 or 3 potatoes, cooked and diced
2 tablespoons olive oil
10 to 12 cooked shrimp
$^1/_2$ cup (about) Tilsiter or Samsø, cut in small cubes
1 teaspoon prepared mustard
1 teaspoon grated onion
Dash of cayenne
1 teaspoon lemon juice
1 anchovy fillet, chopped
1 or 2 hard-cooked eggs, quartered

While potatoes are still warm, toss with oil. Add remaining ingredients (except eggs) in order given, and toss again. Serve in a mound with eggs as garnish. Makes 4 to 6 servings.


## Tomatoes Roquefort

Cut tomatoes in thick slices, top with crumbled Roquefort cheese; sprinkle with olive oil. (Because the cheese is salty, added salt is not usually needed, nor is vinegar needed, because the tomatoes themselves are acidulous.)


## Avocado-Cheese Salad

1 ripe avocado, peeled and diced
2 medium tomatoes, diced; or 6 cherry tomatoes
$^1/_4$ cup cottage cheese
$^1/_4$ cup shredded Swiss
2 chopped scallions
Few thin slices of onion (optional)
$^1/_2$ cup French dressing
Salad greens, 4 to 6 cups

Combine avocado, tomatoes, cottage and Swiss cheese, scallions, onion, and dressing. Marinate until time to serve; then toss with salad greens. Makes 4 to 6 servings.

## Romaine Romano

1 small head romaine lettuce
$^1/_2$ cup creamed cottage cheese
$^1/_4$ cup crumbled Gorgonzola
2 tablespoons olive oil
1 tablespoon basil or tarragon vinegar
Salt and pepper
1 ripe avocado, sliced
1 navel orange, sliced
1 hard-cooked egg, sliced
8 to 10 sliced black olives

Tear apart leaves of romaine and arrange on individual salad plates or on salad platter. Combine cheeses, olive oil, vinegar, salt, and pepper for the dressing, beating to blend well. Arrange slices of avocado, orange, and egg over the romaine. Scatter sliced olives over the top. Pour the dressing over all. Makes 4 to 6 servings.

## Italian Rice Salad

2 large tomatoes
3 cups cooked rice
4 ounces Bel Paese, cubed (1 cup)
$^1/_2$ cup Fontina, cubed
1 jar frozen artichoke hearts in olive oil
1 tablespoon capers
2 anchovy fillets, minced
6 tablespoons olive oil
2 tablespoons lemon juice
Watercress sprigs

To seed the tomatoes, first peel whole tomatoes, then cut in halves, and press each half gently, which forces seeds out. Chop the well-drained, seedless pulp in the salad. Combine with remaining ingredients, form with back of spoon into a mound, and serve garnished with watercress. Makes 4 servings.

## Avocado-Roquefort Salad

1 ripe avocado, sliced
1 navel orange, peeled, sliced, or cut in sections
1 onion, thinly sliced
1 cucumber, partially peeled and sliced
Cherry tomatoes
$^1/_2$ cup Roquefort French Dressing (see Index)

Arrange avocado and orange slices alternately around edge of platter. Place rings from onion slices over them. In center, arrange overlapping cucumber slices. Pile cherry tomatoes on cucumber. Pour Roquefort French Dressing over all. Makes 4 generous servings.

## Potato-Roquefort Salad

8 cups cooked, diced potatoes
2 tablespoons oil
2 teaspoons salt, or to taste
1 teaspoon vinegar
2 cups chopped celery
$^1/_4$ cup minced onion;
    or 2 tablespoons grated onion
4 hard-cooked eggs
$^1/_2$ cup crumbled Roquefort
Freshly ground pepper
$^1/_4$ cup mayonnaise

While potatoes are still warm, toss with oil. Add salt. When potatoes have cooled, add remaining ingredients, but set aside 2 of the eggs for garnish. Mold salad with back of spoon, chill, but remove from refrigerator an hour before serving. Arrange sliced eggs over top. Makes 8 servings.

POTATO-SWISS SALAD: Use $^1/_2$ cup finely diced Swiss Emmentaler or Gruyère instead of Roquefort.

## Lima Salad with Western Dressing

1 package frozen Fordhook limas, cooked
1 pound fresh green beans, broken and cooked until barely
  tender
1 teaspoon grated onion
$1/4$ cup mayonnaise
$1/4$ cup sour cream
2 tablespoons crumbled blue cheese (Roquefort, Gorgonzola,
  Danish, or Wisconsin)
1 tablespoon chili sauce
Salt, pepper

Combine all ingredients, toss, and chill. Serve on curly chicory.
Makes 6 to 8 servings.

## Pineapple-Cheese Slaw

4 cups shredded green cabbage
1 large carrot, scraped and shredded
$1/4$ cup sliced radishes
$1/2$ cup slivered green pepper
1 cup canned pineapple tidbits, drained
$1/2$ cup buttermilk or yogurt
$1/2$ cup mayonnaise
$1/2$ cup finely diced Swiss or Provolone
$1/2$ teaspoon celery seed
Salt to taste

Toss cabbage, carrots, radishes, green pepper, and pineapple
tidbits. Cover, and chill. Combine next four ingredients with
salt to taste, and beat until well blended. Pour salad dressing
over slaw, and toss until well blended and moistened. Serve
with thinly sliced ham, chicken, or tongue. Makes 6 to 8 servings.

# Danish Potato-Cheese Salad

1/2 cup prepared French dressing
2 tablespoons minced or grated onion
1 teaspoon prepared mustard
3 ounces Samsø or Havarti, diced
1 ounce Danish Blue, crumbled
1 pimiento, cut into slivers
2 cups cooked diced potatoes
1 gherkin, sliced lengthwise

Combine French dressing with onion and mustard, add the two cheeses, and marinate about 1/2 hour. Add remaining ingredients. Serve with cold cuts or barbecued frankfurters. Makes 4 servings.

# Macaroni and Cheese Salad

4 cups cooked elbow maracroni
1 teaspoon grated onion
2 tablespoons minced green pepper
2 tablespoons minced pimiento
1/2 cup minced celery
1/2 cup diced Edam or mild Cheddar
1/4 cup mayonnaise
2 tablespoons sour cream
1 teaspoon prepared mustard

Combine all ingredients. Chill before serving. This salad is especially good with baked ham. Makes 4 to 6 servings as a side dish.

# Swiss-Waldorf Salad

3 cups diced tart apples
Lemon juice
1 cup diced celery
2/3 cup coarsely chopped walnuts

¹/₂ cup sour cream
¹/₄ cup mayonnaise
¹/₂ cup Swiss cheese, cut in slivers
3 tablespoons raisins
Dash of salt
Lettuce

Sprinkle apples with lemon juice to prevent darkening. Toss with celery, nuts, sour cream, and mayonnaise; chill. When ready to serve, add cheese, raisins, and salt to taste. Serve on lettuce. Makes 6 servings.

## Orange-Gorgonzola Salad

2 large navel oranges
Few slices onion
2 tablespoons Gorgonzola, crumbled
¹/₃ cup olive oil
¹/₄ teaspoon salt
3 tablespoons red wine vinegar
Shredded romaine lettuce
Freshly ground black pepper

Peel oranges, and slice crosswise. Place in bowl with onion slices, Gorgonzola, oil, salt, and vinegar. Marinate until serving time; then combine with lettuce in salad bowl, grind pepper over the top, and toss lightly. Makes 4 servings.

## Cheese Salad Matelote

¹/₄ pound (1 cup) Tilsiter cheese, shredded
1 green pepper, minced
2 tomatoes, peeled and quartered
1 cucumber, partially peeled and thinly sliced
2 anchovy fillets, chopped
¹/₄ cup olive oil
2 tablespoons vinegar

Combine all ingredients, toss to blend. Makes 4 to 6 servings.

## Pineapple-Cheese Salad Mold

2 envelopes unflavored gelatin
$^1/_2$ cup cold water
$2^1/_2$ cups (1-pound can) crushed pineapple
3 tablespoons lemon juice
$^1/_2$ cup sugar
1 cup heavy cream, whipped
1 cup shredded Cheddar
$^1/_2$ cup chopped walnuts

Soften the gelatin in cold water. Heat the crushed pineapple (do not drain), and stir in the softened gelatin until dissolved. Add the lemon juice and sugar; chill until mixture is partially set. Then fold in the whipped cream, cheese, and nuts. Pour into molds, and chill until set. To serve, unmold and garnish with walnut halves. Makes 6 to 8 servings.

## Stuffed Pears Provolone

12 canned or ripe, fresh pear halves, peeled and cored
Lemon juice
2 3-ounce packages cream cheese, softened
$^1/_2$ cup shredded Provolone
Heavy cream or sour cream
Chicory
Pitted black cherries

Drain canned pear halves. (Brush fresh pears with lemon juice to prevent darkening.) Mix cream cheese with Provolone and enough cream so that the mixture has the consistency of very stiff whipped cream. Spoon mixture into the hollows of 6 pear halves. Press remaining pear halves over cheese mixture. Chill. When ready to serve, stand filled pear upright on a bed of torn pieces of chicory. Garnish with black cherries. Serve with a simple French dressing or mayonnaise blended with whipped cream or sour cream. Makes 6 servings.

## Seafood and Cheese Salad

1 cup (4 ounces) Swiss or natural Gruyère,
  cut into strips
1 cup crabmeat
2 cups cooked shrimp
1 10-ounce package frozen limas, cooked
1 pimiento, in slivers
Few slices onion
³/₄ cup classic or garlic-flavored French dressing
6 to 8 cups (about) salad greens

Combine all ingredients but salad greens; marinate until needed;
then toss with salad greens. Makes 8 servings.

## Tomato Aspic with Cheese Balls

1 envelope unflavored gelatin
¹/₂ cup cold tomato juice
1¹/₂ cups hot tomato juice
¹/₄ teaspoon salt
1 tablespoon lemon juice
1 teaspoon sugar
1 3-ounce package cream cheese
¹/₄ cup grated Parmesan
1 tablespoon minced chives or parsley
1 cup mixed shredded carrot and cabbage

Soften gelatin in cold tomato juice; dissolve with hot juice.
Add salt, lemon juice, and sugar. Pour enough gelatin into 1-
quart ring mold to form film over bottom. Chill until partially
set. Combine cheeses and chives, form into 6 balls. Place these
balls in mold, and chill until gelatin is set. Add two-thirds of
remaining gelatin mixture; chill until partially set. Spread layer
of shredded vegetables over it; then cover with remaining gelatin to fill mold. Chill until very firm. Unmold. Serve with Danish
Blue-Cream Dressing (see Index). Makes 4 to 6 servings.

## Egg and Cheese Salad Mold

1 envelope unflavored gelatin
$^1/_4$ cup cold water
1 can (10$^1/_2$ ounces) condensed tomato soup,
   heated to boiling
2 tablespoons sour cream
$^1/_2$ cup mayonnaise
$^1/_2$ cup chopped celery
$^1/_4$ cup diced green pepper
1 4$^1/_2$-ounce can pitted ripe olives
   or pimiento-stuffed green olives, sliced
1 cup Fontina, soft Monterey Jack, or
   young Manchego, cut in small cubes
3 hard-cooked eggs, chopped

Soften gelatin in cold water. Heat tomato soup, add to gelatin and stir until dissolved. Cool slightly; then stir in sour cream, mayonnaise, chopped celery, and green pepper. Chill until mixture starts to set; then stir in olives, cheese, and eggs, distributing throughout gelatin. Pour into 1$^1/_2$-quart mold, and chill until firm. Unmold on salad greens. Makes 6 to 8 servings.


## Molded Cottage Cheese Salad

1 envelope unflavored gelatin
1 tablespoon sugar
$^1/_2$ teaspoon salt
$^1/_2$ cup water
2 cups creamed cottage cheese
2 tablespoons horseradish
$^1/_2$ cup heavy cream, whipped
2 cups diced apple
$^1/_4$ cup minced green pepper

Place gelatin, sugar, salt, and water in top of double boiler; place over boiling water and stir until gelatin is dissolved. Add remaining ingredients. Turn into 4-cup (1-quart) mold. Chill until firm. Unmold on salad greens. Serve with Roquefort French Dressing (see Index). Makes 6 servings.

# Grapefruit-Cream Cheese Mold

2 envelopes unflavored gelatin
$^1/_2$ cup cold water
1 cup boiling water
$^1/_3$ cup sugar
$^3/_4$ teaspoon salt
2 large grapefruit, peeled and divided into skinned sections;*
    or 1-pound can grapefruit sections and juice
Few drops red food coloring (optional)
1 8-ounce package cream cheese
2 tablespoons light cream
1 tablespoon sugar
Dash of salt
1 cup chopped pecans

Soften the gelatin in the cold water; add the boiling water, stir until gelatin is dissolved. Add $^1/_3$ cup sugar, $^3/_4$ teaspoon salt, grapefruit and juice, and food coloring (if used). Pour half this mixture into a 6-cup ring mold, and refrigerate until set. Beat the cream cheese with the cream, 1 tablespoon sugar, and dash of salt. Stir in the nuts; spread mixture over the set layer of gelatin. Pour the remaining gelatin into the mold, and refrigerate until set. Unmold, and serve with whipped-cream mayonnaise. Makes 6 to 8 servings.

*Note: If fresh grapefruit is used, add $^1/_4$ cup orange juice to gelatin mixture.

# CHEESECAKE AND OTHER DESSERTS

Cheesecake is a word with many meanings. It may refer to a pair of pretty legs in a picture, rococo decor, or too lavish art work — or a deliciously creamy confection that contains not an ounce of cheese!

Even in ancient Greece the original word *tiropeta* meant many things — a honey-sweetened mold of cream cheese chilled in snow, a crust containing a cheese mixture, small, hot cheese-filled pastries consumed as "provocatives to drinking." From the talk of the banqueters in the classic third-century book *The Deipnosophists*, written by an Alexandrian Greek who called himself "Athenaeus," it is clear that every Greek province and city-state in those days had its own special recipe. Some of the "cheesecakes" were mere custards made with eggs and milk — which had their counterpart in the nineteenth-century "lemon-cheese tarts" made with egg yolks and lemon juice. For that matter, consider the "instant cheesecake" sometimes made, in this modern world, of an uncooked "instant pudding" and sour cream.

Pasha, the traditional Easter cheesecake of Russia, is very likely a direct descendant of the chilled, molded cheesecake of early Greece, and there is no question that the Italian *Torta di Ricotta* is a first cousin of the Greek *melopita*, a honey-sweetened cheese mixture in pastry.

Most cheesecakes are made with fresh cheese — cream cheese or cottage cheese or another soft, unripened cheese — as are most other cheese desserts, including sweetened pies and gelatin molds. Among the few exceptions are a syrupy Mexican "bread pudding" in which Monterey Jack is used; several fruit concoctions in which Roquefort, Gorgonzola, or another blue-veined cheese is combined with cream cheese or cream; and a delectable pastry made with Cheddar, which is particularly good when filled with tart greening apples.

Many of the soft ripened dessert cheeses can easily be turned into rich dessert cream toppings — simply by blending in a little confectioners' sugar and cognac. They are superb atop Kirsch-sweetened black cherries or raspberry compote! For such toppings, the delicate *double-crème* or *triple-crème*, delicately flavored dessert cheeses, are especially suitable.

In Italy, a dessert is made of fresh Ricotta simply by adding sugar and cinnamon. Coeur à la Crème in France is always served with strawberries as a sweet.

Only "made" desserts using cheese are given on the following pages. For suggested ways to serve cheese as dessert in itself with demitasse and cognac (or another fine spirit), see Part Three.

### French Cheesecake

$^1\!/_4$ pound (1 stick) butter, softened
4 eggs, separated
1 pound (2 8-ounce packages) cream cheese;
   1 7-ounce package Demi-Suisse, Gervaise, or other
   soft *double-crème* cheese from France
1 cup sifted all-purpose flour
2 tablespoons sugar
1 tablespoon flour
$^1\!/_2$ cup sifted sugar
$^1\!/_4$ cup heavy sweet cream
$^1\!/_4$ cup sour cream
1 teaspoon vanilla
$^1\!/_4$ teaspoon salt

Butter, eggs, and cheese should all be taken from refrigerator at least $^1\!/_2$ hour before preparation. Then to sifted flour add the butter, and work with fingers until well-blended. Work in 2 tablespoons sugar. Press half this pastry dough over bottom of 9-inch spring-form pan or cake pan with removable bottom. Bake in oven preheated to 400° F. about 8 minutes or until lightly browned. Cool. Press remaining pastry dough around edges, chill while preparing filling. Beat the cheese until smooth and fluffy; beat in 1 tablespoon flour and $^1\!/_2$ cup sugar. Stir in egg yolks, cream, and vanilla; blend until smooth. Add salt to egg whites, beat until stiff. Fold into creamed cheese mixture. Pour this mixture into pastry, and bake at 350° F. for 45 minutes or until firm. Let cool at room temperature before turning out of pan. Makes 1 9-inch cake, about 8 rich servings.

# Lindy's Strawberry Cheesecake

COOKIE CRUST:
1 cup sifted flour
$^1/_4$ cup sugar
1 teaspoon grated lemon rind
1 egg yolk
$^1/_2$ cup butter, softened

Blend together flour, sugar, and lemon rind; add egg yolk and butter, and mix with fingers until it forms a smooth dough. Pat or spread on bottom and sides of 9-inch pie pan. Bake at 400° F. for 10 minutes or until lightly browned. Cool. Meanwhile prepare filling.

FILLING:
$1^1/_4$ pounds cream cheese
$^3/_4$ cup sugar
$1^1/_2$ tablespoons flour
$^3/_4$ teaspoon grated orange or lemon rind
$^1/_4$ teaspoon vanilla
3 whole eggs plus 1 egg yolk
2 tablespoons heavy cream

Beat cheese until creamy. Add sugar, flour, grated orange or lemon rind, and vanilla; add eggs one at a time, beating after each addition, then stir in egg yolk. Add cream. Pour into baked, cooled shell. Reduce oven heat to 250° F., place cake in oven, and bake 1 hour or until firm. Cool. When cold, cover with Strawberry Glaze.

STRAWBERRY GLAZE:
1 quart strawberries
$^3/_4$ cup sugar
$^1/_4$ cup cold water
Dash salt
$1^1/_2$ tablespoons cornstarch
1 teaspoon butter
Few drops red food coloring

Wash strawberries and separate larger, more perfect berries for garnish. Chop up less perfect berries, making 1 cup. Mash through food mill or in blender. To crushed berries add sugar, water, salt, and cornstarch. Bring slowly to boil, stirring constantly. Add butter and red food coloring to tint bright red. Cool slightly. Arrange whole berries over top of cake, pointed ends up. Spoon glaze over berries, and chill until firm.

### Pasha (Traditional Russian Easter Sweet)

PASHA:
1 pound pot cheese, farmer's cheese, or Ricotta
Yolks of 2 hard-cooked eggs
$1/4$ pound softened butter
1 3-ounce package cream cheese
$1/2$ pint sour cream
$1/2$ to $3/4$ cup confectioners' sugar
$1/4$ cup finely diced candied fruit or citron
$1/4$ cup finely chopped almonds
Tokay or red Emperor grapes, halved and seeded
2 cups Sabayon Sauce

Force pot cheese and hard cooked egg yolks through sieve. Beat in butter, cream cheese, sour cream, and sugar. The mixture should be very smooth. Stir in fruit and nuts, distributing evenly. Line 1-quart deep mold with cheesecloth, or first rub mold evenly with butter. Press cheese mixture into mold, forcing down hard. Place a plate and a heavy object on top to force it down further. Chill 24 hours. Unmold, and carefully remove cheesecloth (or, if rubbed with butter, loosen from mold by dipping in hot water). Use knife to swirl and smooth sides. Garnish with grapes. Serve with chilled Sabayon Sauce. Makes 8 to 12 rich servings.

SABAYON SAUCE:
2 unbeaten egg yolks
3 tablespoons confectioners' sugar
Grated rind and juice of $1/2$ lemon
$1/4$ cup Rainwater Madeira
1 tablespoon white rum

Place unbeaten egg yolks, sugar, grated lemon rind, and Madeira in top of double boiler. Beat constantly with whisk (or portable electric beater) over hot water until fluffy, smooth, and thickened. Add lemon juice and rum. Chill. Makes 2 cups.

# Refrigerator Cheesecake

CHEESECAKE:
2 envelopes unflavored gelatin
1 cup cold water
3 eggs, separated
$^1/_2$ cup sugar
Grated rind 1 lemon
1 teaspoon lemon juice
3 cups creamed cottage cheese
1 3-ounce package cream cheese, softened
1 teaspoon vanilla or 2 teaspoons brandy or bourbon
1 cup heavy cream, whipped

Soften gelatin in cold water 5 minutes. Add egg yolks, sugar, and lemon rind, and heat in top of double boiler, stirring until gelatin is dissolved and mixture is slightly thickened. Combine cottage and cream cheese, beat together until smooth, and stir into gelatin mixture. Add vanilla or brandy. Beat egg whites until stiff. Beat cream until stiff. Fold each in turn into cheese mixture.

CRUMB TOPPING:
$^1/_2$ cup crushed graham crackers
$^1/_2$ teaspoon cinnamon
4 tablespoons softened butter
1 tablespoon sugar

Combine ingredients. Press into spring-form mold or 8-inch-cake pan with removable bottom. Spoon cheese mixture over crumbs. Chill until very firm, preferably 24 hours. Makes 8 to 10 servings.

# Wisconsin Cheesecake

$2^1/_2$ cups zwieback crumbs (6-ounce package)
$^1/_2$ cup sugar
1 teaspoon cinnamon
$^1/_2$ cup melted butter
4 eggs
1 cup sugar

¹/₈ teaspoon salt
1¹/₂ tablespoons lemon juice
Grated rind ¹/₂ lemon
1 cup light cream
1¹/₂ pounds cottage cheese (2 12-ounce packages)
¹/₄ cup all-purpose flour
¹/₄ cup chopped nuts

Generously butter a spring-form mold or large cake pan with removable bottom. Mix zwieback with ¹/₂ cup sugar, cinnamon, and melted butter; reserve ¹/₂ cup of mixture. Spread remaining mixture on bottom and sides of mold, pressing to form crust. Beat eggs until light, add remaining sugar, salt, lemon juice, and rind. Stir in cream, cottage cheese, and flour. Beat in electric blender or mixer until smooth. Pour into crumb-lined form and cover with reserved zwieback mixture and nuts. Bake at 350° F. for 1 hour until center is set (test with cake tester). Turn off heat, open oven door, and let stay in oven 1 hour longer. Makes 10 to 12 servings.

### Cheese Pie in Chocolate-Wafer Crust

1¹/₄ cups finely crushed chocolate wafers
¹/₃ cup butter, melted
2 8-ounce packages cream cheese, softened
¹/₂ cup sugar
2 eggs, beaten
2 tablespoons Cointreau
1 cup sour cream
2 tablespoons sugar

Mix together wafer crumbs and butter; press over bottom and sides of buttered 9-inch pie pan. Beat cream cheese until fluffy, add ¹/₂ cup sugar gradually, add eggs one at a time, then blend in 1 tablespoon Cointreau. Spread mixture over chocolate crust. Bake 15 minutes in oven preheated to 350° F. Combine sour cream, 2 tablespoons sugar, and 1 tablespoon Cointreau. Spread this mixture as topping over pie. Reduce temperature to 325° F., return to oven, and bake 5 minutes longer. Serve chilled. Makes 8 small but rich servings.

# Pineapple Cheesecake

1 1/2 cups finely crushed vanilla-wafer crumbs
1/4 cup melted butter
1 tablespoon lemon juice
3/4 cup well-drained crushed pineapple
1 pound (2 8-ounce packages) cream cheese
3 eggs, separated
1/2 cup sugar
2 tablespoons flour
1/2 teaspoon salt
2/3 cup evaporated milk
1 teaspoon vanilla
1/4 cup sugar

Combine wafer crumbs, melted butter, and lemon juice. Press over bottom and sides of 9-inch spring-form pan or any pan with removable bottom. Bake at 325° F. for 5 minutes; remove from oven and cool. Place crushed pineapple over bottom crust. Cream the cheese until fluffy; beat in egg yolks, 1/2 cup sugar, flour, and salt. When smooth, beat in undiluted evaporated milk and vanilla. Separately beat egg whites until stiff, beating in 1/4 cup sugar. Fold egg whites into cheese mixture. Pour into pastry. Bake at 325° F. for 50 minutes or until firm in center. Cool; then chill. Serve cold.

WITH GINGER CRUST: Instead of vanilla wafers, make crumbs of gingersnaps.


# Melopita

PASTRY:
1 1/2 cups sifted all-purpose flour
1/4 teaspoon salt
1/2 cup butter
1 egg, well beaten

Preheat oven to 450° F. Blend flour and salt, cut in butter until the size of peas, blend in egg to form dough. Knead with fingers until well blended. Chill. Roll out between sheets of waxed paper; then press with fingers into 8-inch pie pan, making crust stand up around the edge. Chill again for 30 minutes. Place pie shell in hot oven for 10 minutes; then reduce heat to 325° F.

FILLING:
$1/2$ pound Feta
$1/2$ pound Ricotta or farmer's cheese
$1/2$ pound grated Casera, Gruyère, or Swiss
$1/2$ cup honey
$1/4$ teaspoon cinnamon
5 eggs

As soon as crust has been placed in oven, combine cheeses, honey, and cinnamon. Beat to blend well; then beat in eggs one at a time. Add cheese mixture to partially baked crust, return to oven. Bake 50 minutes or until knife inserted in center comes out clean. Cool. Serve cold. Makes 1 8-inch cheese-filled pie, about 6 servings.

### Coeur à la Crème

$1^1/2$ cups (12 ounces) Ricotta or farmer's cheese
1 cup (8-ounce package) cream cheese
$1/2$ cup heavy cream
2 tablespoons softened butter
$1/4$ cup sifted confectioner's sugar (optional)
1 quart strawberries

In blender beat together the Ricotta or farmer's cheese, cream cheese, heavy cream, butter, and sugar until very smooth. Press into 3-cup heart-shaped gelatin mold, which has been rubbed with butter, forcing down as hard as possible with back of spoon. Place plate over top, and weight it with heavy object. Chill in refrigerator overnight. Dip quickly in warm water to unmold, turn out on large, round platter, and smooth surface with knife. Return to refrigerator to keep chilled. Wash the strawberries, using only the most perfect specimens, preferably with stems left on. Surround the Coeur à la Crème with strawberries. To serve, cut portions of the cheese, and serve several strawberries with each. Makes 8 servings.

# Torta di Ricotta

PASTRY:
2 cups sifted all-purpose flour
$1/4$ teaspoon salt
$2/3$ cup butter
1 egg, beaten

Combine flour and salt, cut in butter as for pie crust, then work in beaten egg. Knead until smooth; then press over bottom and sides of 9-inch pie pan, fluting around edges. Chill.

FILLING:
$1^{1}/_{2}$ pounds Ricotta
$1/2$ cup confectioners' sugar
$1/2$ cup shelled, blanched almonds, ground
Grated rind 1 lemon
$1/2$ teaspoon vanilla
4 eggs, beaten

Beat together Ricotta, sugar, almonds, and lemon rind. Beat in vanilla and eggs, one at a time. Pour mixture into chilled pastry. Place in oven preheated to 425° F. for 5 minutes, reduce heat, and bake at 350° F. for 30 minutes longer or until center is firm. Cool. Makes 6 to 8 servings.

## Cherry-Cheese Pie

GRAHAM CRACKER CRUST:
   Prepare crust according to directions on package of graham crackers. Pat into 9-inch pie pan.

FILLING:
12 ounces ($1^{1}/_{2}$ 8-ounce packages) cream cheese
2 eggs
$1/2$ cup granulated sugar
$1/2$ teaspoon vanilla

In blender or electric mixer beat together cream cheese, eggs, sugar, and vanilla. Pour into pie shell. Bake 35 minutes in oven preheated to 350° F. Remove from oven. Cool.

CHERRY GLAZE:     *
1 can pitted sour red cherries, drained

$^1/_2$ cup Cherry Kijafa wine (or drained juice from cherries)
2 teaspoons cornstarch
2 tablespoons sugar
Few drops red food coloring

Drain cherries thoroughly. Blend wine (or cherry juice), cornstarch, and sugar, and cook until clear and thickened. Add cherries and food coloring. Cool slightly; then pour over filling. Makes 6 servings.


### Danish Cheese-Grape Pie

PUMPERNICKEL CRUMB CRUST:
1 loaf (11 ounces) thinly sliced square dark pumpernickel
$^1/_2$ cup butter, melted
$^1/_4$ cup sugar

Dry bread in a slow oven, break into small pieces, and whirl in blender (or crush crumbs with a rolling pin). Blend crumbs, butter, and sugar; press firmly against the bottom and sides of a 9-inch pie plate. Flatten the bottom by pressing with an 8-inch pie plate. Bake the crust in a moderate oven (350° F.) for 15 minutes; cool well before filling.

FILLING:
2 envelopes unflavored gelatin
$^1/_2$ cup cold water
$^1/_4$ pound Danish Blue (1 cup, crumbled)
1 3-ounce package cream cheese, softened
1 cup heavy cream
1 pound seedless green grapes

Soak gelatin in cold water; stir over hot water or low heat until mixture is clear and gelatin dissolved. Mash Danish Blue well; blend with softened cream cheese; stir in gelatin, and mix until well blended. Whip cream stiff, fold into cheese mixture. Pour into baked Pumpernickel Crust. Arrange green grapes, placed upright, thickly over top of cheese filling. Or use red Tokay or black Ribier grapes, in season, split in half and seeded. Chill until firmly set before serving.

# Vatrooshki (Russian Cheese Tarts)

2 packages pie-crust mix (or your own recipe for 2 9-inch pies)
1 pound (16 ounces) creamed cottage cheese
2 tablespoons softened butter
3 egg yolks
1 egg white
2 tablespoons granulated sugar
Pinch of salt
1/2 cup sour cream
Blackberry or red-raspberry jam
About 1/4 cup milk

Prepare pie-crust mix as directed (or your own recipe), rolling out part at a time. Using a small plate (a bread-and-butter plate or a saucer), cut out 12 three-inch circles. Cream together cottage cheese, butter, egg yolks, egg white, sugar, salt, and sour cream. Divide this mixture over 6 of the pastry circles; spoon a little jam over the top of the cheese mixture. Cover with the remaining circles (each of which should have a small hole in the center), moistening inside edges; then seal all around the edges with tines of a fork. Brush top crust with milk. Bake on ungreased baking sheet in oven preheated to 400° F. until crust is golden, about 20 minutes. Makes 6 tarts.

# Cheddar and Apple Pie

PASTRY:
2 cups sifted all-purpose flour
1/4 teaspoon salt
2/3 cup shortening, including 1 tablespoon butter
1/3 cup water

To make pastry, combine flour and salt, chop in shortening and butter until size of peas. Add water a little at a time, toss to blend, then knead with fingers until smooth. Roll out half of pastry at a time to fit 9-inch pie pan.

FILLING:
6 tart apples, peeled, cored, and quartered
1/2 cup sugar

Few drops lemon juice
1/2 cup shredded sharp aged Cheddar

In pastry-lined pan, place the apples; spread sugar over them, and sprinkle with lemon juice. Spread shredded cheese over the apples. Top with upper crust of dough, which has been slit in center. Moisten edges and seal crust, fluting the edges. Bake in oven preheated to 400° F. for 40 minutes or until crust is golden-crisp and apples inside are bubbling. Makes 6 servings.

## Strawberries Roquefort

1 quart strawberries
2 cups (1 pound) creamed cottage cheese
1/2 cup (2 ounces) crumbled Roquefort
2 teaspoons grated orange rind
1/2 cup crushed canned pineapple

Wash strawberries, and hull. Sweeten, if desired. Set aside. Combine remaining ingredients and beat until well blended. Chill both the berries and the Roquefort mixture until ready to serve. Spoon Roquefort mixture into small individual serving dishes, and serve surrounded with strawberries for dipping. Makes 8 servings.

## Peaches Triple-Crème

Top either fresh, frozen, or canned peaches (well-drained) with the following luscious blend:

Scrape the crust from any *double crème* or *triple crème* dessert cheese (such as Brillat-Savarin, Gervaise, Chantilly, Demi-Suisse or Crema Danica). To the creamy-soft cheese, add a tablespoon of fine cognac (like Remy Martin) and a little confectioners' sugar. Beat with spoon until well blended. Spoon about 2 tablespoons over each serving of peaches. This is nectar from heaven.

267

# Apple Pie with Cheddar Crust

PASTRY:
2 cups sifted all-purpose flour
$1/4$ teaspoon salt
$1/2$ cup shortening
$1/2$ cup grated sharp Cheddar
$1/4$ to $1/3$ cup water

To make pastry, combine flour and salt, chop in shortening as fine as peas, then add grated cheese. Add water a tablespoon at a time, using only as much as needed to form a stiff dough. Chill; then roll out half at a time on lightly floured board to make 2 crusts for a 9-inch pie.

FILLING:
6 cups sliced tart apples
$1/2$ cup sugar
Few drops lemon juice
$1/4$ teaspoon cinnamon
1 tablespoon butter

Place bottom crust in pan, and line with apples. Add sugar and cinnamon blended together, lemon juice, and dots of butter. Cover with upper crust, cutting three slits in center; seal edges and flute. Bake at 400° F. for 40 to 45 minutes or until crust is golden crisp and apples are bubbling inside. Serve slightly warm topped by vanilla ice cream, if desired. Makes 1 9-inch pie.

# Blackberry Pie with Cream Cheese Crust

PASTRY:
$1^1/2$ cups sifted flour
$1/2$ teaspoon salt
1 3-ounce package cream cheese, softened
1 egg

Combine flour and salt, and work in cheese with fingers until well blended. Add egg, knead until smooth. Chill at least 30 minutes, divide in half, and roll out each half to fit 8-inch pie pan.

FILLING:
1 pint blackberries

$^{1}/_{2}$ cup sugar
$1^{1}/_{2}$ tablespoons cornstarch
Few drops lemon juice
1 tablespoon butter

Place blackberries in pastry-lined pan; combine sugar and cornstarch, blending well. Sprinkle this mixture over berries. Sprinkle lemon juice over berries; then dot with butter. Cut slits in upper crust, and lay over berries, sealing edges. Bake in oven preheated to 400° F. until crust is delicately golden and berries bubbling inside, about 40 minutes.

### Mexican Cheesecake

This delectable dessert from Mexico is really more a pudding than a cake, puffy and golden and most unusual in flavor.

$1^{1}/_{2}$ cups water
$1^{1}/_{2}$ cups sugar
2 tablespoons butter
4 eggs, separated
$^{1}/_{4}$ cup cognac
8 slices sponge cake*
$^{1}/_{2}$ pound soft Monterey Jack, sliced; or grated hard Jack
   or mild American Cheddar
Cinnamon
1 cup heavy cream, whipped (optional)

Boil water and sugar rapidly together for 3 minutes; add butter; cool. Beat egg whites until stiff. Separately beat yolks until thick and light. Add the sugar syrup to the yolks, beating constantly. Add the cognac. Fold in the egg whites. Arrange 4 slices of the cake in a shallow 2-quart baking dish lined with waxed paper cut to fit. Place half the cheese slices over the cake. Pour over it half the syrup-egg mixture. Repeat with remaining ingredients. Bake in 325° F. oven for 30 minutes or until meringue is firm. Sprinkle with cinnamon while warm. Serve topped with whipped cream if desired. Makes 8 servings.

*Note: Stale leftover plain sponge cake may be used in this recipe with equally good results.

# Raspberry-Cheese Parfait

1 3-ounce package raspberry-flavored gelatin
1 cup hot water
1 10-ounce package frozen red raspberries
1/2 cup Cherry Kijafa wine
1 3-ounce package cream cheese
2 ounces (1/2 cup) Crème de Gruyère
2 tablespoons confectioners' sugar
1 tablespoon brandy or Kirsch

Dissolve gelatin in hot water. Add frozen raspberries and Kijafa; stir until raspberries are defrosted. Chill until partially set. Both cream cheese and Crème de Gruyère should be at room temperature 1 hour before preparation. Beat the cheeses with sugar and brandy in electric blender until smooth. (Add another spoonful of brandy if too stiff.) Spoon the partially set gelatin into parfait or whiskey-sour glasses in layers with the cheese mixture, with the cheese on top. Makes 6 parfaits.

# Lemon-Cream Cheese Pie

1 baked 9-inch pie shell
3 eggs
3/4 cup sugar
1/2 cup lemon juice
2 teaspoons grated lemon rind
3 3-ounce packages cream cheese, softened

Bake the pie shell in the usual way. Cool. Beat the eggs in the top of a double boiler until thick and fluffy. Continue beating over hot water while gradually adding the sugar, lemon juice, and lemon rind. Cook, stirring constantly, until custard is thick and smooth. Meantime, the cream cheese should be soft enough to beat; when custard is smooth, gradually blend cheese into the custard mixture. Cool. Fill the baked pie shell with the cooled mixture. Makes 6 servings.

## Peaches Gorgonzola

In a blender, place 1 ripe fresh peach (chopped) or 2 canned peach halves (well-drained), $1/4$ cup crumbled Gorgonzola, 2 tablespoons heavy cream and 1 tablespoon confectioners' sugar. Beat until smooth. Serve as a topping for sweetened fresh peaches or canned peaches that have been marinated in a little cognac.

## Orange Sherbet Mold

SHERBET MOLD:
3 packages (3 ounces each) orange-flavored gelatin
$2^{1}/_{3}$ cups boiling water
3 cans (11 ounces each) Mandarin oranges and juice
1 pint orange sherbet
3 bananas, sliced

Dissolve gelatin in boiling water. Drain oranges, saving juice. Measure $1^{1}/_{2}$ cups juice, add to gelatin, stir in the sherbet, and chill until partially set. Peel and slice bananas. Arrange banana slices and mandarin sections in mold; add gelatin. Chill until firm. Unmold, serve topped with Roquefort Chantilly as a salad-dessert. Makes 6 to 8 servings.

ROQUEFORT CHANTILLY SAUCE:
$1/2$ cup crumbled Roquefort
$1/4$ cup chopped nuts
1 cup heavy cream, whipped, sweetened
Few drops lemon juice

Stir cheese and nuts into whipped cream. Fold in lemon juice carefully. Serve over Orange Sherbet Mold. (It is also delicious on sponge cake slices.) Makes $1^{1}/_{2}$ cups.

# ndex

273

276

278

279

# The Author and Her Book

BETTY WASON is the author of ten other books including *The Art of Spanish Cooking, Bride in the Kitchen, Dinners That Wait,* and *Cooks, Gluttons & Gourmets.* She has written extensively about travel and world affairs, having served as a CBS correspondent in Greece during the German occupation in 1941.

Her articles have appeared in *Vogue, House & Garden, House Beautiful, Atlantic Monthly* and *American Home.*

Miss Wason was assistant food editor at *McCall's,* editor for the consumer kitchens at General Foods Corporation, and women's editor for the Voice of America. She is a consultant to the Spanish Oil Institute and other firms.

A native of Delphi, Indiana, she holds a B.S. degree in home economics from Purdue University, and is a member of the Overseas Press Club and the American Home Economics Association.